The Founding Fathers

N. York. March 18th. 1787

for you — the pecan Nuts have all been
when I red. by the post about a dozen
by a French Gentleman in a vessel bound
in himself to Paris, or consign them to
despair of being able to possess myself of
my endeavours have been equally un-
maple, notwithstanding the different places
upon a letter to you of some length which I
short notice I had of it, the tediousness of
nable interruptions make it doubtful

The Founding Fathers

JAMES MADISON

A Biography in His Own Words

VOLUME 2

Edited by
MERRILL D. PETERSON

JOAN PATERSON KERR
Picture Editor

NEWSWEEK
New York

ISBN: Clothbound Edition 0-88225-049-3; ISBN: Deluxe Edition 0-88225-050-7
Library of Congress Catalog Card Number 72-92142
Copyright © 1974 by Newsweek, Inc.
All rights reserved. Printed and bound in the United States of America.
Endpapers: Madison to Thomas Jefferson, March 18, 1787;
SOL FEINSTONE COLLECTION, DAVID LIBRARY OF THE AMERICAN REVOLUTION, WASHINGTON CROSSING, PA.

The War of 1812 occurred when Madison was President. An 1813 map records some naval battles.

Chapter 6

To the Revolution of 1800

The contest over the Jay Treaty was the opening gun in the presidential campaign of 1796. It shattered whatever illusions of concord remained in the nation's councils, made political passion a virtue, and split the parties into warring camps. Caught up in the conflict, Madison was nevertheless appalled by it. As long as Washington was President, such was the veneration accorded him that partisanship was not likely to run to violence; but he would soon retire and with him would go the last force for unity. John Adams was the Federalist heir apparent, though Hamilton contested the succession with his favorite, Thomas Pinckney. The Republican candidacy was thrust upon Jefferson by Madison and his friends. Jefferson had wanted Madison himself—"the greatest man in the world"—to run, but Madison would not think of it. Jefferson was older, more popular, and less scarred by the political wars. Besides, Madison intended to retire to Montpelier with his charming bride. The campaign was heated, not between the candidates but between their followers, and the outcome was still uncertain when Madison returned to Congress. As the votes came in, he reported the probable result to Jefferson.

Phila. Decr. 19. 1796

The returns from N. Hampshire Vermont, S.C. & Georga. are still to come in, & leave the event of the Election in some remaining uncertainty. It is but barely possible that Adams may fail of the highest number. It is highly probable, tho' not absolutely certain, that Pinkney will be third only on the list. You must prepare yourself therefore to be summoned to the place Mr. Adams now fills. I am aware of the objections arising from the inadequateness of the importance of the place to the sacrifices you would be willing to make to a greater prospect of fulfilling the patriotic wishes of your friends; and from the

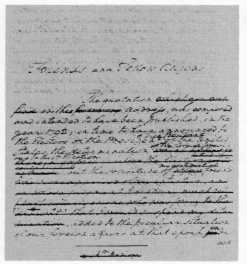

*Draft of Washington's Farewell
Address incorporating Madison's
suggestions and corrections*

irksomeness of being at the head of a body whose sentiments are at present so little in unison with your own. But it is expected that as you had made up your mind to obey the call of your country, you will let it decide on the particular place where your services are to be rendered. It may even be said, that as you submitted to the election knowing the contingency involved in it, you are bound to abide by the event whatever it may. On the whole it seems *essential* that you should not refuse the station which is likely to be your lot. There is reason to believe also that your neighbourhood to Adams may have a valuable effect on his councils particularly in relation to our external system. You know that his feelings will not enslave him to the example of his predecessor. It is certain that his censures of our paper system & the intrigues at New York for setting P [Pinckney] above him have fixed an enmity with the British faction. Nor should it pass for nothing, that the true interest of New England particularly requires reconciliation with France as the road to her commerce. Add to the whole that he is said to speak of you now in friendly terms and will no doubt be soothed by your acceptance of a place subordinate to him. It must be confessed however that all these calculations, are qualified by his political principles and prejudices. But they add weight to the obligation from which you must not withdraw yourself.

Madison's plea was quite unnecessary. If he must serve, Jefferson would prefer the Vice Presidency. "The second office . . . is honorable and easy, the first is but splendid misery." On December 17 he had written to Madison of his long friendship with Adams and said that in the case of a tie vote the choice should go to the New Englander. Moderate Federalists were soothed by the letter, which Madison quietly circulated in Philadelphia, while High Federalists angrily charged Jefferson with hypocrisy and deception. Meanwhile, Jefferson wrote a warm congratulatory letter to Adams, then worried over it lest his expressions of magnanimity and cordiality be disbelieved or convey more than he intended. He finally sent it under cover of his answer to Madison, instructing him to forward or intercept the epistle as he thought best. "If Mr. Adams can be induced to administer the government on its true principles, and to relinquish his bias to an English constitution," Jefferson said, "it is to be considered whether it would not be on the whole for the public good to come to a good understanding with him as to future elections. He is perhaps the only sure barrier against Hamilton's getting in." Madison, always cool to Adams, took alarm at the suggestion of a coalition between moderate Federalists and Republicans and shrewdly suppressed Jefferson's overture.

Philada. Jany. 15. 1797.

The last mail brought me your favor of Jany. 1. inclosing an unsealed one for Mr. A. & submitting to my discretion the eligibility of delivering it. In exercising this delicate trust I have felt no small anxiety, arising by no means however from an apprehension that a free exercise of it could be in collision with your real purpose but from a want of confidence in myself, & the importance of a wrong judgment in the case. After the best consideration I have been able to bestow, I have been led to suspend the delivery of the letter, till you should have an opportunity of deciding on the sufficiency or insufficiency of the following reasons.   1. It is certain that Mr. Adams, on his coming to this place, expressed to different persons a respectful cordiality towards you, & manifested a sensibility to the candid manner in which your friends had in general conducted the opposition to him. And it is equally known that your sentiments towards him personally have found their way to him in the most conciliating form. This being the state of things between you, it deserves to be considered whether the idea of bettering it is not outweighed by the possibility of changing it for the worse. 2. There is perhaps a general air on the letter which betrays the difficulty of your situation in writing it, and it is uncertain what the impression might be resulting from this appearance. 3. It is certain that Mr. A. is fully apprized of the trick aimed at by his pseudo-friends of N.Y. and there may be danger of his suspecting in memento's on that subject, a wish to make this resentment an instrument for avenging that of others.... 4. May not what is said of "the sublime delights of riding in the storm &c." be misconstrued into a reflexion on those who have no distaste to the helm at the present crisis? You know the temper of Mr. A. better than I do: but I have always conceived it to be rather a ticklish one.   5. The tenderness due to the zealous & active promoters of your election, makes it doubtful whether their anxieties & exertions ought to be depreciated by any thing implying the unreasonableness of them. I know that some individuals who have deeply committed themselves, & probably incurred the political enmity at least of the P. elect, are already sore on this head. 6. Considering the probability that Mr. A.s course of administration may force an opposition to it from the Republican quarter, & the general uncertainty of the posture which our affairs may take, there may be real embarrassments from giving written possession to him, of the degree of compliment & confidence which your personal delicacy & friendship have suggested.

I have ventured to make these observations, because I am sure you will equally appreciate the motive & the matter of them; and because I do not view them as inconsistent with the duty & policy of cultivating Mr. Adam's favorable dispositions, and giving a fair start to his Executive career.

The sequel may be briefly told. War with France threatened the Adams administration at its start. The French were now attacking American commerce; Monroe had been angrily recalled by Washington; and diplomatic relations between the two countries were near

collapse. At the time of his inauguration Adams broached to Jefferson the plan of a bipartisan commission to France. Madison was the key to the plan. Would he go to France? Jefferson asked him, and he declined. Doubtless his own personal plans were too well settled to be laid aside for an arduous mission abroad. Even if this were not so, political considerations touching the independence of the Republican party would have led him to the same decision. And had this decision been different, the Hamiltonians in Adams's Cabinet would have vetoed Madison. Thus the spirit of conciliation quickly vanished. Madison's thoughts had turned to home and farm. He wrote to his father as he was about to leave Philadelphia.

> Philada. March 12. 1797
>
> I wrote you by the last mail, and add this by Mr. Jefferson. Lest my last should by any possibility have miscarried, I repeat my request that my name may not be suffered to get on the Poll for the County election. If Mr. Jefferson should call & say any thing to counteract my determination, I hope it will be regarded as merely expressive of his own wishes on the subject, & that it will not be allowed to have the least effect. In declining to go into the Assembly, should there really be a disposition to send me there I am sincere & inflexible. I hope I shall hear from you by the next mail, on the subject of Mordecai & the horses; being extremely anxious now to be on the journey, especially as we are to make visits to Berkeley & Fredk on the way home. At present the roads are made bad by a snow succeeded by rain which has nearly carried it off: but the winds of March will soon put them in order. If the same weather should have happened with you, it will have been a fair opportunity for sowing the Clover seed I sent, & which I hope got to hand in time for the purpose. The greater part of what I sent was purchased for a vessel intended to sail last fall, & cost me 15 dollrs. which with freight &c will exceed the Richmond price. I really think it was an error to be deterred by that price, considering the immense importance of the article, especially in laying a foundation for a meliorating plan of husbandry. The proper remedy for such a disappointment, I am told by a very experienced & intelligent farmer of this neighbourhood, is to sow in the fall on the stubble of the wheat or rye. He says this is his practice whenever he cannot get seed for spring sowing the fields, or when the seed does not take effect, & that the protection & putrefaction of the stuble, ensures a full crop the following year, so that there is no other loss,

The thirty-six gun Philadelphia *(left) was constructed for the quasi war with France during the administration of John Adams (above in an engraving by H. Houston).*

213

Page from the Madison family Bible
recording death of brother Ambrose

than the first fall pasture. I consider this as a valuable hint, to beginners, as it doubles the chance of getting Clover into a rotation.

You will see by the inclosed paper that the last accts. from Paris respecting the negociations for peace & the temper of France towards this Country, are not favorable. This resentment is the fruit of the British Treaty, which many of its zealous advocates begin now to acknowledge was an unwise & unfortunate measure. The accounts are not authentic, & probably not accurate; but coming through so many different channels they are thought to be true in substance.

So long engaged in public life, Madison had little practical knowledge of farming; but with other enlightened men of his time he had become a student of scientific agriculture, the principles of which he would apply to his own lands with considerable success. After the death of his younger brother Ambrose in 1793, the responsibility for management of the family estate fell increasingly to Madison. It was a large estate of some ten thousand acres (half of that being the Montpelier property), which together with approximately one hundred slaves would descend outright to Madison at his father's death. Grain had replaced tobacco as the main cash crop in the Piedmont; so long as armies marched in Europe and American carriers sailed the Atlantic, farming was profitable.

Madison put some of the profits into remodeling Montpelier. A portico of Jefferson's design was added and the entire house was elegantly finished. Dolley Madison presided over the hospitality of the mansion. A British diplomat, Sir Augustus Foster, visited Montpelier in 1807 when Madison was Secretary of State and described her as "a very handsome woman and tho' an uncultivated mind and fond of gossiping, was so perfectly good-tempered and good-humored that she rendered her husband's house as far as depended on her agreeable to all parties." Recalling the visit years later, Foster left this description (not always accurate) of the plantation.

"Notes on the U.S.A." [1833–35]

His house stands upon the Southwest Mountains, as they are called—a range of hills parallel to the Blue Ridge, and about twenty miles removed from it. The house has a fine view of the Ridge and of a well wooded plain that lies in front of it from whence the ascent is so gradual that the house scarcely appears to be upon an elevation. There is a portico to it of the plainest and most massive order of architecture, but which Palladio gives as a specimen of the Tuscan. Mr. Madison himself superintended the building which he had executed by the hands of common workmen to whom he prescribed the proportions to be observed. It is of brick which requires and is intended to be plastered. It occupies about a third part of the length of the house, being forty-seven feet wide, and together with its pediments it is as high as the house, viz., forty feet. There are four columns to this portico, of common bricks diminishing from a third, and having bases as well as plinths....

Mr. Madison has about ten or twelve hundred acres of land at this place which is called Montpellier, and as, from his situation in the republic, he was obliged to be often absent from home, he was under the necessity of trusting to his overseer a great deal. The latter had £60 Virginia currency of £48 sterling per annum, and was furnished with lodging and everything he or his family could want. Mr. Madison assured me that after providing for this overseer, clothing his Negroes, and deducting the expences for repairs, the profits which he derived from the estate did not exceed the overseer's pay.... The expence of a Negro he estimated at twenty-five or thirty dollars a year according to the situation, and you can only calculate, on an average, upon half the number of slaves being fit for service at any given time.

Great depredations are committed, and continue to be committed, unknown to the owners, in the vast extent of their forests, when they remain for a long while absent from their houses in the country. Tan yards being established in the smallest villages the owners of which employ people to go about barking the trees where they are least likely to be detected, and Mr. Madison assured me that for several years an overseer on a neighbouring property had been in the habit of breaking off the branches and tops of his pine trees in order to make lampblack (the smoke of burnt pines collected on canvas being the process employed) which he sold at a considerable profit.

There were wild turkeys in great numbers in the woods about Mr. Madison's place and I very much regretted not having brought my fowling piece as the Secretary of State had none to lend me. Mr. [Thomas] Macon, his brother-in-law [his younger sister Sarah's husband], lived but three miles off on an estate very prettily situated, and there were several other families scattered about in the neighbourhood. The Negro habitations are separate

Nineteenth-century engravings of a Blue Ridge vista (above) and the Madison family homestead

from the dwelling house both here and all over Virginia, and they form a kind of village as each Negro family would like, if they were allowed it, to live in a house by themselves. When at a distance from any town it is necessary they should be able to do all kind of handiwork; and, accordingly, at Montpellier I found a forge, a turner's shop, a carpenter, and wheelwright. All articles too that were wanted for farming or the use of the house were made on the spot, and I saw a very well constructed waggon that had just been completed. The slaves, however, are unwilling to make their own clothes, and during the Revolutionary War, it was very difficult to get them to spin or to card wool. Yet the cloth they did make was superior to the coarser English cloth because they threw the wool of best quality into the stuff in which the English use the worst. The Negro women too preferred by a great deal working in the fields to spinning and sewing. They appeared to me to be a happy thoughtless race of people when under a kind master as was the Secretary of State.

There are some very fine woods about Montpellier, but no pleasure grounds, though Mr. Madison talks of some day laying out space for an English park, which he might render very beautiful from the easy graceful descent of his hills into the plains below. The ladies, however, whom I have known in Virginia, like those of Italy generally speaking, scarcely even venture out of their houses to walk or to enjoy beautiful scenery. A high situation from whence they can have an extensive prospect is their delight and in fact the heat is too great in these latitudes to allow of such English tastes to exist in the same degree at least as in the mother country. A pleasure ground, too, to be kept in order, would in fact be very expensive, and all hands are absolutely wanted for the plantation. Great estates, and consequently great wealth were, it is true, in former days by no means uncommon in Virginia, and I have heard of a Mr. Carter who possessed eighty thousand acres, but the abolition of entails has nearly ruined them all. Many hard cases occurred after the act...was passed for the purpose in 1776, among which I was told by Mr. [John] Randolph of one that was in fact a great act in injustice on the part of Colonel Van, who, having received an estate entailed in 1775, took advantage of the act of the following year,

Guests at Montpelier commented upon the life of the slaves and noted the abundance of wild turkeys.

The Peaks of Otter, two mountains in the Blue Ridge to the south and west of Montpelier, typified the Virginia countryside Madison loved.

and left it away from his sisters to his widow who married again and left the rightful heiresses penniless. At the present day estates are very much subdivided and I believe that even so late as the commencement of the century nobody could be pointed out as possessed of twenty-five thousand acres.

On descending from Mr. Madison's I measured a chestnut tree that was eighteen feet in circumference and I saw several most beautiful umbrella magnolias of which the fruit makes an agreeable bitter that mixed in wine is considered a wholesome draft in hot weather.

It is a very delightful ride of twenty-eight miles from Montpellier to ... Mr. Jefferson's seat at Monticello, the road lying at the foot of the Southwest Ridge.

For nearly a year following Adams's inauguration in 1797, Madison succeeded in placing himself *hors de combat.* The political scene became irresistible by 1798, however. In Madison's opinion, the Adams administration from its beginning had put the nation on a collision course with France. Foreign Minister Talleyrand and the Directory were not blameless; they had decided to follow the British example toward America's neutral commerce and had petulantly rebuffed Monroe's successor as Minister to the French court, Charles C. Pinckney. But Adams was the principal aggressor. Where he might have soothed, he provoked the French; where he might have checked the anglophile Federalists, he entered into their schemes and fastened an insane "war system" on the nation. Madison traced this criminal folly to Adams's apostasy from the principles of 1776, his adulation of the English constitution, and his contempt for the French Revolution. Not only was Adams to blame, but that blame was fundamentally a matter of antirepublican or "monarchical" principle. Madison voiced his opinion to Monroe after the President's saber-rattling speech to Congress in November, 1797.

217

[Montpelier,] Decr. 17. 97

I have not recd. a line from Philada. on the subject of the Speech, or indeed on any other. To me no explanation of the phenomenon is necessary, having been on the ground for observing the progressive apostasy from the principles of our Revolution & Governments, which marked the period of your absence. If events should not be unpropitious to the Monarchical party, you may prepare yourself for still more wonderful indications of its spirit & views. Those who tolerate at present the fashionable sentiments, will soon be ready to embrace & avow them. The active characters who promoted Mr. A. to his station, knowing him to be what he is, can not at bottom have been much averse to his political tenets, and will find in the spirit of party & in personal attachments & animosities, sufficient motives to go all lengths with him. Let us hope however that the tide of evil is nearly at its flood, and that it will ebb back to the true mark of which it has overpassed.

A few months later, in a letter to Jefferson, Madison made an interesting comparison between Adams and George Washington.

[Montpelier, February 18 or 19, 1798]

I am glad to find the public opinion to be taking the turn you describe on the subject of arming. For the public opinion alone can now save us from the rash measures of our hot-heated Executives; it being evident from some late votes of the House of Reps. . . . that a majority there as well as in the Senate are ready to go as far as the controul of their Constituents will permit. There never was perhaps a greater contrast between two characters, than between those of the present President & of his predecessor, altho' it is the boast & prop of the present, that he treads in the steps of his predecessor. The one cool considerate & cautious, the other headlong and kindled into flame by every spark that lights on his passions: the one ever scrutinizing into the public opinion, and ready to follow where he could not lead it: the other insulting it by the most adverse sentiments & pursuits: W. a hero in the field, yet overweighing every danger in the Cabinet. A. without a single pretension to the character of Soldier, a perfect Quixotte as a Statesman: the former cheif Magistrate pursuing peace every where with

French Foreign Minister Talleyrand

sincerity, tho' mistaking the means; the latter taking as much pains to get into war, as the former took to keep out of it. The contrast might be pursued into a variety of other particulars—the policy of the one in shunning connections with the arrangements of Europe, of the other in holding out the U.S. as a makeweight in its Balances of power: the avowed exultation of W. in the progress of liberty every where, & his eulogy on the Revolution & people of France posterior even to the bloody reign & fate of Robespierre—the open denunciations by Adams of the smallest disturbance of the antient discipline order & tranquility of Despotism, &c &c &c.

In the spring of 1798, the XYZ Affair exploded on the country. The three-man commission Adams had sent to France reported that Talleyrand, through his agents (identified only as X, Y, and Z in the dispatches), had demanded a loan and a bribe as the price of treating. Adams laid this nasty business before Congress in March, indignantly announced the end of negotiation, and called for enactment of bold new defense measures. Publication of the dispatches followed. Madison was shocked less by the venality of Talleyrand and his crew, which was not unexampled, than by their stupidity. He was also dismayed by the Federalists' calculated use of this pretext to annihilate the Republicans at home and to ally the country with Britain in war on France. That this was the plan became clearer as Congress laid new taxes, raised a provisional army (with Hamilton second-in-command to Washington), spread delusory fears of French subversion and invasion, enacted the repressive Alien and Sedition Acts, annulled the 1778 treaties of commerce and alliance with France, and embarked upon an undeclared naval war with that power. Several letters to Jefferson that spring charted Madison's reaction to events in Philadelphia.

[Montpelier,] Apl. 22 1798

My last was on the 15th. and acknowledged your preceding letters. I have since recd. that of the 12. under the same cover with the Gazettes; and the instructions & despatches, under a separate cover. The interruptions of company added to the calls of business have not left me time as yet to read over the whole of those papers. A glance at them, with the abstracts given of their intents, fully account for the state of astonishment produced in the public mind. And yet the circumstance that ought to astonish most perhaps, is the publication of them by the Ex. [executive] & Senate. Whatever probability there may be of individual corruption within the pale of the

French Govt. the evidence is certainly very insufficient to support such an attack on its reputation in the face of the world, even if we could separate the measure from its inevitable effect in blasting every chance of accomodation, if it should reach France before terms shall be finally settled. After this stroke in the politics of those two Branches of our Govt. no one who has not surrendered his reason, can believe them sincere in wishing to avoid extremities with the French Republic; to say nothing of the internal views to which they mean also to turn this extraordinary manoeuvre. There has not been time for any impressions on the public sentiment in this quarter, which the Despatches are calculated to make. The first will no doubt pretty much correspond with those made elsewhere; But the final impressions will depend on the further & more authentic developments which cannot be far behind, & wch. may by this time be arrived where you are. I find that in several places the people have turned out with their protests agst. the war measures urged by the Ex. Whether the proceeding will be general is what I cannot pretend to decide. In this County a Petition is to be handed about, which will I presume be pretty fully signed, if sufficiently circulated; unless the disaffected few among us, should be imbolded by the present crisis to circulate along with it, the impressions emanating from the Despatches wch. may stop the hands of wavering or cautious people. Altho' the thermo[me]ter on the mornings of the 15 & 16 inst: was at 31 & 32°. the fruit was not materially injured except in low situations, but having sunk during the night following to 24°. vegitation of every kind seemed to feel the blow. The Peaches & Cherries appear to [be] totally destroyed, and most of the apples. Even the young hickory leaves are in considerable proportion compleatly killed. The weather has since been more natural to the season.

[Montpelier,] May 13, 1798

The successful use of the Despatches in kindling a flame among the people, and of the flame in extending taxes armies & prerogative, are solemn lessons which I hope will have their proper effect when the infatuation of the moment is over. The management of foreign relations appears to be the most susceptible of abuse, of all the trusts committed to a Government, because they can be

A letter Madison wrote a neighbor, trying to track down a pocket-money weighing scale he had lent

concealed or disclosed, or disclosed in such parts & at such times as will best suit particular views; and because the body of the people are less capable of judging & are more under the influence of prejudices, on that branch of their affairs, than of any other. Perhaps it is a universal truth that the loss of liberty at home is to be charged to provisions agst. danger real or pretended from abroad. . . . If he [Adams] finds it thus easy to play on the prepossessions of the people for their own Govt. agst. a foreign, we ought not to be disappointed if the same game should have equal success in the hands of the Directory. We have had little or no rain for a month, and the evil has been increased by much windy & cold weather. The Thermr. yesterday morning was at 38° and the frost such as to kill the leaves of tender trees in low situations. I hope now you will soon be released from the thorny seat in which you are placed, and that I shall not be disappointed of the pleasure of seeing you on your way. You must so arrange your time as to be able to ride a mile while with me to see a Threshing machine I have lately built on Martins place. It is worked & attended by five or six hands at most, and I think promises more for general use than all the other modifications. I shall not describe it, because your own inspection will so soon give you a more perfect idea of it.

The Alien and Sedition Acts, enacted at the height of the war hysteria, seemed to Madison, as to most Republicans, to be aimed at the destruction of the opposition party. The Sedition Act outlawed "any false, scandalous and malicious writing" against the government, Congress, or the President. Every Republican newspaper was threatened. The Alien Act gave the President power to expel all foreigners deemed "dangerous to the peace and safety of the United States." This was meant for Frenchmen and Irishmen, who were almost invariably allied with the Republican cause. A companion measure, the Naturalization Act, raised the period of residency for American citizenship from five to fourteen years. The alien bill was before the Senate when Madison vented his wrath to Jefferson.

[Montpelier,] May 20. 1798

The Alien bill proposed in the Senate is a monster that must for ever disgrace its parents. I should not have supposed it possible that such an one could have been engendered in either House, & still persuade myself, that it can not possibly be fathered by both. It is truly to be

*An act passed by the Fifth Congress
"respecting alien enemies" in 1798*

deplored that a standing army should be let in upon us by the absence of a few sound votes. It may however all be for the best. These addresses to the feelings of the people from their enemies, may have more effect in opening their eyes, than all the arguments addressed to their understandings by their friends. The President also seems to be co-operating for the same purpose. Every answer he gives to his addressers, unmasks more & more his principles & views. His language to the young men of Ph[il]a. is the most abominable & degrading that could fall from the lips of the first magistrate of an independent people, & particularly from a Revolutionary patriot. It throws some light on his meaning when he remarked to me, "that there was not a single principle the same in the American & French Revolutions".... The abolition of Royalty was it seems not one of his Revolutionary principles. Whether he always made this profession is best known to those who knew him in the year 1776. The turn of the elections in N.Y. is a proof that the late occurrences have increased the noise only & not the number of the Tory party.... I forgot to acknowledge the pamphlet containing the last despach from the Envoys .... It is evidently more in the forensic than Diplomatic stile and more likely in some of its reasonings to satisfy an American Jury, than the French Government.

When Jefferson stopped at Montpelier on his return from Philadelphia early in July, he was full of gloom yet somehow confident that the evils of war and taxes and oppressive legislation would draw forth the republican spirit of the people and produce their own remedy. But during the summer months he decided a more radical cure was needed. Because of the war party's hold on the federal government, this could only originate in the states. Apparently without consulting Madison, he drafted what became the Kentucky Resolutions of 1798. The resolutions introduced by Madison's old friend George Nicholas and adopted by the Kentucky legislature set forth the compact theory of the Union, declared the Alien and Sedition Acts unconstitutional, and, without going to the length of "nullification" as Jefferson had proposed, urged concerted state action for their repeal. Madison saw Jefferson's draft at Monticello in October and agreed to prepare similar resolutions for introduction in the Virginia assembly. A man of cooler judgment and a more cautious politician, Madison adhered to Jefferson's reasoning but steered clear of his bold conclusion: that in the case of federal usurpation of powers a nullification by the state authorities is "the rightful remedy." The Virginia Resolutions of 1798 simply declared the right and duty of the legislature to interpose its authority when in its opinion certain federal laws were unconstitutional and to call upon the sister states to join in securing their repeal. The resolutions were followed by an address, also of Madison's authorship, defending the action.

"Address to the People"
[January 23, 1799]

FELLOW-CITIZENS,—Unwilling to shrink from our representative responsibility, conscious of the purity of our motives, but acknowledging your right to supervise our conduct, we invite your serious attention to the emergency which dictated the subjoined resolutions....

It would be perfidious in those entrusted with the guardianship of the State sovereignty, and acting under the solemn obligation of the following oath, "I do swear that I will support the Constitution of the United States," not to warn you of encroachments which, though clothed with the pretext of necessity, or disguised by arguments of expediency, may yet establish precedents which may ultimately devote a generous and unsuspicious people to all the consequences of usurped power.

Encroachments springing from a government whose organization can not be maintained without the co-operation of the States, furnish the strongest excitements upon the State Legislatures to watchfulness, and impose upon them the strongest obligation to preserve unimpaired the line of partition....

Exhortations to disregard domestic usurpation, until foreign danger shall have passed, is an artifice which may be forever used, because the possessors of power, who are the advocates for its extension, can ever create national embarrassments, to be successively employed to soothe the people into sleep, whilst that power is swelling, silently, secretly, and fatally. Of the same character are insinuations of a foreign influence, which seize upon a laudable enthusiasm against danger from abroad, and distort it by an unnatural application, so as to blind your eyes against danger at home.

The sedition act presents a scene which was never expected by the early friends of the Constitution. It was then admitted that the State sovereignties were only diminished by powers specifically enumerated, or necessary to carry the specified powers into effect. Now, Federal authority is deduced from implication; and from the existence of State law, it is inferred that Congress possess a similar power of legislation; whence Congress will be endowed with a power of legislation in all cases whatsoever, and the States will be stripped of every right reserved, by the concurrent claims of a paramount Legislature.

The sedition act is the offspring of these tremendous pretensions, which inflict a deathwound on the sovereignty of the States....

It is vicious in the extreme to calumniate meritorious public servants; but it is both artful and vicious to arouse the public indignation against calumny in order to conceal usurpation. Calumny is forbidden by the laws, usurpation by the Constitution. Calumny injures individuals, usurpation, States. Calumny may be redressed by the common judicatures; usurpation can only be controlled by the act of society. Ought usurpation, which is most mischievous, to be rendered less hateful by calumny, which, though injurious, is in a degree less pernicious?

RESOLUTIONS

OF

VIRGINIA AND KENTUCKY,

PENNED BY

MADISON AND JEFFERSON,

IN RELATION TO THE

ALIEN AND SEDITION LAWS:

AND

DEBATES

IN THE

HOUSE OF DELEGATES OF VIRGINIA,

IN DECEMBER, 1798,

ON THE SAME.

RICHMOND:
PUBLISHED BY ROBERT I. SMITH.
Samuel Shepherd & Co. Printers.
1832.

*Title page to a later publication
of the Virginia and Kentucky
Resolutions in opposition to the
Alien and Sedition Acts of 1798*

But the laws for the correction of calumny were not defective. Every libellous writing or expression might receive its punishment in the State courts, from juries summoned by an officer, who does not receive his appointment from the President, and is under no influence to court the pleasure of Government, whether it injured public officers or private citizens. Nor is there any distinction in the Constitution empowering Congress exclusively to punish calumny directed against an officer of the General Government; so that a construction assuming the power of protecting the reputation of a citizen officer will extend to the case of any other citizen, and open to Congress a right of legislation in every conceivable case which can arise between individuals....

... Remember that precedents once established are so much positive power; and that the nation which reposes on the pillow of political confidence, will sooner or later end its political existence in a deadly lethargy. Remember, also, that it is to the press mankind are indebted for having dispelled the clouds which long encompassed religion, for disclosing her geniune lustre, and disseminating her salutary doctrines.

The sophistry of a distinction between the liberty and the licentiousness of the press is so forcibly exposed in a late memorial from our late envoys to the Minister of the French Republic, that we here present it to you in their own words:

"The genius of the Constitution, and the opinion of the people of the United States, cannot be overruled by those who administer the Government. Among those principles deemed sacred in America, among those sacred rights considered as forming the bulwark of their liberty, which the Government contemplates with awful reverence and would approach only with the most cautious circumspection, there is no one of which the importance is more deeply impressed on the public mind than the liberty of the press. That this *liberty* is often carried to excess; that it has sometimes degenerated into *licentiousness,* is seen and lamented, *but the remedy has not yet been discovered. Perhaps it is an evil inseparable from the good with which it is allied; perhaps it is a shoot which cannot be stripped from the stalk without wounding vitally the plant from which it is torn. However desirable those measures might be which might*

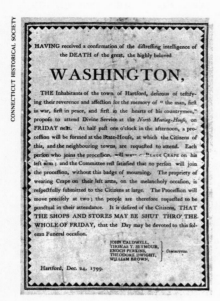

HAVING received a confirmation of the distressing intelligence of the DEATH of the great, the highly beloved

WASHINGTON,

THE Inhabitants of the town of Hartford, desirous of testifying their reverence and affection for the memory of " the man, first in war, first in peace, and first in the hearts of his countrymen," propose to attend Divine Service at the *North Meeting-House*, on FRIDAY next. At half past one o'clock in the afternoon, a procession will be formed at the State-House, at which the Citizens of this, and the neighbouring towns, are requested to attend. Each person who joins the procession, will wear a BLACK CRAPE on his left arm; and the Committee rest satisfied that no person will join the procession, without this badge of mourning. The propriety of wearing Crape on their left arms, on the melancholy occasion, is respectfully submitted to the Citizens at large. The Procession will move precisely at two; the people are therefore requested to be punctual in their attendance. It is desired of the Citizens, THAT THE SHOPS AND STORES MAY BE SHUT THRO' THE WHOLE OF FRIDAY, that the Day may be devoted to this solemn Funeral occasion.

JOHN CALDWELL,
THOMAS Y. SEYMOUR,
ENOCH PERKINS,   } *Committee.*
THEODORE DWIGHT,
WILLIAM BROWN,

Hartford, Dec. 24, 1799.

Broadside issued in Hartford, Connecticut, on death of George Washington on December 14, 1799

correct *without enslaving the press, they have never yet been devised in America.* No regulations exist which enable the Government to suppress whatever calumnies or invectives any individual may choose to offer to the public eye, or to punish such calumnies and invectives otherwise than by a legal prosecution in courts which are alike open to all who consider themselves as injured."

As if we were bound to look for security from the personal probity of Congress amidst the frailties of man, and not from the barriers of the Constitution, it has been urged that the accused under the sedition act is allowed to prove the truth of the charge. This argument will not for a moment disguise the unconstitutionality of the act, if it be recollected that opinions as well as facts are made punishable, and that the truth of an opinion is not susceptible of proof. By subjecting the truth of opinion to the regulation, fine, and imprisonment, to be inflicted by those who are of a different opinion, the free range of the human mind is injuriously restrained. . . .

All the preceding arguments, arising from a deficiency of constitutional power in Congress, apply to the alien act; and this act is liable to other objections peculiar to itself. If a suspicion that aliens are dangerous constitute the justification of that power exercised over them by Congress, then a similar suspicion will justify the exercise of a similar power over natives; because there is nothing in the Constitution distinguishing between the power of a State to permit the residence of natives and of aliens. It is, therefore, a right originally possessed, and never surrendered, by the respective States, and which is rendered dear and valuable to Virginia . . . because her peculiar situation renders the easy admission of artisans and laborers an interest of vast importance.

But this bill contains other features, still more alarming and dangerous. It dispenses with the trial by jury; it violates the judicial system; it confounds legislative, executive, and judicial powers; it punishes without trial; and it bestows upon the President despotic power over a numerous class of men. Are such measures consistent with our constitutional principles? And will an accumulation of power so extensive in the hands of the Executive, over aliens, secure to natives the blessings of republican liberty?

If measures can mould governments, and if an uncontrolled power of construction is surrendered to those who administer them, their progress may be easily foreseen, and their end easily foretold. A lover of monarchy, who opens the treasures of corruption by distributing emolument among devoted partisans, may at the same time be approaching his object and deluding the people with professions of republicanism. He may confound monarchy and republicanism, by the art of definition. He may varnish over the dexterity which ambition never fails to display, with the pliancy of language, the seduction of expediency, or the prejudices of the times; and he may come at length to avow that so extensive a territory as that of the United States can only be governed by the energies of monarchy; that it cannot be defended, except by standing armies; and that it cannot be united except by consolidation.

Measures have already been adopted which may lead to these consequences. They consist—

In fiscal systems and arrangements, which keep a host of commercial and wealthy individuals imbodied, and obedient to the mandates of the treasury.

In armies and navies, which will, on the one hand, enlist the tendency of man to pay homage to his fellow-creature who can feed or honor him; and on the other, employ the principle of fear, by punishing imaginary insurrections, under the pretext of preventive justice.

In the extensive establishment of a volunteer militia, rallied together by a political creed, armed and officered

War on the high seas actually broke out between France and the United States in 1798. The American Constellation *captured the French frigate* L'Insurgente *in February, 1799, causing great excitement.*

IRVING S. OLDS COLLECTION, NEW-YORK HISTORICAL SOCIETY

by executive power, so as to deprive the States of their constitutional right to appoint militia officers, and to place the great bulk of the people in a defenceless situation.

In swarms of officers, civil and military, who can inculcate political tenets tending to consolidation and monarchy both by indulgencies and severities; and can act as spies over the free exercise of human reason.

In destroying, by the sedition act, the responsibility of public servants and public measures to the people, thus retrograding towards the exploded doctrine "that the administrators of the Government are the masters, and not the servants, of the people," and exposing America, which acquired the honour of taking the lead among nations towards perfecting political principles, to the disgrace of returning first to ancient ignorance and barbarism. . . .

In transferring to the Executive important legislative powers; particularly the power of raising armies, and borrowing money without limitation of interest.

In restraining the freedom of the press, and investing the Executive with legislative, executive, and judicial powers, over a numerous body of men.

And, that we may shorten the catalogue, in establishing, by successive precedents, such a mode of construing the Constitution as will rapidly remove every restraint upon Federal power.

Let history be consulted; let the man of experience reflect; nay, let the artificers of monarchy be asked what further materials they can need for building up their favorite system.

These are solemn but painful truths; and yet we recommend it to you not to forget the possibility of danger from without, although danger threatens us from within. Usurpation is indeed dreadful; but against foreign invasion, if that should happen, let us rise with hearts and hands united, and repel the attack with the zeal of freemen who will strengthen their title to examine and correct domestic measures, by having defended their country against foreign aggression.

Pledged as we are, fellow-citizens, to these sacred engagements, we yet humbly and fervently implore the Almighty Disposer of events to avert from our land war and usurpation, the scourges of mankind; to permit our

EXPOSITION
OF THE
FEDERAL CONSTITUTION.

CONTAINED IN THE
REPORT
OF THE COMMITTEE OF THE
VIRGINIA HOUSE OF DELEGATES;
TO WHOM WERE COMMITTED
THE PROCEEDINGS,
OF SUNDRY OF THE OTHER STATES,
IN ANSWER TO THE
RESOLUTIONS OF THE GENERAL ASSEMBLY,
Of the 21st Day of December, 1798,
COMMONLY CALLED
MADISON'S REPORT.

TO WHICH IS SUBJOINED
A SERIES OF PAPERS UNDER THE SIGNATURE OF
HAMPDEN,
(Originally published in the Richmond Enquirer of June, 1819.)
BEING A CRITIQUE ON THE OPINION
OF THE
SUPREME COURT OF THE UNITED STATES,
IN THE
CASE OF THE BANK LAW.

RICHMOND, VA.
PRINTED BY THOMAS RITCHIE.
1819.

A reprint of Madison's 1799 report justifying the Virginia Resolutions

fields to be cultivated in peace; to instil into nations the love of friendly intercourse; to suffer our youth to be educated in virtue, and to preserve our morality from the pollution invariably incident to habits of war; to prevent the laborer and husbandman from being harassed by taxes and imposts; to remove from ambition the means of disturbing the commonwealth; to annihilate all pretexts for power afforded by war; to maintain the Constitution; and to bless our nation with tranquillity, under whose benign influence we may reach the summit of happiness and glory, to which we are destined by *nature* and *nature's God.*

In thus rushing to the defense of civil liberties, the Republican leaders ran the risk of provoking a crisis of union. This was not their intention. Their appeal to states' rights was only a tactic in the larger strategy of liberty; and they were pursuing, as Jefferson said, "a political resistance for political effect." The effect was slow in coming. The Sedition Act terrorized public opinion. Vigorously enforced by the administration with the aid of compliant judges and juries, it decimated the Republican press and clogged political avenues of change. Petitions for its repeal poured into Congress, with no other effect than to stiffen Federalist resolution. And several state legislatures, also Federalist dominated, vindicated the Alien and Sedition Acts in rebuff of the Virginia and Kentucky Resolutions. Jefferson concluded that the two states should renew their protests. Writing to Madison in midsummer, he even suggested that the states announce their intention, should the usurpations persist, of seceding from the Union.

This was too much for Madison. On a sultry Sunday afternoon he rode to Monticello and with little difficulty calmed his friend's feelings. Jefferson receded from the threat of secession, "not only in deference to his [Madison's] judgment, but because we should never think of separation but for repeated and enormous violations, so these, when they occur, will be cause enough of themselves." Kentucky, in 1799, briefly repeated its earlier protest. The Virginia assembly, where Madison was once again a delegate, adopted a lengthy report from his pen expounding the theory of federal union and vindicating human rights. Meanwhile, the initial cause of the controversy, the crisis with France, was on its way to a peaceful settlement, John Adams having broken with the High Federalists and dispatched a new trio of envoys to France. Jefferson was back in Philadelphia when Madison wrote to him from Richmond.

Richmond Decr. 29. 1799

My promise to write to you before your leaving Albemarle was defeated by a dysenteric attack which laid me

William Branch Giles

up for about a week, and which left me in a state of debility not yet thoroughly removed. My recovery has been much retarded by the job of preparing a vindication of the Resolutions of last Session agst. the replies of the other States, and the sophistries from other quarters. The Committee made their report a few days ago, which is now in the press and stands the order of the day for thursday next. A sett of Resolutions proposed by Mr. [William B.] Giles, instructing the Senators to urge the repeal of the unconstl. acts, the disbanding of the army, and the proper arrangement of the Militia, are also in the press and stand the order of the same day for the same Committee. It is supposed that both these papers, the latter perhaps with some modifications, will go through the H. of Delegates. The Senate, owing to inattention & casualties, is so composed as to render the event there not a little uncertain. . . . There is a report here that the Legislature of N. Carolina now in Session, have voted the Resolutions of Virginia under their table. The report is highly improbable, and I do not believe it. But it is impossible to calculate the progress of delusion, especially in a State where it is said to be under systematic management, and where there is so little either of system or exertion opposed to it. We had a narrow escape yesterday from an increase of pay to the members, which would have been particularly unseasonable & injurious both within & without the State. It was rejected on the third reading by a small majority; and was so much a favorite, with the distant members particularly, that I fear it has left them in rather an ill humour.

The late course of foreign events has probably made the same impression every where. If it should not render France less anxious to meet our advances, its good effects will be felt every way. If our Executive & their Envoys be sincere in their pacific objects, it will perhaps supply by their increased anxiety what may be lost on the other side. But there can be little confidence after what has been seen, that the negociation would be influenced by this temper of the Envoys, instead of that which perverted it in the hands of their predecessors. This possibility of failure in the diplomatic experiment, will present the most specious obstacle to an immediate discharge of the army. It would be useful for the Assembly to know how this matter is viewed where you are.

Richmond Jany. 4. 1800.
My last covered a copy of the Report on the Resolutions of last year. I now inclose a copy of certain resolutions moved by Mr. Giles, to which he means to add an instruction on the subject of the intercource law which has been so injurious to the price of our Tobo [tobacco]. It is not improbable that the Resolutions when taken up, may undergo some mollifications in the spirit & air of them. The Report has been under debate for two days. The attacks on it have turned chiefly on an alledged inconsistency between the comment now made, and the arguments of the last Session, and on the right of the Legislature to interfere in any manner with denunciations of the measures of the Genl. Govt. The first attack has been parried by an amendment admitting that different constructions may have been entertained of the term "States" as "parties" &c but that the sense relied on in the report must be concurred in by all. It is in fact concurred in by both parties. On examination of the debates of the last Session, it appears that both were equally inaccurate & inconsistent in the grounds formerly taken by them. The attack on the right of the Legislature to interfere by declarations of opinion will form a material point in the discussion. It is not yet known how far the opposition to the Report will be carried into detail.

THE PROVIDENTIAL DETECTION

A Federalist cartoon of 1800 shows a watchful eye and American eagle preventing Jefferson from making a burnt offering of the Constitution on an "Altar of Gallic Despotism."

Although the Sixth Congress, elected at the peak of the war frenzy, was overwhelmingly Federalist, all the signs in 1800 pointed to that "revolution of opinion" Jefferson and Madison had been awaiting for two years. In both Philadelphia and Richmond politicians were jockeying for position in the coming presidential contest. Republicans again united behind Jefferson, while Adams, in his bid for reelection, faced insurgency within the ranks. All the accumulated passion and fury of a decade of party conflict poured into the campaign; no one doubted that the outcome would determine the fate of republican government on the continent for a long time to come. Except within the Virginia Republican organization, Madison took little part in the campaign. He was in ill health and seems not to have stirred from Montpelier, having returned from Richmond early in the year.

Republicanism triumphed. By early December the electoral vote could be confidently predicted: 73 for Jefferson, 65 for Adams. Jefferson dashed off a letter to his running mate, Aaron Burr of New York, congratulating him on his election as Vice President. Unfortunately, as he soon discovered, Burr also received 73 electoral votes, which threw the choice into the House of Representatives where the Federalists were in control. (Prior to the Twelfth Amendment in 1804—the direct result of the electoral tie in 1800—ballots were cast only for President, the Vice Presidency going to the runner-up.) The Republicans had been on guard against just such a possibility, however remote. A Republican elector in some state would discard his vote for Burr, thereby preventing a tie with Jefferson. The result might have been secured in the Virginia "college of electors." But Burr had charged the Virginia Republicans with bad faith for failing to support him when he was second on the Republican ticket four years earlier. Madison, therefore, demanded a unanimous vote for the New Yorker in Virginia, being assured by Burr's friends that votes would be thrown away from him in New York or elsewhere. Burr failed to deliver on this promise to place Jefferson's election beyond hazard, and Republican electors north and south played Alphonse and Gaston to each other.

From the new capital on the Potomac, Jefferson informed Madison that "an absolute parity" between the Republican candidates seemed certain. "This has produced great dismay and gloom on the Republican gentlemen here, and equal exultation on the Federalists." Madison, in reply, shared his anxiety.

[Montpelier,] Jany. 10, 1801.

I find that the vote of Kentucky establishes the tie between the Repub: characters, and consequently throws the result into the hands of the H. of R. Desperate as some of the adverse party there may be, I can scarcely allow myself to believe that enough will not be found to frustrate the attempt to strangle the election of the people, and smuggle into the Chief Magistracy the choice creature of a faction. It would seem that every individual member, who has any standing or stake in society, or any portion of virtue or sober understanding must revolt at the tendency of such a manouvre. Is it possible that Mr. A[dams] shd. give his sanction to it if that should be made a necessary ingredient? Or that he would not hold it his duty or his policy, in case the present House should obstinately refuse to give effect to the Constn., to appoint, which he certainly may do before his office expires as early a day as possible, after that event, for the succeeding House to meet, and supply the omission. Should he disappt. a just expectation in either instance, it will be an omen, I think, forbidding the steps towards which you seem to be meditating. I would not wish to discourage any attentions which friendship, prudence, or benevolence may suggest in his behalf, but I think it not improper to remark, that I find him infinitely sunk in

YALE UNIVERSITY ART GALLERY

Aaron Burr, the Republican vice-presidential candidate in 1800, received the same number of electoral votes as did Jefferson.

By Yesterday's Mails.

Highly Important and Interesting.

PENNSYLVANIA.   PHILAD. FEB. 14.
BY EXPRESS.
WASHINGTON, Feb. 11, half past 3, afternoon.
ACCORDING to the rule of proceedings established by the House, they proceeded to the Senate Chamber, where (by Mr. *Nicholas* and Mr. *Rutledge*, the tellers on the part of the House, and Mr. *Wells* on the part of the Senate) the votes were counted and the result declared by the Vice-President, as follow:—

For THOMAS JEFFERSON,   73
    AARON BURR,   73
    JOHN ADAMS,   65
    C. C. PINCKNEY,   64
    JOHN JAY,   1

The tellers declared there was some informality in the votes of *Georgia*, but believing them to be the true ones, reported them as such.

The Vice-President then, in pursuance of the duty enjoined upon him, declared, that *Thomas Jefferson* and *Aaron Burr* being equal in the number of Votes, it remained for the House of Representatives to determine the choice.

The two Houses then separated, and the House of Representatives returned to their chamber, where seats had been previously prepared for the members of the Senate. A call of the members of the House, arranged according to States, was then made; upon which it appeared, that every member was present except Gen. *Sumpter*, who is unwell, and unable to attend. Mr. *Nicholson* of *Maryland*, was also unwell but attended and had a bed prepared for him in one of the committee rooms, to which place the ballot box was carried to him, by the tellers appointed on the part of the State.

The Columbian Centinel *of Boston reported the electoral deadlock.*

the estimation of all parties. The follies of his administration, the oblique stroke at his Predecessor in the letter to [Tench] Coxe ... are working powerfully agst. him, added to these causes is the pamphlet of H[amilton, an open *Letter Concerning the Public Conduct and Character of John Adams*] which, tho' its recoil has perhaps more deeply wounded the author, than the object it was discharged at, has contributed not a little to overthrow the latter staggering as he before was in the public esteem.

On the supposition of either event, whether of an interregnum in the Executive, or of a surreptitious intrusion into it, it becomes a question of the first order, what is the course demanded by the crisis. Will it be best to acquiesce in a suspension or usurpation of the Executive authority till the meeting of Congs. in Decr. next, or for Congs. to be summoned by a joint proclamation or recommendation of the two characters havg a majority of votes for President. My present judgment favors the latter expedient. The prerogative of convening the legislature must reside in one or other of them; and if both concur, must substantially include the requisite will. The intentions of the people would undoubtedly be pursued. And if, in reference to the Constn: the proceeding be not strictly regular, the irregularity will be less in form than any other adequate to the emergency; and will be in form only rather than substance; whereas the other remedies proposed are substantial violations of the will of the people, of the scope of the Constitution, and of the public order & interest. It is to be hoped however that all such questions will be precluded by a proper decision of nine States in the H. of R.

The Federalist scheme to force an interregnum or to elect Burr was at length defeated. On the thirty-sixth ballot in the House of Representatives, Jefferson was elected. Madison had agreed to become Secretary of State in any government Jefferson might head. He had no intention of changing his mind, though his own feeble health and the declining state of his seventy-seven-year-old father combined to give him pause. Near the end of February his father died, which delayed Madison's departure. He sent Jefferson his apologies, along with his opinion of Adams's wholesale appointment of Federalist judges in the final hours of his administration.

Inventory of the estate of Madison's father, who died in February, 1801

[Montpelier, February 28, 1801]

Your favor of the 1st. instant was to have been acknowledged a week ago, but the irregularity of the post occasioned by high waters has delayed it to the present opportunity. I have now to acknowledge your two subsequent ones of the 12th. & 19th. In compliance with the last, I had proposed to leave home in a few days, so as to be with you shortly after the 4th. of March. A melancholy occurrence has arrested this intention. My father's health for several weeks latterly seemed to revive, and we had hopes that the approach of milder seasons would still further contribute to keep him with us. A few days past however he became sensibly worse, and yesterday morning rather suddenly, tho' very qui[e]tly the flame of life went out. It is impossible for me now to speak of my movements with precision. Altho' the exact degree of agency devolving on me remains to be known, a crowd of indispensible attentions must necessarily be due from me. In this posture of things I can only say that I shall wait the return of this post after this reaches, by which I hope to learn whether your intended continuance at Washington will admit, and the state of things will require, my being there before you leave it. By this information I shall be governed, unless imperiously controuled by the circumstances here.

The conduct of Mr. A. is not such as was to have been wished or perhaps expected. Instead of smoothing the path for his successor, he plays into the hands of those who are endeavoring to strew it with as many difficulties as possible; and with this view does not manifest a very squeamish regard to the Constn. Will not his appts. to offices, not vacant actually at the time, even if afterwards vacated by acceptances of the translations, be null?

The result of the contest in the H. of R. was generally looked for in this quarter. It was thought not probable that the phalanx would hold out agst. the general revolt of its partizans out of doors & without any military force to abet usurpation. How fortunate that the latter has been witheld; and what a lesson to America & the world, is given by the efficacy of the public will when there is no army to be turned agst. it!

Chapter 7

Secretary of State

The city of Washington was but a decade young in 1801. Sprawled along the Potomac between Georgetown and Alexandria, the embryo capital of three thousand people boasted few of the amenities of civilization. Men scoffed at its pretensions and groaned under its discomforts. Two "shining objects" relieved the dreary scene: the President's House, gleaming under its coat of whitewash, and a mile and a half away, the boxlike torso of the unfinished Capitol, its north wing alone awkwardly dominating the summit of Capitol Hill. Settlements clustered around these cardinal points, which were connected by a treacherous roadway through forest and marsh, Pennsylvania Avenue. Good houses were scarce. The Madisons, arriving on May 1, first stayed with the President, and not until the succeeding fall were they permanently installed in a large new brick house two blocks to the east.

The entire staff of the State Department, which was located in the same executive quarter of the city, consisted of one chief clerk, seven clerks, and a messenger. The department had certain "home office" responsibilities —registration of patents, supervision of the census, custody of public documents, printing of the laws, and so on. But Madison quickly found, as had his predecessors, that foreign affairs were all-consuming. He had never set foot outside the United States—he never would—and he had no diplomatic experience; still, he was uniquely qualified for the post of Secretary of State. He had a clear conception of the national interest and understood the intricate relationship of policy objectives to the balance of forces both in the Atlantic world and at home. He possessed a good head for business and those personal qualities of quiet dignity, tactful reserve, and dogged perseverance that were wanted in diplomacy. Above all, he knew the mind of the President. In law and in practice the Chief Executive had full responsibility for the conduct of foreign affairs. Jefferson, even more than his predecessors, would be his own Secretary of State. In every previous case— that of Jefferson himself, of Edmund Randolph, and of Timothy Pickering—

this subordination of the office had produced conflict with the President. But in the case of Jefferson and Madison it would work beautifully because of the perfect friendship, harmony, and trust between them.

Coming into executive employment for the first time since he had served on the governor's council in Virginia more than twenty years before, Madison had little time for anything outside the line of official duty. Of course he entered into the social life of the village capital, over which Dolley Madison presided as the surrogate First Lady of the widower President; but he sharply curtailed his private correspondence and curbed the partisan feelings that had impelled him for so long in opposition. Jefferson, in his inaugural address, had appealed for an end to political fanaticism and a restoration of harmony and affection. "We are all republicans: we are all federalists." He had made it equally evident, however, that the Republicans came into power dedicated to reform. In the administration's attempt to strike a balance between reconciliation and reform, Madison's weight was generally thrown into the former scale. More than any other American statesman, he could claim to be both "federalist" and "republican," and with these credentials he became the leading voice of moderation in the President's Cabinet.

The first test of administration policy came on the matter of patronage. Republicans looking to reform called for wholesale removal of Federalist officeholders, while the reconcilers urged a moderate course. Madison, significantly, removed none of the Federalist clerks in his department, persuaded Jefferson to retain Rufus King as Minister to Great Britain, and gave little satisfaction to Republicans craving the spoils of office. His stance is suggested in a letter to the Virginia party leader, Wilson Cary Nicholas.

An 1808 print by William Birch shows the Capitol under construction, its two wings bridged by an eagle.

Washington July 10. 1801

I can not at so late a day acknowledge your two favors... without an explanation which I am sure your goodness will accept as an apology. Having brought with me to this place a very feeble state of health, and finding the mass of business in the Department, at all times considerable, swelled to an unusual size by sundry temporary causes; it became absolutely necessary to devote the whole of my time & pen to any public duties, and, consequently to suspend my private correspondence altogether, notwithstanding the arrears daily accumulating. To this resolution I have thus far adhered. I must now endeavor to make some atonement for the delay and your case is among the first that is suggested both by obligation & inclination.

That one of your letters which is confidential has been imparted to no person whatever. The P. O. Genl. continues in the hands of Col. H. [Joseph Habersham] who though not perhaps sufficiently in the views of the

An early engraving of Washington,
looking down Pennsylvania Avenue

Administration, is much respected personally, & is warmly espoused politically also by some of the purest and most weighty of our friends. It will be difficult to make a satisfactory arrangement for this Dept. that will not involve translations &c. which will prevent a real vacancy. Besides this I am inclined to believe that the P. would be afraid to draw on Virga. agst. competitions which wd. abound from other States. The Indivi[du]al spoken of by you would, as you must be well assured, be perfectly desired as an associate in the public business, on every consideration, unless it be that of robbing another important station of his services.

Little has occurred which you have not found in the Newspapers. The task of removing, and appointing officers, continues to embarrass the Ex. and agitate particular parts of the Union. The degree, the mode & the times of performing it, are often rendered the more perplexing by the discord of information & counsel received from different persons whose principles & views are the same. In Connecticut the fever & murmur of discontent at the exercise of this power is the greatest. The removal of [Elizur] Goodrich [the customs collector at New Haven] & appt. of a respectable Repubn. have produced a Remonstrance to the President in the strongest terms that decorum would tolerate. The spirit in that State is so perverse that it must be rectified by a peculiar mixture of energy and delicacy. The Secyship. of the Navy is still unfilled.

The prospect in foreign affairs was brighter than it had been for years. An uneasy *detente* prevailed with Britain, while a new treaty with France, known as the Convention of 1800, removed the immediate source of difficulty with that power. Writing to Jefferson as early as January, Madison had been optimistic.

Toussaint L'Ouverture, leader of the rebel blacks in Santo Domingo

[Montpelier,] Jany 10, 1801.
France has sufficiently manifested her friendly disposition, and what is more, seems to be duly impressed with the interest she has in being at peace with us. G.B., however intoxicated with her maritime ascendancy, is more dependent every day on our commerce for her resources, must for a considerable length of time look in a great degree to this Country, for bread for herself, and absolutely for all the necessaries for her islands. The prospect of a Northern Confederacy of neutrals cannot fail, in several ways, to inspire caution & management toward the U.S. especially as, in the event of war or interruption of commerce with the Baltic, the essential article of naval Stores can be sought here only. Besides these cogent motives to peace and moderation, her subjects will not fail to remind her of the great pecuniary pledge they have in this Country, and which under any interruption of peace of commerce with it, must fall under great embarrassments, if nothing worse.

After eight years of war, peace was in the offing in Europe. The preliminary articles of the Peace of Amiens would be signed in October. Hopes for smooth sailing were jarred, however, by rumors of Spain's retrocession of Louisiana to France. So long as that vast province—with the port of New Orleans and the Floridas to the east—remained in the hands of Spain, the United States was content. For these Spanish dominions must fall, like ripe fruit from the tree, whenever the Americans were ready for them. Moreover, under the terms of Thomas Pinckney's 1795 treaty with Spain, the Americans enjoyed free navigation of the Mississippi and the privileges of the port. But French possession of Louisiana, and possibly the Floridas too, was another matter, signaling the rebirth under Napoleonic auspices of French empire in the New World. Napoleon had already embarked on the reconquest of Santo Domingo, the richest of the French colonies, then in control of rebel blacks led by Toussaint L'Ouverture; and Louisiana was part of his grand design in North America. At first Jefferson and Madison refused to take alarm. If the bargain had in fact been made, Napoleon's plans were involved in so many difficulties that they might never materialize. The reconquest of Santo Domingo would not be easy work. Whether or not the Floridas were included in the cession was unknown, but without them Louisiana would be of doubtful value to France. And

France dared not risk confrontation with the United States on the Mississippi lest she find herself again at war in Europe. Considerations such as these lay behind the surprisingly mild instructions Madison gave to Robert R. Livingston, newly appointed Minister to France, in the fall. Although Livingston was to urge reasons against the cession, he should do nothing that would "unnecessarily irritate our future neighbors, or check the liberality which they may be disposed to exercise in relation to the trade and navigation through the mouth of the Mississippi."

In the negotiations that led to the Louisiana Purchase nearly twenty months later, Jefferson called the tune and Madison played it. How much he may have influenced Jefferson's moves is uncertain; but on the record his part was to press the American case on Louis Pichon, the French chargé d'affaires, who in turn transmitted every perturbation to Talleyrand in Paris. He was also to carry out Jefferson's policy in instructions to American ministers abroad. Jefferson struck a bold new course in April, 1802. In a letter addressed to Livingston but left open for the benefit of its courier, Pierre Dupont de Nemours, through whom its sentiments would be conveyed to the First Consul himself, Jefferson gave stern warning to France. "There is on the globe one single spot, the possessor of which is our natural and habitual enemy. It is New Orleans, through which must pass the produce of three-eights of our territory, and from its fertility it will ere long yield more than half our whole produce and contain more than half our inhabitants.... The day France takes possession of New Orleans fixes the sentence which is to restrain her forever within her low water mark. It seals the union of two nations who in conjunction can maintain exclusive possession of the ocean. From that moment we must marry ourselves to the British fleet and nation." While Jefferson flourished this thunderbolt, Madison wrote more officially to Livingston in Paris, mentioning for the first time the possibility of a purchase.

Louisiana planter's house near the sought-after port of New Orleans

Washington, May 1st. 1802

The Cession of Louisiana to France becomes daily more and more a source of painful apprehensions. Notwithstanding the Treaty of March 1801 [which confirmed the retrocession], and notwithstanding the general belief in France on the subject, and the accounts from St Domingo that part of the armament sent to that island were eventually destined for Louisiana, a hope was still drawn from your early conversations with Mr Talleyrand that the French Government did not mean to pursue the object. Since the receipt of your last communications, no hope remains but from the accumulating difficulties of going thro' with the undertaking, and from the conviction you may be able to impress, that it must have an instant and powerful effect in changing the relations between France and the United States. The change is obvious, and the more it can be developed in candid and friendly appeals to the reflections of the French Government, the more it will urge it to revise and abandon the project. A mere neighbourhood could not be friendly to the harmony which both countries have so much an interest in cherishing: but if a possession of the mouth of the Mississippi is to be added to other causes of discord, the worst events are to be apprehended. You will consequently spare no efforts that will consist with prudence and dignity, to lead the Councils of France to proper views of this subject, and to an abandonment of her present purpose. You will also pursue by prudent means the enquiry into the extent of the Cession, particularly whether it includes the Floridas as well as New Orleans; and endeavor to ascertain the price at which these, if included in the Cession, would be yielded to the United States. I cannot in the present state of things be more particular on this head, than to observe that in every view it would be a most precious acquisition, and that as far as the terms could be satisfied by charging on the acquisition itself, the restitutions, and other debts to American Citizens, great liberality would doubtless be indulged by this Government. The President wishes you to devote every attention to this object, and to be frequent and particular in your communications relating to it.

Some days later Madison wrote to Charles Pinckney, the Minister to Spain, to cover himself on that flank.

[Washington,] May 11th. 1802

We are still without a line from you since your arrival at Madrid, and feel an increasing solicitude to hear from you on the subject of Louisiana. The latest information from Paris has confirmed the fact that it was ceded by a Treaty prior to that of March 1801; and notwithstanding the virtual denial of the Cession in the early conversations between Mr Livingston and the [French] Minister of Foreign Relations, a refusal of any explanations at present, seems to admit that the Cession has taken place. Still there are chances of obtaining a reversal of the transaction. The repugnance of the United States to it is and will be pressed in a manner that cannot be without some effect. It is known that most of the French states-

Robert R. Livingston, a New York Republican, was Minister to France.

men best informed on the subject, disapprove of it. The pecuniary difficulties of the French Government must also be felt as a check; whilst the prospect of a protracted and expensive war in St. Domingo must form a very powerful obstacle to the execution of the project. The Counsels of England appear to have been torpid on this occasion. Whether it proceed from an unwillingness to risk a fresh altercation with France, or from a hope that such neighbourhood between France and United States would lead to collisions which might be turned to her advantage, is more than I can decide. The latter consideration might justly have great weight with her, but as her eyes may be more readily turned to the immediate and certain purposes to be answered to her rival, it is to be presumed that the policy of England will contribute to thwart the acquisition. What the intentions of Spain may be, we wait to learn from you. Verbal information from inofficial sources has led us to infer that she disowns the instrument of Cession, and will vigorously oppose it. Should the Cession actually fail from this or any other cause, and Spain retain New Orleans and the Floridas, I repeat to you the wish of the President that every effort and address be employed to obtain the arrangement by which the Territory on the East Side of the Mississippi including New Orleans may be ceded to the United States, and the Mississippi made a common boundary, with a common use of its navigation, for them and Spain. The inducements to be held out to Spain, were intimated in your original instructions on this point. I am charged by the President now to add, that you may not only receive and transmit a proposition of guaranty of her territory beyond the Mississippi, as a condition of her ceding to the United States the Territory including New Orleans on this side, but in the case it be necessary may make the proposition yourself, in the forms required by our Constitution. You will infer from this enlargement of your authority, how much importance is attached to the object in question, as securing a precious acquisition to the United States, as well as a natural and quiet boundary with Spain. . . .

Charles Pinckney of South Carolina was the American Minister to Spain.

FREE LIBRARY OF PHILADELPHIA

As the months passed and Jefferson and Madison summered in Virginia and returned to Washington in the fall, the problem of the Mississippi seemed no closer to resolution. The administration ardently wished a pacific settlement, whether with gold or boundary guarantees or both. Peace, said Jefferson, "is the most important of all things to us." Of next importance was time, which in this affair as in all things was believed to be on the American side. Napoleon had yet to make good his policy; no French expedition sailed for New Orleans; and war clouds again gathered in Europe. The clock was turned ahead dramatically in October, however. Madison's dispatch to Pinckney explained the situation.

[Washington,] November 27th. 1802

A letter from a confidential citizen at New Orleans, of which a copy is inclosed, has just informed us, that the Intendant at that place, by a proclamation from which an extract is also inclosed, had prohibited the deposit of American effects, stipulated by the Treaty of 1795; and as the letter is interpretted that the river was also shut against the external commerce of the U. States from that port. Whether it be the fact or not, that this latter prohibition has also taken place, it is evident that the useful navigation of the Mississippi essentially depends on a suitable depository for the articles of commerce that a privation of the latter is equivalent to a privation of both.

This proceeding is so direct and palpable a violation of the Treaty of 1795, that in candor it is to be imputed rather to the Intendant solely, than to instructions of his Government. The Spanish Minister takes pains to impress this belief and it is favoured by private accounts from New Orleans mentioning that the Governor did not concur with the Intendant. But from whatever source the measure may have proceeded the President expects that the Spanish Government will neither lose a moment in countermanding it, nor hesitate to repair every damage which may result from it. You are aware of the sensibility of our Western citizens to such an occurrence. This sensibility is justified by the interest they have at stake. The Mississippi is to them every thing. It is the Hudson, the Delaware the Potomac and all the navigable rivers of the Atlantic States formed into one stream. The produce exported thro' that channel last year amounted to $1,622,672 from the Districts of Kentucky and Mississippi only, and will probably be fifty [per] Cent more this year (from the whole Western Country, Kentucky alone has exported for the 1st half of this year $591,432 in value) a great part of which is now or shortly will be afloat for New Orleans and consequently exposed

Napoleon Bonaparte by Lefèvre

to the effects of this extraordinary exercise of power. Whilst you presume therefore in your representations to the Spanish Government, that the conduct of its officer, is no less contrary to its intentions, than it is to its good faith, you will take care to express the strongest confidence, that the breach of the Treaty will be repaired in every way which justice and a regard for a friendly neighbourhood may require.

An 1803 permit of passage, signed by Madison and Jefferson, according neutral status to the ship O'Cain

I have communicated the information received from New Orleans to the Chevalier D'Yrujo [Minister of Spain to the United States], with a view to obtain his immediate interposition, as you will find by the inclosed copy of a letter to him. He readily undertakes to use it with all the effect he can give it by writing immediately on the subject to the local authority at New Orleans.... It is to be hoped that the Intendant will be led to see the error which he has committed, and to correct it, before a very great share of its mischief will have happened. Should he prove as obstinate as he has been ignorant or wicked, nothing can temper the irritation and indignation of the Western Country but a persuasion that the energy of their own Government will obtain from the justice of that of Spain, the most ample redress.

The immediate crisis of closure was quietly resolved through the intercession of the Spanish envoy, Yrujo. Meanwhile, in order to still the clamor at home and exploit the crisis for maximum effect abroad, Jefferson appointed James Monroe minister extraordinary to join Livingston in negotiations for the purchase of New Orleans and the Floridas, supposing the Floridas were France's to sell. On March 2, 1803, Madison sketched the articles of the plan and authorized a purchase price of upward of ten million dollars. The time chosen for the experiment, he pointed out to the envoys, was one in which the grave danger of collision on the Mississippi had been strikingly brought into view. "The sensibility and unanimity in our nation which have appeared on this occasion, must convince France that friendship and peace with us must be precarious until the Mississippi shall be made the boundary between the United States and Louisiana; and consequently render the present moment favorable to the object with which you are charged." A later letter to Monroe and Livingston covered the last resort: the overture to Britain that Jefferson had earlier threatened.

[Washington,] April 18, 1803

The reasonable and friendly views with which you have been instructed by the President to enter into negocia-

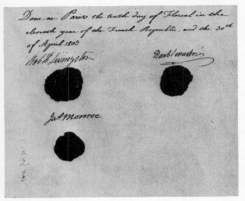

Signatures of Livingston, Monroe, and François de Barbé-Marbois, French Finance Minister, on purchase treaty

tions with the French Government, justify him in expecting from them an issue favorable to the tranquillity and to the useful relations between the two Countries. It is not forgotten, however, that these views, instead of being reciprocal, may find, on the part of France, a temper adverse to harmony, and schemes of ambition, requiring, on the part of the United States, as well as of others, the arrangements suggested by a provident regard to events. Among these arrangements, the President conceives that a common interest may recommend a candid understanding and closer connection with Great Britain; and he presumes that the occasion may present itself to the British Government in the same light. He accordingly authorises you ... to open a confidential communication with Ministers of the British Government, and to confer freely and fully on the precautions and provisions best adapted to the Crisis, and in which that Government may be disposed to concur; transmitting to your own, without delay, the result of these consultations.

The threat of this overture, combined with more compelling circumstances, made its execution unnecessary. Napoleon's dream of New World empire faded fast in the early months of 1803. Santo Domingo was lost. Spain would not yield the Floridas. War was again imminent in Europe and Napoleon turned his imperious gaze eastward toward Egypt, the Levant, and India. He could not defend Louisiana while marching to the east or risk American hostility in this new venture. "Irresolution and deliberation are no longer in season," he declared on April 11. "I renounce Louisiana." Monroe arrived in Paris the next day and the purchase treaty was quickly arranged. It was not the bargain the Americans had sought. It included the whole of Louisiana—the immense uncharted country between the Mississippi and the Rocky Mountains or beyond—together with New Orleans, but not the Floridas, for the price of approximately fifteen million dollars. Fortunately, Livingston and Monroe were guided by the spirit rather than the letter of their instructions. Madison warmly congratulated them not long after the treaty reached Washington.

[Washington,] July 29th. 1803
In concurring with the disposition of the French Government to treat for the whole of Louisiana, altho' the western part of it was not embraced by your powers, you were justified by the solid reasons which you give for it, and I am charged by the President to express to you his entire approbation of your so doing.

This approbation is in no respect precluded by the silence of your Commission and instructions. When these were made out, the object of the most sanguine was limited to the establishment of the Mississippi as our boundary. It was not presumed that more could be sought by the United States either with a chance of success, or perhaps without being suspected of a greedy ambition, than the Island of New Orleans and the two Floridas, it being little doubted that the latter was or would be comprehended in the Cession from Spain to France. To the acquisition of New Orleans and the Floridas the provision was therefore accommodated. . . .

. . . In truth the communications in general between Mr Livingston and the French Government, both of prior and subsequent date, manifested a repugnance to our views of purchase which left no expectation of any arrangement with France by which an extensive acquisition was to be made, unless in a favorable crisis, of which advantage should be taken. Such was thought to be the crisis which gave birth to the extraordinary commission in which you are joined. It consisted of the state of things produced by the breach of our deposit at New Orleans, the situation of the French Islands, particularly the important Island of St Domingo; the distress of the French finances, the unsettled posture of Europe, the increasing jealousy between G Britain and France, and the known aversion of the former to see the mouth of the Mississippi in the hands of the latter. These considerations it was hoped might so far open the eyes of France to her real interest and her ears to the monitory truths which were conveyed to her thro' different channels, as to reconcile her to the establishment of the Mississippi as a natural boundary to the United States; or at least to some concessions which would justify our patiently waiting for a fuller accomplishment of our wishes under auspicious events. The crisis relied on has derived peculiar force from the rapidity with which the complaints and questions between France and Great Britain ripened towards a rupture and it is just ground for mutual and general felicitation that it has issued under your zealous exertions, in the extensive acquisition beyond the Mississippi.

With respect to the terms on which the acquisition is made, there can be no doubt that the bargain will be regarded as on the whole highly advantageous.

Artist's later rendition of the American flag raising in New Orleans

A fresco by Brumidi in the United States Capitol shows Livingston and Monroe negotiating the purchase of Louisiana with Barbé-Marbois.

The Louisiana Purchase gave Madison tremendous satisfaction. It planted the Americans on both banks of the Mississippi, all but eliminated European colonialism from the continent, buttressed the nation's power and independence, fixed its destiny westward, and secured room to grow in freedom for generations to come. Unlike Jefferson, he was little troubled by constitutional objections to this revolution in the American Union. From the acquisition of Louisiana, which he had not expected, he returned his attention to the more immediate objective, the Floridas. The boundaries of Louisiana were obscure. He asked Livingston and Monroe what "pretensions" the United States had to claim West Florida to the Perdido River, the present-day boundary between Alabama and Florida. Jefferson soon made that claim, determined to finesse West Florida from Spain. East Florida was also wanted, though the United States would pay two million dollars for it and throw half of Texas into the bargain. Monroe was expected to proceed to Madrid after finishing his business in Paris. Madison thought the crisis peculiarly favorable, as he wrote to Monroe.

[Washington,] July. 29 1803

You will be at no loss for the arguments most likely to have weight in prevailing on Spain to yield to our wishes. These Colonies, separated from her other territories on this Continent, by New Orleans, the Mississippi, and the whole of Western Louisiana are now of less value to her than ever; whilst to the United States, they retain the peculiar importance derived from their position, and their relations to us thro' the navigable rivers running from the U States into the Gulph of Mexico. In the hands of Spain they must ever be a dead expence in time of peace, indefensible in time of War, and at all times a source of irritation and ill blood with the United States. The Spanish Government must understand in fact that the United States can never consider the amicable relations between Spain and them definitively and permanently secured, without an arrangement on this subject, which will substitute the manifest indications of nature, for the artificial and inconvenient state of things now existing.

The advantage to be derived to your negotiations from the war which has just commenced, will certainly not escape you. Powerful, and it might be presumed, effectual use may be made of the fact, that Great Britain meant to seize New Orleans with a view to the anxiety of the United States to obtain it; and of the inference from that fact, that the same policy will be pursued with respect to the Floridas. Should Spain be engaged in the war it cannot be doubted that they will be quickly occupied by a British force, and held out on some condition or other, to the United States. Should Spain be still at peace, and wish not to lose her neutrality, she should reflect that the facility and policy of seizing the Floridas must strengthen the temptations of G. Britain to force her into the war. In every view, it will be better for Spain, that the Floridas should be in the hands of the United States, than of Great Britain; and equally so, that they should be ceded on beneficial terms by herself, than that they should find their way to us thro' the hands of Great Britain.

The Spanish Government may be assured of the sincere and continued desire of the United States to live in harmony with Spain; that this motive enters deeply into the solicitude of their Government for a removal of the danger to it, which is inseparable from such a neighbourhood as that of the Floridas; and that having, by a late Convention with G. Britain, adjusted every territorial question and interest with that Nation, and the Treaty with France concerning Louisiana having just done the same with her, it only remains that the example be copied into an arrangement with Spain, who is evidently not less interested in it than we are.

Cartoon of a hornet, Napoleon, stinging prairie dog Jefferson into coughing up two million dollars for East and West Florida

The opportunity passed, however, as more urgent business—the impressment of American seamen—called Monroe to London to replace Rufus King, who was retiring. Relations with Spain rapidly deteriorated. The Floridas negotiation was resumed in 1805, when Monroe finally joined Pinckney in Madrid; but it came to nothing then and dragged on for years. Spain would neither bite Madison's carrot nor jump at his stick.

The war in Europe slowly brought affairs with Britain into the foreground. The first British minister accredited to Jefferson's Republican administration, Anthony Merry, arrived in November, 1803. Merry and his imperious lady were appalled by Washington—drearier and more barbaric, they thought, than the worst parts of Spain. Madison took him in full regalia to be presented to the President, who was found, on Merry's account, "not merely in undress, but *actually standing in slippers down at the heels*, and both pantaloons, coat, and under-clothes indicative of utter slovenliness and indifference to appearances, and in a state of negligence actually studied." A day or two later Jefferson entertained the Merrys at dinner. The Madisons were present together with most of the tiny Washington diplomatic corps. When dinner was announced, Jefferson offered his arm to Dolley Madison, heedless of her demurring whispers, "Take Mrs. Merry," and escorted her to the place at his right. Mrs. Merry was seated well down the table, while her poor husband scurried to find what seat he could. "This will be cause of war," the Marchioness Yrujo muttered. Four days later the Merrys were similarly affronted as guests of the Secretary of State. And so it went. The Merrys were humiliated by Jefferson's introduction of the democratic custom of the country, pell-mell, into official society. The minister poured his heart out to his government, thereby threatening to turn a social spat into an international incident. It did not come to that, but Madison was obviously concerned and kept Monroe informed in London. In the private letter that follows he relates the next act in this diplomatic comic opera.

Washington Feby 16. 1804

In a private letter by Mr. Baring I gave you a detail of what had passed here on the subject of Etiquette. I had hoped that no farther jars would have ensued as I still hope that the good senses of the British government respecting the right of the government here to fix its rules of intercourse and the sentiments and manners of the country to which they ought to be adapted will give the proper instructions for preventing like incidents in future. In the mean time a fresh circumstance had taken place which calls for explanations.

The President desirous of keeping open for cordial civilities whatever channels the scruples of Mr. M[err]y might not have closed asked me what these were understood to be and particularly whether he would come and take friendly and familiar dinners with him. I undertook to feel his pulse thro' some hand that would do it the least impropriety. From the information obtained I inferred that an invitation would be readily accepted and with the less doubt as he had dined with me (his lady declining) after the offence originally taken. The invitation was accordingly sent and terminated in the note

Our Country by BENSON J. LOSSING, 1877

Nineteenth-century engraving shows Jefferson's mode of dress that so shocked the British minister.

from him to me & my answer herewith inclosed. I need not comment on this display of diplomatic superstition, truly extraordinary in this age and country. We are willing to refer it to the personal character of a man accustomed to see importance in such trifles and over cautious against displeasing his government by surrendering the minutest of his or its pretentions. What we apprehend is that with these causes may be mingled a jealousy of our disposition toward England and that the mortifications which he has inflicted on himself are to be set down to that account. In fact it is known that this jealousy particularly since the final adjustment with France exists or is affected in a high degree and will doubtless give its colour to the correspondence of the legation with its government. To apply an antidote to this poison will require your vigilant and prudent attention. It can scarcely be believed that the British Govt. will not at once see the folly committed by its representative especially in the last scene of the farce and that it will set him to right in that respect. But it may listen with a different ear to suggestions that the U.S. having now less need of the friendship of Britain may be yielding to a latent enmity toward her. The best of all proofs to the contrary would be the confidential communications you possess, if it were not an improper condescension to disclose them for such a purpose. Next to that is the tenor of our measures, and the dictates of our obvious policy; on our appeal to both of which you may found the strongest assurances that the Govt. of the U.S. is sincerely and anxiously disposed to cultivate harmony between the two nations. The President wishes you to lose no opportunity and to spare no pains that may be necessary to satisfy the British Administration on this head and to prevent or efface any different impressions which may be transmitted from hence.

I collect that the cavil at the *pêle mêle* here established turns much on the alledged degradation of Ministers & Envoys to a level with chargés d'affaires. The truth is, & I have so told Mr. Merry that this is not the idea; That the President did not mean to decide any thing as to their comparative grades or importance; that these would be estimated as heretofore; that among themselves they might fix their own ceremonies, and that even at the Presidents table they might seat themselves in any subordination they pleased. All he meant was that no seats were to be designated for them, nor the order in which they might happen to sit to be any criterion of the respect paid to their respective commissions or Countries. On public occasions, such as Inaugural Speech &c. the Heads of Depts. with foreign ministers, and others invited on the part of the Govt. would be in the same *pêle mêle* within the space assigned them. It may not be amiss to recollect that under the old Congress, as I understand, and even in the ceremonies attending the introduction of the Govt. the foreign ministers were placed according to the order in which their Govts. acknowledged by Treaties the Independence of the U. States. In this point of view the *pêle mêle* is favorable both to G.B. and to Spain.

Madison approved of the new etiquette, even if he lacked Jefferson's zeal for it. The secretary of the British legation, Augustus Foster, said that a dinner at the Madisons was "more like a harvest-home supper, than the entertainment of the Secretary of State." In a capital so lacking in other diversions, a heavy burden of entertainment fell on the President and the Secretaries. The dry and stiff personality Madison exposed to the public seemed to mellow in the social circle. Men found him affable, good-humored, and full of anecdote. A vivid description of Madison as he appeared at this time is contained in a recollection by Edward Coles, who would later become his private secretary.

[December 23, 1854]

In his dress, he was not at all eccentric, or given to dandyism, but always appeared neat & genteel & in the costume of a well-bred & tasty old school gentleman. I have heard in early life he sometimes wore light-colored clothes. But from the time I first knew him, wh. was when he visited at my Fathers when I was a child, I never knew him to wear any other color than black; his coat being cut in what is termed dress fashion; his breeches short, with buckles at the knees, black silk stockings, and shoes with strings or long fair boot tops when out in cold weather, or when he road on horseback of which he was fond. His hat was of the shape and fashion usually worn by gentlemen of his age. He wore powder on his hair, which was dressed full over the ears, tied behind, and brought to a point above the forehead, to cover in some degree his baldness.... In height he was about five feet six inches, of small and delicate form, of

rather a tawny complexion, bespeaking a sedentary and studious man; his hair was originally of a dark brown color; his eyes were bluish, but not of a bright blue; his form, features, and manner were not commanding, but his conversation exceedingly so and few men possessed so rich a flow of language, or so great a fund of amusing anecdotes, which were made the more interesting from their being well-timed and well-told. His ordinary manner was simple, modest, bland, and unostentatious, retiring from the throng and cautiously refraining from doing or saying anything to make himself conspicuous.

Dolley's sister Anna Payne Cutts

In the summer of 1805 the Madisons traveled from Washington to Philadelphia, where the aptly named Dr. Philip Physick promised to cure Dolley of an ulcerated tumor near her knee, an ailment that had kept her almost completely immobilized since May. On the morning of their arrival in Philadelphia, Dolley wrote to her sister Anna.

[Philadelphia, July 29, 1805]

I feel as if my heart is bursting—no Mother, no Sister—but fool that I am, here is my beloved Husband sitting anxiously by me and who is my unremitting nurse. But you know how delicate he is—I tremble for him. On our way one night he [was] taken very ill with his old bilious complaint. I thought all was over with me. I could not fly to him and aid him as I used to do. But heaven in its mercy restored him next morning and he would not pause until he heard my fate from Doctr. P.

[Philadelphia,] Wednesday 31st. July [1805]

My dear sister. We are at excellent lodgings in Lenson Street, & I feel quite like another being. My knee is better. Doct. P. has splintered it, that is fixed a bark nearly a yd. long & with a bandage has bound it so tight that I cannot even lift it from the bed—not a step can I take—but this process is to cure it without any thing, we hope, & the Doct. thinks. I'm in no pain but from the fixed position. I have had all the world to see me. ... We have invitations to the House of one Dozen gentry but withstand all to be [at ease here]....

Madison in his customary black suit

Under Dr. Physick's care Dolley's leg began to heal. But by the end of October she was still too ill to travel and Madison was forced to return to Washington alone. The separation occasioned a rare exchange of letters between the devoted couple, who were seldom apart.

[Philadelphia,] 23d: October 1805

A few hours only have passed since you left me my beloved, and I find nothing can releave the oppression of my mind but speaking to you in this *only* way.

The Doctor called before you had gone far and with an air of sympathy wished you could see how much better the knee appeared. I could only speak to assure him it felt better. Betsey Pemberton and Amy [Dolley's maid] are sitting beside me and seem to respect the grief they know I feel, at even a short separation from one who is all to me. I shall be better when Peter [the coachman] returns, not that any length of time could lessen my just regret, but an assurance that you are well and easy will contribute to make me So. I have sent the books and note to Mrs: Dallas. B. Pemberton puts on your hat to divert me, but I cannot look at her.

24th: of October. What a sad day! The watchman announced a cloudy morning at one o'clock, and from that moment I found myself unable to sleep from anxiety for thee my dearest husband—detention cold and accident seemed to menace thee! ...

25th: This clear cold morning will favor your journey and enliven the feelings of my darling! I have nothing new to tell you. Betsey and myself sleep quietly together and the knee is mending. I eat very little and sit precisely as you left me. The doctor during his very short visits, talks of you, he says he regards you more than any man he ever knew and nothing could please him so much as passing his life near you—sentiments so congenial with one's own, and in *such cases*, like dew drops on flowers, exhilarate as they fall!

Adieu, my beloved, our hearts understand each other. In fond affection thine

DOLLY P. MADISON

Philadelphia Novr: 1st: [1805]

I have great pleasure, my beloved in repeating to you what the Doctor has just now said, that the knee would be well in one day more and in two or three I might begin to ride—so that I may reasonably hope that a fortnight more will be the extent of my stay in Philadelphia. I am so impatient to be restored to you.

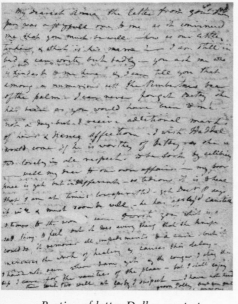

Portion of letter Dolley wrote to her sister, Anna Cutts, August 19, 1805, beginning "My dearest Anna"

I wish you would indulge me with some information respecting the war with Spain and disagreement with England, as it is so generally expected here that I am at a loss what to surmise. You know I am not much of a politician but I am extremely anxious to hear (as far as you may think proper) what is going forward in the Cabinet—on this subject, I believe you would not desire your wife the active partizan, such as her neighbor Mrs: T, nor will there be the slightest danger whilst she is conscious of her want of talents, and her diffidence in expressing her opinions [on matters] always imperfectly understood by her sex....

Kiss my child for me and remember me to my friends. ...Adieu, my dear husband, Peter brings me no letters which really unfits me for writing more to any one,

Your ever affectionate

D.

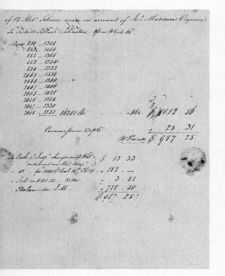

In November, 1805, Madison was asked to return some books he had borrowed from the Library of Congress (above); below, a bill of sale "made an account of Jas. Madison Esquire" for tobacco he had sold in Richmond.

[Washington, November 6, 1805]
Yours of the 1st. instant, my dearest gives me much happiness, but it can not be compleat till I have you again secure with me. Let me know the moment you can of the time you will set out that I may make arrangements for paying the Dr &c. My Tob[acc]o has been sold in Richd; but unfortunately the bills are not yet come on....Your question as to our [situation] in regard to Spain & England is puzzling. As one gets into ill humor it is possible the other may change her circumstance....Your friends are all well except Capt T [Thomas Tingey] who has been in extreme danger but is mending. Mrs T also has been unwell. I enclose a letter from Payne [Dolley's son, now fourteen years old]....

Your [own]

Affec

J.M.

The beginning of Jefferson's second administration in 1805 had coincided with William Pitt's return to power in Britain and the formation of the Third Coalition of European nations against Napoleon. All Europe was now engulfed in war; the United States was the last neutral of consequence. The Royal Navy, supreme on the seas, stepped up its harassment of American commerce; the impressment of American seamen soared to new heights; privateers infested American waters and plundered American trade. On July 23 a British admiralty court abruptly reversed the country's policy on the neutral carrying trade from enemy colonies. The decision in the case of the ship *Essex* marked a return to strict interpretation of the Rule of 1756, under which a trade closed in time of peace could not be opened in time of war. In 1793 Britain had enforced this rule with devastating effect against American carriers between French and Spanish colonies and the Continent. Since then the Americans had learned to evade the restriction by inserting an American port in the trade, landing the goods and paying the duties, then reexporting the "neutralized" cargoes to Europe. The admiralty courts came to accept the principle of the "broken voyage" as legitimizing the trade. In 1805 more than one-half of American exports were in fact reexports. The trade floated American prosperity. Now the *Essex* decision declared the trade fraudulent and made it subject to seizure and condemnation. Madison was still in Philadelphia attending his sick wife when he learned of this blow to American neutrality. He wrote to Monroe, who had just returned from defeat in Madrid to face a new crisis in London.

Philada. Sep. 24, 1805

The decision in the Admiralty Courts of G.B. disallowing the sufficiency of landing, and paying duties on, Colonial produce of belligerent Colonies, re-exported from ports of the U.S., to protect the produce agst. the British Cruisers & Courts, has spread great alarm among merchants & has had a grevious effect on the rate of commerce. From the great amt. of property afloat subject to this new & shameful depredation, a dreadful sence of distress may ensue to our commerce. The subject was brought to attention by the case of the Aurora, which gives rise to the observations & instructions contained in my letter of 12 April last. I omitted in that letter to refer you to a case in Blackstone's reports, when Ld. Mansfield says, that it was a rule settled by the Lords of appeals that a transhipment off a central port, was equivalent to the landing, of goods from an enemy's colony, and that in the case of a landing there could be *no color* for seizure. As Mr. Kings correspondence may not be in London I think it not amiss to remind you of what passed with the British Govt. in 1801, in consequence of such seizures as are now sanctioned. A copy of the doctrine transmitted by the Govt. to the Vice admy. Courts as the law for their guidance is inclosed. If such a condemnation out of their own mouths has no effect, all meanings will be lost; and absolute submission, or some other resort in vindication of our neutral rights, will be the only alternative left.

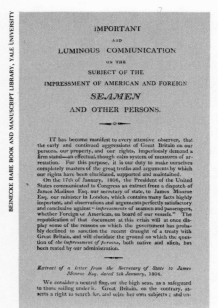

IMPORTANT
AND
LUMINOUS COMMUNICATION
ON THE
SUBJECT OF THE
IMPRESSMENT OF AMERICAN AND FOREIGN
SEAMEN
AND OTHER PERSONS.

IT has become manifest to every attentive observer, that the early and continued aggressions of Great Britain on our persons, our property, and our rights, imperiously demand a firm stand—an effectual, though calm system of measures of arrestation. For this purpose, it is our duty to make ourselves completely masters of the great truths and arguments by which our rights have been elucidated, supported and maintained. On the 17th of January, 1806, the President of the United States communicated to Congress an extract from a dispatch of James Madison Esq. our secretary of state, to James Monroe Esq. our minister in London, which contains many facts highly important, and observations and arguments perfectly satisfactory and conclusive against "*impressments* of seamen and passengers, whether Foreign or American, on board of our vessels." The republication of that document at this crisis will at once display some of the reasons on which the government has probably declined to sanction the recent draught of a treaty with Great Britain, and will elucidate the ground on which the question of *the impressment of persons*, both native and alien, has been rested by our administration.

Extract of a letter from the Secretary of State to James Monroe Esq. dated 5th January, 1804.

We consider a neutral flag, on the high seas, as a safeguard to those sailing under it. Great Britain, on the contrary, asserts a right to search for, and seize her own subjects ; and un-

Printed text of an 1804 letter from Madison to James Monroe in London on impressment of American seamen

I hope you will have recd. the instructions above referred to, and that your interposition will have had a good effect. I am engaged in a pretty thorough investigation of the original principle, to which so many shapes are given, namely, that "a trade not open in peace is not lawful in war," and shall furnish you with the result as soon as my remarks are digested. If I am not greatly deceived, it will appear that the principle is not only agst. the law of nations, but one which G.B. is precluded from assuming by the most conclusive facts & arguments derived from herself.

Madison's "pretty thorough investigation" resulted in a long diplomatic paper which marshaled all the authorities from Grotius through Vattel to show that the Rule of 1756 had no standing in international law. Close examination of treaties over a long period proved that Britain had often recognized the trade she now condemned. Indeed, her conduct had always been dictated by expediency. Force was the true foundation of the rule. "The question no longer is, whether the trade be right or wrong in itself, but on which side the superiority of force lies? The law of nations, the rights of neutrals, the freedom of the seas, the commerce of the world, are to depend, not on any fixed principle of justice, but on the comparative state of naval armaments." And why did Britain now return to strict enforcement of the old rule? Not to cut off supplies from her enemies, which might be justified militarily, but to force a dangerous rival, the United States, from the colonial trade and to monopolize it for herself even to the point of supplying her own enemies. Madison's argument was devastating. In law and learning and logic it showed him at his best; but it also disclosed the awful vulnerability of a statesman who could thus wrap himself in the heavy gray pedantry of the law. Britain was not interested in Madison's debater's points. Originally intended to be an official state paper, the report was withdrawn, and although published as a thick pamphlet and distributed to congressmen, it fell of its own weight. John Randolph, Madison's particular enemy in the House, contemptuously dismissed it as "a shilling pamphlet hurled against eight hundred ships of war."

The wave of captures following the *Essex* decision caused an uproar among the coastal merchants. Congress, in response, called for an extraordinary mission to Britain to seek a comprehensive settlement and backed this up with a Nonimportation Act triggered for nine months hence. Madison was cool to the plan. A settlement must take the form of a treaty, with concessions on both sides, and he wanted no successor to the Jay Treaty, the commercial articles of which had expired. Two years earlier he had committed to Monroe the project of a convention limited to neutral rights and impressment. Only military contraband and effectual blockade were to be admitted as exceptions to the freedom of neutral commerce. Impressment was to be virtually outlawed. This problem was peculiar to Anglo-American relations. In order to man her navy and recover her absconding subjects, Britain claimed the right to take seamen from American vessels on the high seas. In the process thousands of American citizens were cruelly pressed into His Majesty's service. Impressment assaulted the very existence of American nationality. Its abolition was made an ultimatum in any settlement with Britain. On Madison's recommendation Jefferson named William Pinkney of Maryland to join Monroe in the negotiations. Pinkney's Federalist background gave dissident Republicans, like Randolph, further opportunity to damn the administration's temporizing politics, which were charged to Madison. The instructions to Monroe and Pinkney ran to seven thousand words, including Madison's observations on the proposed treaty.

[Washington, May 17, 1806]

The 4th Article, besides the stipulation on the subject of contraband, relates to two other Subjects;   1. that of free Ships free goods,   2. that of a trade with enemies Colonies.

1.   With respect to the first, the principle that a neutral flag covers the property of an enemy, is relinquished, in pursuance of the example of the Russian Treaty, on which the article is modelled.... The importance of that principle to the security of neutral Commerce, and to the freedom of the Seas, has at all times been felt by the United States; and although they have not asserted it as the established law of Nations, they have ever been anxious to see it made a part of that law. It was with reluctance of course that a contrary stipulation was authorized, and merely as a means of obtaining from Great Britain the recognition of a principle now become of more importance to neutral Nations possessing mercantile Capital, than the principle of "free Ships free goods." It is to be particularly kept in view therefore that such a contrary stipulation is to be avoided if possible; and, if unavoidable, that the stipulation be so modified as to interfere as little as possible with the spirit and policy of any provisions in favor of the principle which may be likely to be introduced into a treaty of peace among the present belligerent powers of Europe....

2.   The vast importance of the Colonial Trade, with the circumstances and the excitement which have taken place since the date of the original instructions to Mr. Monroe, will require that the neutral right on this subject

John Randolph by Gilbert Stuart

Pictorial Field Book of the War of 1812
(Extra Illustrated) BY BENSON J. LOSSING, 1868

While William Pinkney (above) and Monroe were negotiating neutral commercial rights, a bill of lading (below) for goods shipped to Madison from Marseilles in 1806 excepted liability for "Danger of the Seas."

MANUSCRIPT DIVISION, LIBRARY OF CONGRESS

be provided for in an appropriate article, and in terms more explicit than are used in the article under review. As the right in this case, turns on the general principle, that neutrals may lawfully trade, with the exceptions of blockades and contraband, to and between all ports of an enemy, and in all articles, although the trade shall not have been open to them in time of peace, particular care is to be taken, that no part of the principle be expressly or virtually abandoned, as being no part of the law of Nations. On the contrary it is much to be desired that the general principle in its full extent, be laid down in the stipulation; but as this may not be attainable and as too much ought not to be risked by an inflexible pursuit of abstract right . . . you are left at liberty, if found necessary, to abridge the right in practice . . .; not omitting to provide that in case Great Britain should by her Treaties or instructions leave to any other nation the right in a greater extent than it is stipulated to the United States, they may claim the enjoyment of it in an equal extent.

The abuses which have been committed by Great Britain under the pretext that a neutral trade, from enemy Colonies, through neutral ports, was a direct trade, render it indispensable to guard against such a pretext by some express declaration on that point. The most that can be conceded on the part of the United States is, that *the landing of the goods, the securing the duties, and the change of the Ship,* or preferably, the landing of the goods alone, or with the securing the duties, shall be requiste to destroy the identity of the voyage and the directness of the trade; and that the ordinary documents of the Custom House Officers, shall be sufficient evidence of the facts or fact.

A satisfactory provision on this subject of trade with enemy Colonies, is deemed of so much consequence to the rights and interests of the United States . . . that as was enjoined with respect to the provision against impressment, no stipulation is to be entered into not consistent with a continuance of that act, unless the provision with respect to the Colonial trade be also obtained.

Napoleon's victories on the Continent and a new ministry in London suddenly raised Madison's hopes for the negotiations. By his calculation, certainly, the American commissioners held the winning hand.

He was, therefore, mortified by the treaty they signed on December 31, 1806. Jefferson angrily refused even to submit it to the Senate. Britain stood firm on impressment, offering only informal assurances of caution and forbearance in the practice. The warmth of Madison's feelings may be seen from his remarks to an American friend in England, George Joy.

> Washington May 22, 1807
>
> The Treaty signed with the British Commissrs. has not recd. the approbation of the President. Full justice is done to the talents & exertions of ours; but the terms admitted on the other side, do not satisfy the expectations on this. The case of impressments, particularly, having been brought to a formal issue, & having been the primary object of an Extry. Mission, a Treaty could not be closed which was silent on that subject; a subject which, whenever it shall no longer be seen thro' the mist with which practice enveloped rights, must excite wonder that the patience of the U.S. has remained so long unexhausted. That an officer from a foreign ship should pronounce any person he pleased, covered by the American flag on the high seas, to be not an Amn. Citizen, but a British subject, & carry this interested decision on the most important of all questions to a freeman, into execution on the spot, is so anomalous in principle, so grievous in practice, and so abominable in abuse, that the pretension must finally yield to sober discussion & friendly expostulation.

There were numerous other objections to the Monroe-Pinkney Treaty. Its commercial articles were unsatisfactory, despite British concessions on the reexport trade. In a note attached to the treaty Britain demanded, as a condition of compliance on her part, American retaliation against Napoleon's recent Berlin Decree, which declared lawful prize of all traffic with Britain. While Napoleon straddled the Continent and while the Florida purchase hung on his good offices with Spain, Jefferson and Madison would not be bullied into war against France.

So the treaty was returned for renegotiation. Madison penned new instructions. After detailed analysis of each article, he concluded with an essay on the natural advantages the United States possessed for the vindication of its cause against Britain. He believed now, as in 1794 and in 1789, that in any quarrel with the United States Britain must lose because her vital interests—in the West Indies, in the American market for her manufactures, in her dependence on American food and raw materials—could be mortally wounded, while those of the United States were invulnerable.

[Washington,] May 20th — 1807

There are considerations moreover which cannot be without weight with a prudent Cabinet, however composed. They must know that, apart from the obstacles which may be opposed here to the use of British manufactures, the United States, by a mere reciprocation of the British navigation and Colonial laws, may give a very serious blow to a favorite system, a blow that would be felt perhaps as much too in its example, as in its immediate operation. Should this policy be adopted by the United States, as it respects the British West Indies, the value of those possessions would be either speedily lost, or be saved no otherwise than by a compliance with the fair reciprocity claimed by this Country. It can no longer be unknown to the most sanguine partisan of the Colonial Monopoly, that the necessaries of life and of cultivation, can be furnished to those Islands from no other source than the United States; that immediate ruin would ensue if this source was shut up; and that a gradual one would be the effect of even turning the supplies out of the present direct channel, into a circuitous one thro' neutral ports in the West Indies. . . .

It ought to occur moreover to the British Government that its marine may become as dependant as its Colonies on the supplies of the United States. As an auxiliary resource for naval stores, this Country must be at all times important to Great Britain. But it will be the sole and therefore an essential one in case that of the Baltic and even of the Black sea, should fail. And it may be justly remarked that a prohibition of this branch of our exports wd be a less sacrifice than that of any other important one; inasmuch as some of the articles of which it consists, being necessary to ourselves, and of an exhaustable nature, make it a problem whether the regulation would not in itself accord with our permanent interests.

Lastly it should not be forgotten that the United States are one of the Granaries which supply the annual deficit of the British harvests. The northern part of Europe, the usual concurrent resource is in a situation that must disable it, for some time, whatever the course of events may be, to spare any of its stock of food; nor can any substitute, other than the redundant harvests of the United States, be relied on to make up that deficiency. Add to this prospect, the possibility of an unfavorable

Nineteenth-century representation of the "British right of search"

season requiring enlarged importations of bread from the only source that can furnish it, and the risk of losing this would be an evil which no provident Counsels would neglect to guard against, by any measures equitable in themselves, or even by concessions neither dishonorable nor materially injurious.

On the other hand Great Britain having been led by her peculiar system to carry her commercial exclusions and restrictions to the utmost limit permitted by her immediate wants, would find no countervailing resources to be turned against the United States. She could not prohibit the importation of our productions. These are necessaries which feed her people, which supply her manufactories, which keep up her Navy, and which, by direct and indirect contributions to her revenue and credit strengthen all her faculties as a great power. As little could she prohibit the exportation of her manufactures to the United States. This is the last evil she would think of inflicting on herself. If it withheld from us the means of enjoyment, it would take from her own people the means of existence.

Would war be a better resort? That it would be a calamity to the United States is so well understood by them that peace has been cherished in the midst of provocations which scarcely permitted honor to listen to interest, to reason or to humanity. War they will continue to avert by every policy which can be reconciled with the essential duties which a nation owes to itself. But what will be the gain and the loss to Great Britain by a choice of this resort? The spoils of our defenceless commerce might enrich her greedy cruizers, and flatter the sentiment of national wealth. A temporary spasm might, at the same time, be produced in the affairs of the United States. But these effects weigh little against the considerations which belong to the opposite scale. To say nothing of the hostile use that might be made against Great Britain of 50,000 seamen, not less hardy or enterprizing than her own, nor of her vulnerable possessions in our neighbourhood, which tho' little desired by the United States, are highly prized by her, nor of the general tendency of adding the United States to the mass of nations already in arms against her; it is enough to observe, that a war with the United States involves a complete loss of the principal remaining market for her manufactures, and of the principal, perhaps the sole, remaining source of, supplies without which all her faculties must wither. Nor is it an unimportant circumstance, tho' it seems to have engaged little of her attention, that in the loss would be included, all the advantages which she now derives from the neutrality of our flag, and of our ports, and for which she could find no substitutes in distributing her manufactures, and even her fish to their necessary markets, and in obtaining the returns which she wants. The more these collateral advantages are enquired into, the more important will the interest appear which Great Britain has in preserving them.

These are views of the subject, which, tho' not to be presented to Great Britain with an air of menace or defiance, equally forbidden by respect to ourselves, and to her, may find a proper way to her attention. They merit hers as well as ours; and if they ought to promote on both sides, a spirit of accommodation, they show at the same time that Great Britain is not the party which has the least interest, in taking counsel from them.

Commodore James Barron

Whatever small chance remained for the treaty was blasted by the British attack on the U.S.S. *Chesapeake*. On June 22, 1807, just off Norfolk, the *Chesapeake* was hailed by the H.M.S. *Leopard* and ordered to submit to search for British seamen. When the American commander, Commodore James Barron, refused to submit, the *Leopard* poured broadsides into the defenseless frigate, killing three and wounding eighteen before its flag was struck. Four alleged deserters were then removed and the *Chesapeake* limped back to port. As the country rose in thunderous indignation, Madison sent Monroe his instructions.

[Washington,] July 6 1807

The documents herewith inclosed from No. 1 to No. 9 inclusive explain the hostile attack with the insulting pretext for it, lately committed near the Capes of Virga. by the British ship of war the Leopard on the American frigate the Chesapeake. No. 10 is a copy of the Proclamation issued by the President interdicting, in consequence of that outrage, the use of our waters and every other accomodation, to all British armed ships.

This enormity is not a subject for discussion. The immunity of a National ship of war from every species and purpose of search on the high seas, has never been con-

After the Leopard *(at left in the picture below) poured broadsides into the* Chesapeake, *the British seized four alleged deserters (above).*

tested by any nation. G.B. would be second to none in resenting such a violation of her rights, & such an insult to her flag. She may bring the case to the test of her own feelings, by supposing that instead of the customary demand of our mariners serving compulsively even on board her ships of war, opportunities had been seized for rescuing them in like manner, whenever the superiority of force or the chance of surprize might be possessed by our ships of war.

But the present case is marked by circumstances which give it a peculiar die. The seamen taken from the Chesapeake had been ascertained to be native Citizens of the U. States; and this fact was made known to the bearer of the demand, and doubtless, communicated by him to his commander [prior] to the commencement of the attack. It is a fact also, affirmed by two of the men with every appearance of truth that they had been impressed from American vessels into the British frigate from which they escaped, and by the third, that having been impressed from a British Merchant ship, he had accepted the recruiting bounty under that duress, and with a view to alleviate his situation, till he could escape to his own Country. Add that the attack was made during a period

of negotiations, & in the midst of friendly assurances from the B. Government.

The printed papers herewith sent will enable you to judge of the spirit which has been roused by the occasion. It pervades the whole community, is abolishing the distinctions of party, and regarding only the indignity offered to the sovereignty & flag of the nation, and the blood of Citizens so wantonly and wickedly shed, demands in the loudest tone, an honorable reparation.

With this demand you are charged by the President. The tenor of his proclamation will be your guide in reminding the British Govt. of the uniform proofs given by the U.S. of their disposition to maintain faithfully every friendly relation; of the multiplied infractions of their rights by British naval Commanders on our Coasts & in our harbours; of the inefficacy of re-iterated appeals to the justice & friendship of that Govt., and of the moderation on the part of the U.S. which re-iterated disappointment had not extinguished; till at length no alternative is left but a voluntary satisfaction on the part of G.B. or a resort to means depending on the U.S. alone.

The nature & extent of the satisfaction ought to be suggested to the British Govt. not less by a sense of its own honor than by justice to that of the U. States. A formal disavowal of the deed, and restoration of the four seamen to the Ship from which they were taken, are things of course. Beyond these, the U States have a right to expect and require every solemnity of form & every other ingredient of retribution & respect, which, according to usage & the sentiments of mankind, are due in the strongest cases to the insulted rights & sovereignty of a nation. And it is the particular instruction of the President, that you do not allow it to be supposed, that any satisfaction of an inferior character, will be accepted by the U.S.

Should it be alledged as a ground for declining or diminishing the satisfaction in this case, that the U.S. have themselves taken it by the interdict contained in the Proclamation, the answer will be obvious. The interdict is a measure not of a reparation, but of precaution; and would besides be amply justified by occurrences prior to the extraordinary outrage in question.

The exclusion of all armed ships whatever from our

Broadside headlined "British Barbarity and Piracy!!" recounts a later naval incident described as "Leopard Outspotted."

This 1808 broadside was the work of
Massachusetts Federalists who felt
the French were the real enemies.

waters is in fact so much required by the vexations and
dangers to our peace experienced from their visits, that
the President makes it a special part of the charge to you,
to avoid laying the U.S. under any species of restraint
from adopting that remedy. Being extended to all Belligerent nations, none of them could of right complain;
and with the less reason, as the policy of all nations has
limited the admission of foreign ships of war into their
ports, to such numbers as being inferior to the naval
force of the Country, could be readily made to respect
its authority & laws.

Jefferson, although he had only to nod to take the country
to war, deliberately cooled the crisis and awaited British response to his
demands. The Tenth Congress convened in the fall. Partly at Madison's
instigation, the President adopted a high tone toward Britain and called for
accelerated military preparations. Meanwhile the country's position became
intolerable. Not only did Britain refuse to make amends for the *Chesapeake*
affair; she also prepared new orders in council which would place the entire
European continent under blockade. American commerce would be coerced
into the monopolistic British system—again licensed, taxed, and "colonized"
by George III. Napoleon, for his part, announced the extension of the Berlin
Decree to the Americans, previously exempted. Between the emperor's
tightening Continental System and the British orders American commerce
was caught in the jaws of a vise, a maniacal war of blockades from which
there seemed to be no appeal to reason and justice.

Thus it was that Jefferson recommended and Congress enacted on
December 22 the Embargo Act shutting off American foreign commerce
and navigation. Combined with the Nonimportation Act against Britain,
only now put into effect, the embargo launched the system of "commercial
coercion" Madison as well as Jefferson had long advocated. That the United
States might, by withholding its trade, force justice on the marauding powers
of Europe, especially Britain, was an idea as old as the nation itself. To no
other idea had Madison clung so tenaciously during twenty years. The
experiment would at last be made in a situation fraught with peril.

With the internal history of the embargo—the enforcement, the economic deprivations, the political opposition—Madison had little to do. These
problems fell to Jefferson and Secretary of the Treasury Albert Gallatin.
But the embargo was essentially an instrument of American diplomacy,
which was Madison's province. Once its effects were felt abroad, Madison
believed, either France would recede from her decree in order to force
American conflict with Britain, or the stoppage of American trade would
prove so ruinous to Britain as to bring her to justice. It was the same old

neutral game, playing off one European empire against the other for America's benefit, but the stakes were higher than before. The diplomatic strategy took form in the spring of 1808. Pinkney in London, where he had succeeded Monroe, and John Armstrong, the minister in Paris, would each demand revocation of the obnoxious decrees, at the same time holding out the idea that compliance by one power would invite American hostilities against the other if it persisted in its edicts. The following is taken from Madison's instructions to Armstrong.

[Washington,] May 2d. 1808

The conditions on which the suspending authority is to be exercised will engage your particular attention. They appeal equally to the justice and the policy of the two great belligerent powers now emulating each other in violations of both. The President counts on your best endeavors to give to this appeal all the effect possible with the French Government. Mr Pinkney will be doing the same with that of Great Britain. The relation in which a recall of its retaliating decrees by either power, will place the United States to the other, is obvious; and ought to be a motive to the measure proportioned to the desire which has been manifested by each, to produce collisions between the U States and its adversary; and which must be equally felt by each to avoid one with itself.

Should wiser Councils or increasing distresses induce Great Britain to revoke her impolitic orders against neutral commerce, and thereby prepare the way for a removal of the Embargo as it applies to her, France could not persist in the illegal part of her decrees, if she does

Jefferson, prodded by Napoleon in the cartoon below right, informs dismayed citizens the ports must be closed to the British; below left, a turtle named "Ograbme" (embargo spelled backward) snaps at smuggler loading sugar on a British ship.

*Cartoon of Jefferson and Madison
dragging a ship into dry dock at
Napoleon's instigation; Congress
hotly debates the embargo at right.*

not mean to force a contest with the United States. On the other hand should she set the example of revocation Great Britain would be obliged, either by following it, to restore to France the full benefit of neutral trade which she needs, or by perservering in her obnoxious orders after the pretext for them had ceased, to render collisions with the United States inevitable.

In every point of view therefore it is so clearly the sound policy of France to rescind so much at least of her decrees as trespass on neutral rights, and particularly to be the first in taking the retrograde step, that it cannot be unreasonable to expect that it will be immediately taken.

The repeal of her decrees is the more to be expected, above all if Great Britain should repeal or be likely to repeal hers, as the plan of the original decree at Berlin did not extend to a violation of the freedom of the seas, and was restricted to a municipal operation nearly an entire year notwithstanding the illegal British orders of Jany 1807, and as a return of France to that restricted scope of her plan, would so immaterially diminish its operation against the British commerce, that operation being so completely in the power of France on land, and so little in her power on the high seas.

But altho' we cannot of right demand from France more than a repeal of so much of her decrees as violate the freedom of the seas, and a great point will be gained by a repeal of that part of them, yet as it may not have the effect of inducing a repeal of the whole illegal system of the British Government which may seek pretexts, or plead a necessity for counteracting the unprecedented and formidable mode of warfare practiced against her, it will be desirable that as little room as possible should be left for this remaining danger to the tranquil enjoyment of our commercial rights.

These overtures failed. Napoleon, instead of snatching at the bait, made a mockery of the embargo. George Canning, the British Foreign Secretary, reacted with contempt. There was no accounting for Napoleon, but Madison blamed Canning's obstinacy on treacherous Federalist opposition to the embargo. Despite the mounting discontents of British merchants and manufacturers and workers, the government at Westminster adhered to its edicts in the delusory expectation planted by the madcap Federalists of producing a political revolution, perhaps even disunion, in the United States. Be that as it may, the discontents on American shores were no less real, and more compelling, than those in Britain. Madison's own reckoning of the "noble experiment" may be gleaned from his letters to Pinkney over several months.

Washington May 1. 1808

The colonizing & taxing features of the B. orders have so effectually re-inforced the other charges agst. them, that the public mind every where is rallying to the policy of the Embargo; and there can be no doubt that the efforts to render it unpopular are re-coiling on the authors of them. It has been somewhat eluded, but the last supplimental act will probably give it due effect. An indignation agst. the smugglers is moreover beginning to co-operate with those charged with its execution.

The B. Govt. may therefore calculate on the efficacy as well as the duration of the measure unless a repeal of its orders should obtain an exercise of the Power vested in the P. to open our ports in that event. To this prudent course it must be strongly impelled by the distresses of the W. Indies, the discontents at home, the alienation of our habits from her manufactures, and the vigorous means tak[en] to provide sub[s]titutes of our own; and by the apprehension that France may entitle herself to a removal of the Embargo as it applies to her, and thus expose G.B. to the dilemma of appearing to be forced into the measure by that example, or of encountering the consequences of adhering to her system after all pretext for it shall be at an end.

Washington July 21. 1808

Great efforts have been made to render the Embargo unpopular, and to promote evasions & violations of it. These efforts have not ceased & have not been without a certain degree of effect. With the means used by our own Citizens have been united great exertions from the Canadian & N. Scotia borderers. On the lakes combinations have been formed on both sides of the boundary, and it is believed, tho' not as yet proved, that a British party passed the boundary and carried away by force a quantity of Potash &c.... It is certain also that no inconsiderable quantities of provisions have been smuggled into the W. Indies. The Measure however cannot but have had a powerful effect in that quarter. The general price even of provisions shews it. And with respect to lumber so indispensible to their situation & pursuits, there is reason to believe that scarcely any supplies whatever have found their way. So that on the whole, connecting the Embargo with the Orders in Council, the W. India. interest has no reason to exult in the policy of the latter. Within ourselves, the body of the people have borne the privations with a firmness which leaves no doubt of their perserverence as long as they shall see the alternative with submission to the foreign Edicts. The sense of Natl. honor & independence seems to be entering deeper & deeper into the mass of the people, and the operation of the retaliating system on the onstanding navigation affords daily evidence of the good fortune of that which has been saved from the danger.

If the B. Orders continue much longer they will certainly have more than a temporary effect on B. manufactures. It is astonishing what a zeal for homespun has been excited, and I am persuaded that altho calculations may carry the extent and permanency of the substitutes in some cases too far, it will be found that the looms & wheels set up will be continued after the crisis is over in a degree beyond any idea entertained beyond the Atlantic....

George Canning

A storm of protest against the Embargo Act rolled over New England in the fall, providing Federalists with ammunition in their campaign against the act and against Madison who, with Jefferson's support, had emerged as the preeminent Republican candidate for President in the

1808 elections. Fearing that Federalist opposition would undermine the administration's position abroad, Madison wrote again to Pinkney as Congress convened.

Lord Erskine, British Minister to the United States, by Gilbert Stuart

Washington November 9th. 1808.
The conduct of the British cabinet in rejecting the fair offer made to it, and even sneering at the course pursued by the U.S., prove at once a very determined enmity to them, and a confidence that events were taking place here which would relieve it from the necessity of procuring a renewal of commercial intercourse by any relaxation on its part. Without this last supposition it is difficult to believe that, with the prospect at home and abroad in Europe, so great a folly would have been committed. As neither the public nor Congress have yet had time to disclose the feelings which result from the posture now given to our relations with Great Britain, I cannot speak positively on that subject. I shall be much disappointed, however, if a spirit of independence and indignation does not strongly reinforce the past measures with others which will give a severity to the contest of privations at least, for which the British government would seem to be very little prepared in any sense of the word. It was perhaps unfortunate, that all the intelligence from this country, previous to the close of your correspondence with Mr. Canning, was from a quarter and during a period most likely to produce miscalculations of the general & settled dispositions. You will see in the newspapers sufficient evidence of the narrow limits to which discontent was confined; and it may reasonably be expected that the counter-current will be greatly strengthened by the communications now going forth to the public.

Washington Decr. 5. 1808
Congs. seemed to be sufficiently determined, as you will observe, to resist the unjust and insulting Edicts of the Belligerents, and differ only as to the mode best suited to the case. The disposition to prefer war to the course hitherto pursued, is rather gaining than losing ground; and is even promoted by the efforts of those most opposed to war with G.B. who concur in deciding agst. submission, and at the same time contend that withdrawing from the Ocean is submission. It is very questionable however whether a preference of war, to be

269

commenced within the present Session, is so general in Congs, or so much looked for by the nation, as to recommend the measure. Whether in case, the measure should be declined, any such substitute, providing for war, during the recess, as I have intimated in one of my last letters, will be acceptable, is more than I can undertake to say; nothing of the sort having been even brought into Conversation.

I find by conversation with Mr Erskine [the British minister] that he is himself favorably impressed by the documents laid before Congs. as to the fairness of our Conduct towards the two belligerents, and that he is willing I should believe that the impression will be the same [fo]r his Govt. As it may be conceived by him, however, to be politic to lull our feelings & suspicions, I am the less sure, that he calculates on any change in the Councils of his Govt. likely to do justice to those of this Govt.

As to the state of the public mind here, you will sufficiently collect it from the printed information now forwarded. I can not believe that there is so much depravity or stupidity in the Eastern States as to countenance the reports that they will separate from their brethren rather than submit no longer to the suspension of their commerce. That such a project may lurk within a Junto, ready to sacrifice the rights interests & honor of their Country, to their ambitious or vindictive views, is not to be doubted; but that the body of an intelligent people devoted to commerce & navigation with few productions of their own, and objects of unceasing jealousy to G.B. on acct. of their commerce & navigation, should be induced to abandon the Southern States for which they are the merchants & carriers, in order to enter into an Alliance with G.B. seems to be impossible.

Cartoon showing the death of the "terrapin policy," the embargo

By the end of November it was clear that Madison had won the election, despite opposition from left and right: from the Randolph faction of Republicans who believed he had betrayed the cause and who took up Monroe, alienated because of the rejected British treaty, as their candidate; and from eastern Federalists who accused him of selling out the nation to Napoleon. The vote of the electors in December was 122 for the Secretary of State and 47 for his Federalist opponent, Charles Cotesworth Pinckney. Although he lost four of five New England states and part of New York,

Madison's victory was still a vote of confidence in him and in the administration he had served. But the embargo issue remained, and the outgoing administration seemed incapable of leadership. In the early months of 1809 congressional opposition climaxed with a proposal to repeal the embargo and to enact in its place a milk-and-water nonintercourse law reopening trade with all the world except Britain and France. The President-elect kept William Pinkney informed of these late developments.

"Happy is the land, Who hails thee vested with the chief command" reads part of a poem by William Ray to Madison on March 22, 1809.

Washington Feby 11. 1809

My official letter by this conveyance leaves little of importance to be added to its contents. You will see with regret the difficulty experienced in collecting the mind of Congress to some proper focus. On no occasion were the ideas so unstable and so scattered. The most to be hoped for at present is that a respectable majority will finally concur in taking a course not essentially dishonoring the resolution not to submit to the foreign Edicts. The last vote taken, as stated in reports of their proceedings, 60 odd agst. 50 odd [for], implies that a non-intercourse with G.B. & F. including an Embargo on Exports to those two Nations, will be substituted for the general Embargo existing. And it is not improbable that 8 or 10 of the minority who prefer a simple adherence to the latter, will on finding it cannot be retained, join in the non-intercourse proposed. It is impossible however to foretell the precise issue of such complicated views.

If the non-intercourse as proposed, should be adopted, it will leave open a trade to all the Continent of Europe, except France....

The repeal of the Embargo has been the result of the opinion of many that the period prescribed by honor to that resort agst. the tyrannical Edicts agst. our trade, had arrived; but principally from the violence exerted agst. it in the Eastern quarter, which some wished to assuage by indulgence, and others to chastise into an American Spirit by the lash of British Spoliations. I think this effect begins to be anticipated by some who have been most clamorous for the repeal. As the Embargo is disappearing, the orders & decrees come into view, with the commercial & political consequences which they cannot fail to produce. The English market will at once be glutted; and the continental market particularly for the Sugar & Coffee in the Eastern Wharehouses will be sought at every risk. Hence Captures and clamors agst.

the authors of them. It can not I think be doubted that if the Embargo be repealed & the orders be enforced, that war is inevitable, and will perhaps be clamored for in the same quarter which now vents its disappointed love of gain agst. the Embargo.

There is reason to believe that the disorganizing spirit in the East, is giving way to the universal indignation of the parties elsewhere agst. it. It is explained in part also by the course of events abroad which lessens the prospect of British support, in case of a Civil war.

Finally on March 1, 1809, amidst much confusion, the embargo was repealed and the Nonintercourse Act was adopted, as Madison reported to Pinkney.

Washington Mar. 17. 1809
You will learn by the communications from the Dept. of State, that the discussions of Congs. on our foreign relations had an issue less operative than was at one time looked for. The aversions to war, the inconveniences produced by or charged on the embargo, the hope of favorable changes in Europe, the dread of civil convulsions in the East, and the policy of permitting the discontented to be reclaimed to their duty by losses at sea, had each a share in producing the Non-intercourse Act. Certain it is that no measure was ever adopted by so great a proportion of any public body which had the hearty concurrence of so small a one; and it seems to be as little satisfactory out of doors, as it was within.

Madison firmly believed, as did Jefferson and Pinkney, that the embargo would have succeeded had it been given a little more time. Repeal pulled the rug from under the British opposition to the orders in council just as it was aiming the knockout blow. Unfortunately, in this "contest of privations" time had run out at home. Madison's faith in the policy blinded him to the harsh realities of domestic discord and distress which could no longer be ignored except at grave peril to the nation itself. But defeat of "peaceable coercion" might have been tolerable for Madison had it been succeeded by a strategy of force, perhaps beginning with letters of marque or reprisal. The embargo had always been justified as the only alternative to submission or war. When its sequel was neither, but a halfway measure no one believed in, the credibility of American diplomacy was undermined and the future clouded in the extreme.

Chapter **8**

Gathering Storm Clouds

Inauguration Day, March 4, 1809, "from its commencement to its close, was marked by the liveliest demonstrations of joy," according to the *National Intelligencer*, the administration newspaper in Washington. James Madison in his carriage, escorted by a troop of cavalry, arrived at the Capitol at noon and entered the splendid new chamber of the House of Representatives overflowing with people. Led to the front of the hall, he found Jefferson, feeling like "a prisoner released from his chains," seated to his right and Chief Justice John Marshall, who would administer the oath of office, to his left. Madison's brief address was commonplace—a piece of Republican homespun to match the suit of American cloth he wore in patriotic salute to the infant manufactures spawned by the embargo. After taking the oath, the new President left the hall to the roar of guns and proceeded to his home on F Street, which was thrown open to all and sundry. The day's festivities concluded with an inaugural ball at Long's Hotel. Margaret Bayard Smith, whose husband edited the *National Intelligencer*, wrote this breezy report in a personal letter.

> Saturday, March [4], 1809.
> To-day after the inaguration, we all went to Mrs. Madison's. The street was full of carriages and people, and we had to wait near half an hour, before we could get in,—the house was completely filled, parlours, entry, drawing room and bed room. Near the door of the drawing room Mr. and Mrs. Madison stood to receive their company. She looked extremely beautiful, was drest in a plain cambrick dress with a very long train, plain round the neck without any handkerchief, and beautiful bonnet of purple velvet, and white satin with white plumes. She was all dignity, grace and affability. Mr. Madison shook my hand with all the cordiality of old

Certificate of the tally of the electoral ballots, dated February 8, 1809, naming Madison the President and George Clinton Vice President

acquaintance. . . .

. . . The crowd was immense both at the Capitol and here, thousands and thousands of people thronged the avenue. The Capitol presented a gay scene. Every inch of space was crowded and there being as many ladies as gentlemen, all in full dress, it gave it rather a gay than a solemn appearance,—there was an attempt made to appropriate particular seats for the ladies of public characters, but it was found impossible to carry it into effect, for the sovereign people would not resign their privileges and the high and low were promiscuously blended on the floor and in the galleries.

Mr. Madison was extremely pale and trembled excessively when he first began to speak, but soon gained confidence and spoke audibly. From the Capitol we went to Mrs. M's., and from there to Mr. Jefferson's. . . .

Sunday morning. Well, my dear Susan, the chapter draws to a close. Last night concluded the important day, in which our country received a new magistrate. . . . The room was so terribly crowded that we had to stand on the benches; from this situation we had a view of the moving mass; for it was nothing else. It was scarcely possible to elbow your way from one side to another, and poor Mrs. Madison was almost pressed to death, for every one crowded round her, those behind pressing on those before, and peeping over their shoulders to have a peep of her, and those who were so fortunate as to get near enough to speak to her were happy indeed. As the upper sashes of the windows could not let down, the glass was broken, to ventilate the room, the air of which had become oppressive, but here I begin again at the end of the story. Well, to make up for it I will begin at

The President's House during the administration of James Madison

274

"Madison's March," which serenaded Madison and "his Lady" on March 4, 1809, his first Inauguration Day

the beginning. When we went there were not above 50 persons in the room, we were led to benches at the upper fire place. Not long afterwards, the musick struck up Jefferson's March, and he and Mr. [Isaac] Coles [Jefferson's private secretary] entered. He spoke to all whom he knew, and was quite the plain, unassuming citizen. Madison's March was then played and Mrs. Madison led in by one of the managers and Mrs. [Anna] Cutts [Dolley's sister] and Mr. Madison, she was led to the part of the room where we happened to be, so that I accidently was placed next her. She looked a queen. She had on a pale buff colored velvet, made plain, with a very long train, but not the least trimming, and beautiful pearl necklace, earrings and bracelets. Her head dress was a turban of the same coloured velvet and white satin (from Paris) with two superb plumes, the bird of paradise feathers. It would be *absolutely impossible* for any one to behave with more perfect propriety than she did. Unassuming dignity, sweetness, grace. It seems to me that such manners would disarm envy itself, and conciliate even enemies. The managers presented her with the first number, — "But what shall I do with it," said she, "I do not dance." "Give it to your neighbor," said Capt. Tingey. "Oh no," said she, "that would look like partiality." "Then I will," said the Capt. and he presented it to Mrs. Cutts. I really admired this in Mrs. M. Ah, why does she not in all things act with the same propriety? She would be too much beloved if she added all the virtues to all the graces. She was led to supper by the French Minister, Mrs. Cutts by the English Minister, she sat at the centre of the table, which was a cressent, the French and English ministers on each hand, Mrs. Cutts the next on the right hand, Mrs. [Robert] Smith [wife of the Secretary of State] the next on the left and Mr. Madison on the other side of the table opposite Mrs. M....Mr. Jefferson did not stay above two hours; he seemed in high spirits and his countenance beamed with a benevolent joy. I do believe father never loved son more than he loves Mr. Madison, and I believe too that every demonstration of respect to Mr. M. gave Mr. J. more pleasure than if paid to himself. Oh he is a good man! And the day will come when all party spirit shall expire, that every citizen of the United States will join in saying "He is a good man." Mr. Madison, on the contrary, seemed spiritless and exhausted. While he was standing by me I said, "I wish with all my heart I had a little bit of seat to offer you." "I wish so too," said he, with a most woe begone face, and looking as if he could scarcely stand,—the managers came up to ask him to stay to supper, he assented, and turning to me, "but I would much rather be in bed" said he. Immediately after supper Mr. and Mrs. M. withdrew, the rest of the company danced until 12, the moment the clock struck that hour, the musick stopped, and we all came home tired and sick. "And such," said I as I threw myself on the bed, "such are the gaiety and pleasures of the world!"

The Madisons at once moved into the President's House and Dolley launched her remarkable career as First Lady. Large, bustling, vivacious, fashionable, "Queen Dolley" was everything her husband was not. Under her management the President's House, rudely furnished in Jefferson's time, acquired touches of elegance. So did the entertainment. The Wednesday afternoon "drawing rooms" recalled President Washington's celebrated levees (which Jefferson had abolished), though free of their stiffness and formality. In 1811 young Washington Irving stepped into "the blazing splendor" of this weekly salon. "Here I was most graciously received," he wrote, "found a crowded collection of great and little men, of ugly old women and beautiful young ones, and in ten minutes was hand in glove with half the people in the assemblage. Mrs. Madison is a fine, portly, buxom dame, who has a smile and pleasant word for everybody. Her sisters, Mrs. Cutts and Mrs. [Lucy Payne] Washington, are like the two merry wives of Windsor: but as to Jemmy Madison—ah poor Jemmy!—he is but a withered little apple-john." Dolley created an aura of glamour even around the Presidency of James Madison.

The unprecedented unity and harmony in the executive that Jefferson had maintained for eight years broke down at once under Madison. Contemplating no change of policy from the previous administration, he wanted as few changes of personnel as possible. Albert Gallatin was slated for the State Department; but when his enemies in Congress protested, Madison abandoned the plan, kept Gallatin in the Treasury, and gave the post to Robert Smith, formerly Secretary of the Navy, whose brother Samuel headed the troublesome faction in the Senate. The first of several bad decisions Madison made in the choice of his official family, it splintered the administration from the start. Smith's talent for intrigue exceeded his talent for diplomacy, so Madison continued to handle the important affairs of the State Department. More inept than Smith, though free of guile, were William Eustis and Paul Hamilton, appointed to the posts of War and Navy, respectively. Caesar Rodney stayed on as Attorney General. During eight years Jefferson had had three attorneys general but only one secretary in each of the four departments. During the same term Madison ran through as many attorneys general and fourteen secretaries. Weakness and discord in the Cabinet reflected, of course, Madison's own deficiencies of personality and leadership. Congress, too, escaped the President's control. Adhering rigidly to the constitutional separation of powers, Madison was reluctant to lead Congress. Jefferson, too, had bowed ceremoniously to the doctrine, but seeing that the alternative was chaos had controlled Congress through the unofficial apparatus of party leadership. Lacking Jefferson's political talents, Madison adopted a passive role toward Congress, which gained in power and prestige as the Presidency declined.

Foreign affairs virtually monopolized the President's agenda. He had no confidence in the Nonintercourse Act as an instrument of American neutrality. A trade legally open to all the world except Britain and France was, in fact, open to those nations as well, especially to a Britain that ruled the seas. France had every right to complain and did, while Britain was relieved of the pressure of the embargo and yet free to plunder American shipping as before. Madison was therefore pleasantly surprised in April by the offer of the British minister, David Erskine, to revoke the orders in council in exchange for normal trade between the two countries. Madison at once proclaimed the trade open and on the effective date, June 10, six hundred ships sailed confidently for Britain. Napoleon might be expected to reciprocate. Perhaps then the embargo had succeeded after all, for Erskine's instructions antedated the Nonintercourse Act. Madison sent Jefferson the good news.

Pencil drawing of young Washington Irving in 1805 by John Vanderlyn

Washington Apl. 24. 1809

You will see in the newspapers the result of the advances made by G.B. Attempts were made to give shapes to the arrangement implying inconsistency and blame on our part. They were however met in a proper manner & readily abandoned; leaving these charges in their full force, as they now bear on the other side. The B. Cabinet must have changed its course under a full conviction that an adjustment with this country, had become essential; & it is not improbable that this policy may direct the ensuing negociation; mingling with it, at the same time, the hope that it may embroil us with France. To this use it may be expected the Federalists will endeavor to turn what is already done, at the coming session of Congs. The steps deemed proper to give the proceeding a contrary turn will not be omitted. And if France be not bereft of common sense, or be not predetermined on war with us, she will certainly not play into the hand of

277

Monticello, Jefferson's home

her Enemy. Besides the general motive to follow the example of G.B. she cannot be insensible of the dangerous tendency of prolonging the commercial sufferings of her allies, particularly Russia, all of them already weary of such a state of things, after the pretext of enforcing it shall have ceased. She must be equally aware of the importance of our relations to Spanish America, which must now become the great object of Napoleons pride & ambition.

Jefferson hailed this "triumph of our forbearing and yet perservering system." Federalists, on the other hand, acclaimed the new President for boldly reversing Jefferson's course. Madison alluded to this mischievous and mistaken view of the matter in a subsequent letter to his friend at Monticello.

Washington May 30. 1809

The newfangled policy of the federal party, you will have noticed, has made a considerable figure in the newspapers. Some of the Editors are resuming the Old cant, and the others will doubtless soon follow the example. Nothing could exceed the folly of supposing that the principles & opinions manifested in our foreign discussion, were not, in the main at least, common to us; unless it be the folly of supposing that such shallow hypocrisy could deceive any one. The truth is, the sudden & unlooked for turn of the B. Cabinet, has thrown the party entirely off the Center. They have at present no settled plan. There is reason to believe that the leaders are soured towards England, and much less disposed than heretofore to render our interests subservient to hers. Expressions have been used by one at least of the Essex Cabinet [a group of New England Federalists], whether sincerely or insidiously may not be absolutely certain, from which it is inferred that a disposition exists in that quarter not even to continue the non-intercourse Act agst. France. Certain it is, that the desire of war with her is no longer manifested; and the deficiency of the English markets excites a keen appetite for a trade with the continent; and that a real uneasiness is felt lest the negociations with G.B. should end in sacrifices on our part, which they have been reproaching the Administration for not being ready to make. As one proof of their present feelings, the federal leaders shew a marked alienation from Erskine. The Elections in Massts. as well as in N.H. and N.Y. have issued unfavorably. But the smallness of the majority, and the overstrained exertions it has required, seem to depress rather than flatter the successful party. No confidence is felt in the permanency of the triumph.

Madison was at Montpelier near the end of July when he learned from Gallatin that Britain's Foreign Secretary Canning had repudiated the Erskine agreement. In his friendship for the United States the envoy had, in truth, violated his instructions. That something was amiss had been suggested by the new British order of April 26 which substituted the fiction of a far-flung blockade of the Continent—from Holland to Italy—for the harsh restrictions of the earlier system. Even if an improvement, the blockade contradicted the Erskine agreement and still interfered with neutral trade. Replying to Gallatin, Madison speculated on the reason for this latest act of British "fraud and folly."

Montpellier July 28. 1809

The conduct of the B. Govt. in protesting the arrangement of its Minister surprizes one in spite of all their examples of folly. If it be not their plan, now that they have filled their magazines with our supplies, and ascertained our want of firmness in witholding them, to adopt openly a system of monopoly & piracy, it may be hoped that they will not persist in the scandalous course in which they have set out. Supposing Erskine to have misunderstood or overstrained his instructions, can the difference between our trading directly & indirectly with Holland, account for the violent remedy applied to the case? Is it not more probable that they have yielded to the clamors of the London Smugglers in Sugar and Coffee, whose numbers & impudence are displayed in the scandalous & successful demand from their Govt. that it should strangle the lawful trade of a friendly nation lest it should interfere with their avowed purpose of

By the Virtue, Firmness and Patriotism of
JEFFERSON & MADISON,
Our Difficulties with England are settled—our Ships have been preserved, and our Seamen will, hereafter, be respected while sailing under our National Flag.

Heading of a proclamation issued by Madison in April, 1809, declaring prematurely that difficulties with England had been settled

The Life and Letters of Dolly Madison
BY ALLEN C. CLARK, 1914

Madison's stepson, John Payne Todd

carrying on a smuggling trade with their Enemies. Such an outrage on all decency, was never before heard of, even on the shores of Africa [by the Barbary pirates]. I have a private letter of late date from London, which says it was whispered that the Ministry were inclined to swallow the pill sent them; but that the King considered himself as insulted in what related to Berkley [Admiral George C. Berkeley, the responsible British officer in the *Chesapeake-Leopard* affair, whose punishment Madison had said was "due from His Britannic Majesty to his own honor"] and positively refused his consent. This is not impossible, and may assist in explaining the phenomenon. Still, I can not but hope...that things may take another turn, under the influence of the obvious & striking considerations which advise it. The sudden disavowal of Erskine by the Ministry took place in a moment of alarm...and the confusion is strongly marked on the expedient resorted to. Whilst they acknowledge the obligation to save the Amn. Merchts. from the snare, they not only leave it open for those not going directly from the U.S. but take no notice of the Mediterranean ports opened by the arrangement & shut by their decree. This is another presumption that the Holland market alone was in their thoughts, & that on acct. of the Smugglers who awed them.

In answer to a letter to Mr. [Robert] Smith, I have made a few observations on the several points for consideration; declining a return to Washington, as not necessary, but awaiting the result of your consultations on that as on other subjects. I venture to hope that my return will not be found necessary; the less so as you will be able to bring with you so full a view of the state of things, and the sentiments of your colleagues, that my decision as far as necessary, may be made as well here as at Washington.

The crisis was such, however, that Madison was forced to make the tiring journey to Washington in the August heat, staying just long enough to proclaim the restoration of nonintercourse with Britain. While at the capital, Madison wrote to his wife.

[Washington, August, 1809]
I hope you receid., my dearest, a letter written by the last mail. I write this in haste just to tell you that P[ayne]

& myself are well; & that I am making exertions to get thro' the necessary business, with a hope of setting out on my return tomorrow. It is very possible however that I may be detained till friday morning. I send you all the foreign news in the inclosed papers. That from France has a better complexion than preceding accts. of her temper towards the U.S. The tone of Cannings speech also is a little different from the arrogance of his instructions to Mr. Erskine. Payne writes. I must refer to his letter for what I am prevented from adding. . . .

The bright promises of April shriveled in August. Anglo-American relations were in a worse state than before. The *Chesapeake* affair dragged on, impressment was still at issue, the orders in council still "colonialized" American trade, and the Erskine imbroglio frayed tempers on both sides. Back home in Virginia, Madison wrote to Jefferson.

Montpellier Aug. 16. 1809

I got home from my trip to Washington on Saturday last; having remained there three days only. You will have seen in the Procln. issued, the result of [our] consultation on the effect of what has passed on our relations with G.B. The enforcement of the non-intercourse act agst. her, will probably be cri[ticiz]ed by some friends and generally assailed by our adversaries, on the ground that the power given to the Ex. being special, was exhausted by the first exercise of it; and that the power having put out of force the laws to which it related, could under no possible construction restore their operation. . . .

Erskine is in a ticklish situation with his Govt. I suspect he will not be able to defend himself agst. the charge of exceeding his instructions, notwithstanding the appeal he makes to sundry others not published. But he will make out a strong case agst. Canning, and be able to avail himself much of the absurdity and evident inadmissibility of the articles disregarded by him. He can plead, also that the difference between his arrangmt. & the spontaneous order of Apl. 26. is too slight to justify the disavowal of him. . . .

We are looking out for Mr. & Mrs. Gallatin every day. Untill they arrive, and we learn also the periods of your being at & absent from Home, we do not venture to fix a time for our proposed visit to Monticello.

English mug honoring "Maddison"

Erskine was recalled, to be succeeded by Francis James Jackson, whose tone and temper were altogether different. Believing the United States the injured party in the Erskine matter, Madison expected an explanation from Jackson. Instead the minister accused Smith and Madison of conniving in Erskine's violation of instructions. Midway in this dialogue, Madison reported to William Pinkney in London.

Washington Ocr. 23. 1809

You will see in the communications from the Dept. of State what has passed with Mr. Jackson. No reply to Mr. S.s answer has yet been made. It appears that the B. Govt. continues to be equally ignorant of our character, & of what it owes to its own. . . . For it is impossible not to see that the avowed object is no longer to retaliate on an enemy, but to prevent our legitimate commerce from interfering with the London Smugglers of Sugar & Coffee. How can a nation expect to retain the respect of Mankind whose Govt. descends to so ignoble a career?

What will be the future course of Mr. Jackson, or that of his Govt. or of Congs. I do not undertake to anticipate, farther than that Congs. will in some form or other keep up a counteraction to the misconduct of both Belligerents. As to Mr. J. it can not be supposed that he has any effective authority to overcome the difficulties before him. Altho' we continue sincerely anxious to facilitate his doing so, yet no[t] a little indignation is felt, at the mean & insolent attempt to defraud the U.S. of the exculpatory explanation dictated by the respect due to them; and particularly at the insinuation in Jackson's answer that this Govt. colluded with Mr. E. in violating his instructions.

You will observe by the Gazettes that Mr. Onis, appointed by the Spanish Junta [controlled by Britain], is just arrived here as a Minister Plenipo: of Ferdinand; and that efforts are made to turn the question of his being received, to party purposes. The principle of neutrality on one hand, and on the other, the limited authority of the Executive . . . could never permit the reception of Mr. Onis in the actual state of things in Spain. . . .

The public opinion or rather that of the discontented party has already undergone a considerable change in favor of the system pursued in our foreign relations, and the change is still going on. In Maryld. & Vermont, the fact is shewn by the late elections. And all accts. from the Eastward prognosticate that the next elections in Massts. N.H. & R. Island, will reverse those which took place during the fever which the Embargo was made to produce. Reflection alone would probably have brought about such a change. But it has been hastened by the disappointment of all parties, as to the Conduct of G.B. on the subject of Mr. Erskine's arrangement; and by the severe experience, that a trade limited to the B. dominions is but a mouthfull and not as the people were told it wd. be a bellyfull. The shipments to the W. Inds. have been ruinous. In the Mediterranean the losses, owing to captures, recaptures & markets glutted from Engd. will not be less than 25 or 30 per Ct. In the Baltic, & the N. of Europe, the speculations are still more entirely blasted. The lumber merchts. who struck at the great demand in England have been successful; and the others have been saved from loss, by the expected consequence of the Disavowal of Mr. Erskine.

The most remarkable feature in our internal prospects is the astonishing progress of manufactures, more especially in the Household way. Throughout the middle, S. & W. countries, they have taken a lasting root; it being found, that with the aid of the machineries accomodated to the family scale & of habit, cloathing & many other articles can be provided both cheaper & better than as heretofore. Passion is spur also to interest in the case. Nor is necessity without its influence; for in truth, the planters & farmers being deprived of the customary markets & prices for their produce, can no longer pay for their customary supplies from abroad.

New-York, Oct. 4.

SPANISH AFFAIRS.

Late last night the Spanish frigate Cornelia, capt. Don John Roderigues de Arias, arrived at the quarantine ground. She sailed from Cadiz on the 20th of August. This vessels has brought out his excellency Don Lewis de Onis, minister plenipotentiary and envoy extraordinary from his Catholic majesty Ferdinand the 7th to the United States of America. Also Don Bartholomew Rengenet, consul from his Catholic majesty for Philadelphia, their ladies, daughters and domestics, and Mr. Richard Bailey, of this city.

Article in the October 9, 1809, issue of the National Intelligencer *of Washington, D.C., announcing arrival of the Chevalier d'Onis from Cadiz*

Jackson's arrogance was not to be tolerated. After little more than a month, the talks were broken off, the minister dismissed and handed his passport. He struck out for a happier political clime, New England, where he was lionized by Anglomen, while back in Washington Congress condemned his "outrageous and insolent" conduct. The diplomatic rupture distressed Madison's old friend, George Logan, of Philadelphia. As good a Quaker as he was a Republican, Logan went to Washington to plead his cause and on his return home, apparently dissatisfied with the President's posture, wrote to him imploring peace. In his own mind Logan had already appointed himself the envoy of peace, intending to repeat in this crisis with Britain the intervention he had undertaken in 1798 with France—a mission that had produced the Logan Act making such personal diplomacy a crime. Madison, in reply to Logan, credited his good intentions but at the same time justified the administration's course toward Britain.

George Logan of Philadelphia

Washington Jany 19th 1810

I have received your favour of the 10th. Your anxiety that our country may be kept out of the vortex of war, is honourable to your judgement as a patriot, and to your feeling as a man. The same anxiety is, I sincerely believe, felt by the great body of the nation, & by its public councils; most assuredly by the Executive Branch of them. But the question may be decided for us, by actual hostilities against us, or by proceedings, leaving no choice but between absolute disgrace & resistance by force. May not also manifestations of patience under injuries & indignities, be carried as far, as to invite this very dilemma?

I devoutly wish that the same disposition to cultivate peace by means of justice which exists here, predominated elsewhere, particularly in G.B. But how can this be supposed, whilst she persists in proceedings, which comprise the essence of hostility; whilst...we see her converting the late reconciliation through one of her Ministers, into a source of fresh difficulties & animosities, thro' another. For in this light must be viewed, her disavowal of Mr. Erskine, and the impressions made thro' his successor. Had the disavowal been deemed essential to her interests, a worse plaister could not have been devised for the wound necessarily inflicted here....

Notwithstanding all these grounds of discontent & discouragement, we are ready as the B. Govt. knows, to join in any new experiment, (& thro' either our diplomatic channel there, or hers here) for a cordial & comprehensive adjustment of matters between the two countries.

Let reparation be made for the acknowledged wrong commited in the case of the Chesapeak, a reparation so cheap to the wrongdoer, yet so material to the honour of the injured party; & let the orders in Council, already repealed as to the avowed object of retaliation, be repealed also as an expedient for substituting an illicit commerce, in place of that to which neutrals have, as such, an incontestible right. The way will then be opened for negotiation at large; and if the B. Govt. would bring into it the same temper as she would find in us; & the same disposition to insist on nothing inconsistent with the rule of doing as she would, or rather as she *will* be done by, the result could not fail to be happy for both.

Permit me to remark that you are under a mistake in supposing that the Treaty concluded by Messr. M[onroe] & P[inkney] was rejected because it did not provide that free ships should make free goods. It never was required nor expected that such a stipulation should be inserted.... Let me add that the acceptance of that Treaty would have very little changed the actual situation of things with G.B. The orders in council would not have been prevented but rather placed on stronger grou[n]d; the case of the Chesapeak, the same as it is; so also the case of impressments, of fa[c]titious blockades &c all as at present, pregnant sources of contention & ill humour.

From this view of the subject, I cannot but persuade myself, that you will concur in opinion, that if unfortunately, the calamity you so benevolently dread, should visit this hitherto favoured country, the fault will not lie where you would wish it not to lie.

Nathaniel Macon, Chairman of the House Committee on Foreign Affairs

Madison hoped to avoid war, but war was preferable to submission, and he mildly suggested that Congress look to the country's defenses. The Nonintercourse Act would expire with the current session. Although no one advocated its renewal, neither the administration nor Congress could agree on an alternative system to economic coercion. At Gallatin's initiative, Nathaniel Macon, Chairman of the House Committee on Foreign Affairs, introduced what became known as Macon's Bill. Essentially a navigation act, it would permit American ships to ply the seas at their own risk but close American ports to all British and French vessels. Madison thought well of the measure. After four months of wearisome debate, however, Macon's Bill died to be succeeded by Macon's Bill No. 2, enacted at the session's close. The last of a succession of experiments to vindicate American neutrality by commercial sanctions, the act reopened trade with both belligerents but provided that if either government revoked its edicts the President might prohibit intercourse with the other. According to one historian the act was "equivalent to alliance with England" inasmuch as it surrendered American commerce to the nation that controlled the Atlantic sea lanes. Doubtless Napoleon would see it in that light. Although Madison disliked the measure, he decided to make the best of it. Writing to Pinkney, who was pleased that Lord Wellesley had been named to replace Canning in the Foreign Ministry, Madison touched on the impasse over Jackson and then speculated at length on the fate of the new policy.

Washington May 23d 1810

You will learn from the Department of State, as you must have anticipated, our surprise that the answer of

Lord Wellesley, to your very just and able view of the case of Jackson, corresponded so little with the impressions of that Minister manifested in your first interviews with him. The date of the answer best explains the change; as it shows that time was taken for obtaining intelligence from this country, and adapting the policy of the answer to the position taken by the advocates of Jackson. And it must have happened that the intelligence prevailing at that date was of the sort most likely to mislead. The elections which have since taken place in the Eastern States, and which have been materially influenced by the affair of Jackson and the spirit of party connected with it, are the strongest of proofs, that the measure of the Executive coincided with the feelings of the Nation. In every point of view the answer is unworthy of the source from which it comes.

From the manner in which the vacancy left by Jackson is provided for, it is infered that a sacrifice is meant of the respect belonging to this Government, either to the pride of the British Government, or to the feelings of those who have taken side with it against their own. On either supposition, it is necessary to counteract the ignoble purpose. You will accordingly find that on ascertaining the substitution of a Chargé, to be an intentional degradation of the diplomatic intercourse on the part of Great Britain, it is deemed proper that no higher functionary should represent the United States at London....

The Act of Congress transmitted from the Department of State, will inform you of the footing on which our relations to the Belligerent powers were finally placed. The experiment now to be made, of a commerce with both, unrestricted by our laws, has resulted from causes which you will collect from the debates, and from your own reflections. The new form of appeal to the policy of Great Britain and France on the subject of the Decrees and Orders, will most engage your attention. However feeble it may appear, it is possible that one or other of those powers may allow it more effect than was produced by the overtures heretofore tried.... Among the inducements to the experiment of an unrestricted commerce now made, were two which contributed essentially to the majority of votes in its favor; first a general hope, favored by daily accounts from England, that an adjustment of differences there, and thence in France, would

Lord Wellesley

Columbia teaches "Mounseer Beau"
Napoleon and laggard John Bull a new
lesson—to respect free trade and
seamen's rights—in an 1813 cartoon.

render the measure safe & proper; second, a willingness in not a few, to teach the advocates for an open trade, under actual circumstances, the folly, as well as degradation of their policy. At the next meeting of Congress, it will be found, according to present appearances, that instead of an adjustment with either of the Belligerents, there is an increased obstinacy in both; and that the inconveniences of the Embargo, and non-intercourse, have been exchanged for the greater sacrifices as well as disgrace, resulting from a submission to the predatory systems in force. It will not be wonderful therefore, if the passive spirit which marked the late session of Congress, should at the next meeting be roused to the opposite point; more especially as the tone of the Nation has never been as low as that of its Representatives, and as it is rising already under the losses sustained by our Commerce in the Continental ports, and by the fall of prices in our produce at home, under a limitation of the market, to Great Britain. Cotton I perceive is down at 10 or 11 cents in Georgia. The great mass of Tobacco is in a similar situation. And the effect must soon be general, with the exception of a few articles which do not at present, glut the British demand. Whether considerations like these will make any favorable impression on the British Cabinet, you will be the first to know. Whatever confidence I may have in the justness of them, I must forget all that has past before I can indulge very favorable expectations. Every new occasion seems to countenance the belief, that there lurks in the British Cabinet, a hostile feeling towards this Country, which

287

will never be eradicated during the present Reign; nor overruled, whilst it exists, but by some dreadful pressure from external or internal causes.

With respect to the French Govt. we are taught by experience to be equally distrustful. It will have however the same opportunity presented to it, with the British Govt., of comparing the actual state of things, with that which would be produced by a repeal of its Decrees; and it is not easy to find any plausible motive to continue the former as preferable to the latter. A worse state of things, than the actual one, could not exist for France, unless her preference be for a state of War. If she be sincere either in her propositions relative to a chronological revocation of illegal Edicts against Neutrals, or to a pledge from the United States not to submit to those of Great Britain, she ought at once to embrace the arrangement held out by Congress. . . .

During the past year Napoleon had seized ten million dollars worth of American ships and cargoes in reprisal for the Nonintercourse Act. Considering the American trade as identical with the British, he made any Yankee vessel liable to seizure and sequestration in ports under French control. The practice was "legalized" by the Rambouillet Decree of March, 1810. Strictly in terms of maritime losses, France had become the greater enemy of American neutrality. Nevertheless, Madison continued to hold that "the original sin against neutrals lies with Great Britain" and that she remained the greater threat. France might pillage but she could not monopolize or colonize American trade. So Madison refused to shift the balance of American resistance from Britain to France.

Napoleon knew how to play the game for his benefit, and now, in August, he seized upon the invitation extended by Macon's Bill No. 2. On his order the Duke of Cadore, Foreign Minister, told John Armstrong, U.S. Minister to France, that the Berlin and Milan Decrees were revoked as of November 1, it being understood that Britain would lift her orders and sham blockades or that the United States would force her to reform. Madison learned of the Cadore letter by way of Pinkney and did not wait for confirmation. Historians disagree on whether he allowed himself to be duped by Napoleon or, rather, shrewdly adopted the fiction of French repeal in order to force the issue with Britain. At any rate, he took the letter at face value, interpreted the French repeal as unconditional, and on November 2 proclaimed nonintercourse with Britain subject to repeal of her orders within ninety days. At the same time, with Britain and France warring in Spain, he jumped at the chance to annex West Florida, which was already predominantly settled by Americans. Announcing possession of the area by the United States, Madison ordered Governor William Claiborne of the Orleans Territory to enter West Florida and to establish a civil government there. In writing to Armstrong, he discussed this latest chapter in the collapse of Spanish empire as well as the Cadore letter.

Washington Oct. 29th 1810

You will learn from the Department of State that altho' no direct authentication of the repeal of the French decrees has been received from you, a proclamation issues on the ground furnished by your correspondence with Mr. Pinkney. It is to be hoped that France will do what she is understood to be pledged for, and in a manner that will produce no jealousy or embarrassment here. We hope in particular that the sequestred property will have been restored.... The course which G.B. will take, is left by Wellesley's pledge, a matter of conjecture. It is not improbable that the orders in Council will be revoked and the sham blockades be so managed if possible, as to irritate France against our non-resistance without irritating this Country to the resisting point. It seems on the whole that we shall be at issue with G.B. on the ground of such blockades, and it is for us a strong ground.

You will see also the step that has been produced by the posture of things in W. Florida. If France is wise she will neither dislike it herself, nor promote resentment of it in any other quarter. She ought in fact, if guided by prudence and good information, to patronize at once, a general separation of S. America from old Spain. This event is already decided, and the sole question with France is whether it is to take place under her auspices, or those of Great Britain. The latter ... is taking her measures with reference to that event; and in the mean time, is extorting commercial privileges [from West Florida residents] as the recompence of her interposition. In this particular her avarice is defeating her interest. For it not only invites France to outbid her; but throws in seeds of discord which will take effect the moment peace or safety is felt by the party of whom the advantage is taken.... It merits the consideration of France also, that in proportion as she discourages, in any way, a free intercourse of the U.S. with their revolutionary neighbours, she favors the exclusive commerce of her rival with them; as she has hitherto favored it with Europe,

Federalist handbill of 1811 warned that the French decrees had not been repealed and that American ships were still being detained.

289

by her decrees against our intercourse with it. As she seems to be recovering from the one folly, it may be hoped she will not fall into the other.

Britain yielded nothing, and Congress enacted into law the nonintercourse proclaimed by Madison. Napoleon, far from giving thought to reparations, continued his seizures, justified now on local customs regulations which, unlike the old decrees, were outside the scope of international law though their effect was the same. Britain insisted the French decrees were still in force. The United States insisted they were repealed. In this deadlock one country must yield or war must ensue. Whatever the truth of the matter, Madison stuck to the idea of repeal because it got him out of the scrape with France, rescued the nation from the disgraceful submission of the last two years, and restored peaceable coercion of Britain. Federalists, and some Republicans too, said the policy connived in Napoleonic fraud and deceit; they also denounced it as unconstitutional and destructive of commerce. Resolutions and addresses poured into the President from the eastern towns. To one of them, from New Haven, he sent his quiet answer.

Washington May 24. 1811.

I have recd. fellow Citizens, the petition which you have addressed to me representing the inconveniences experienced from the existing non-importation law, and soliciting that the National Legislature may be speedily convened.

It is known to all that the Commerce of the U.S. has, for a considerable period, been greatly abridged & annoyed by Edicts of the Belligerent powers; each professing retaliation only on the other; but both violating the clearest rights of the U.S. as a neutral nation. In this extraordinary state of things, the Legislature willing to avoid a resort to war, more especially during the concurrent aggressions of two great Powers, themselves at war, the one with the other, and determined on the other hand agst. an unqualified acquiescence, have endeavored by successive and varied regulations affecting the commerce of the parties, to make it their interest to be just.

In the Act of Congress out of which the existing non-importation has grown, the state of Commerce was no otherwise qualified than by a provision, that in case either of the Belligerents should revoke its unlawful Edicts, and the other should fail to do the same, our ports should be shut to the vessels & merchandize of the latter. This provision...was equally presented to

Invoice for pipes (casks) of wine ordered by Madison and Dolley's sister Lucy Washington in 1811

An 1811 cartoon portrays the refusal of Congress to renew the charter of the Bank of the United States.

the attention of both. In consequence of the communication the French Government declared that its Decrees were revoked. As the British Government had expressed reluctance in issuing its orders, and repeatedly signified a wish to find in the example of its adversary, an occasion for putting an end to them, the expectation was the more confident, that the occasion would be promptly embraced. This was not done; and the period allowed for the purpose having elapsed, our ports became shut to British Ships and merchandize....

If appeals to the justice of the Belligerents, through their interests, involve privations on our part also, it ought to be recollected that this is an effect inseparable from every resort, by which one nation can right itself agst. the injustice of others.

If sacrifices made for the sake of the whole result more to some than to other districts or descriptions of Citizens, this also is an effect, which tho always to be regretted, can never be entirely avoided. Whether the appeal be to the sword, or to interruptions or modifications of customary intercourse, an equal operation on every part of the Community never happens....

In estimating the particular measure which has been adopted by the national Councils, it may be reasonably expected therefore, from the candor of enlightened Citizens, that with the peculiarity of the public situation, they will be impressed also with the difficulty of selecting the course most satisfactory, and best suited to diminish its evils or shorten their duration: that they will keep in mind that a resort to war must involve necessary restrictions on commerce; and that were no measure whatever opposed to the Belligerent acts against our Commerce, it would not only remain under the severe restrictions now imposed by foreign hands, but new motives would be given for prolonging and invigorating them.

Feuding in Congress and in the Cabinet rocked the administration in 1811. The treasury faced declining revenues from the ban on British imports, yet additional funds were wanted for the country's defenses. Congress continued to starve the army and navy, however, and also defeated the bill to renew the charter of the Bank of the United States. Madison did not lift a finger to help Gallatin save the Bank, upon which the Secretary depended heavily and without which, in his opinion, the government could not finance a war. Old Republican feelings against the Bank, this last monument of Federalism, contributed to its demise, but much of the opposition was simply opposition to Gallatin. His enemies were not limited to "The Invisibles"—the followers of Senator Samuel Smith and his intriguing brother, the Secretary of State. But this faction was especially virulent, and it aimed to knock Gallatin out with the Bank. He did, in fact, threaten to resign. But Madison could not afford to lose him. His hand forced at last, he demanded Robert Smith's resignation. Smith chose to be fired, however, and then to smear the administration in the press. His publication (Madison called it "wicked") included the charge of executive collusion with France. The Cabinet crisis shook public confidence in the administration. To repair the public injury, and a painful personal one as well, Madison prevailed upon James Monroe to forget his old grudge (resulting from the rejection in 1807 of his treaty with Britain) and to become Secretary of State. Although Monroe entered the office half convinced Madison was the anglophobe his enemies portrayed, he soon fell in with the President's foreign policy.

During the summer the Virginia triumvirs—Jefferson, Madison, and Monroe—surveyed the diplomatic impasse, and the President returned to Washington in the fall all but finally committed to war. His message to the new Congress on November 5 was a call to arms. He reported the failure of the round of diplomacy commenced on the arrival of the latest British envoy, Sir Augustus Foster. Foster took the hard line: either the United States must make war on Napoleon's Continental System or submit its commerce to British orders. It was, Madison told Congress, "an indispensable condition of the repeal of the British orders, that commerce should be restored to a footing, that would admit the productions and manufactures of Great Britain . . . into markets shut against them by the Enemy; the United States being given to understand that, in the mean time, a continuance of their non-importation act, would lead to measures of retaliation." British privateers and cruisers hovered on American coasts and preyed on American carriers. Britain denied redress for old injuries and persisted in measures that amounted to commercial war on the United States. "With this evidence of hostile inflexibility in trampling on rights which no Independent Nation can relinquish, Congress will feel the duty of putting the United States into an armour, and an attitude demanded by the crisis, and corresponding with the national spirit and expectations."

The message appealed to the rising war fever. The West was especially volatile. News of the Battle of Tippecanoe reached the capital just as Congress commenced. This bloody encounter between frontier Americans and stubbornly resisting Indians in the Northwest was charged to British support of the Shawnee chief Tecumseh and his defensive confederacy. It sparked demands to take Canada, thereby ending the Indian menace, expelling the British, and satiating western land hunger. The Twelfth Congress soon gave

Battle of Tippecanoe, 1811

voice to these demands. Overwhelmingly Republican, it included a number of militant young patriots, primarily westerners—Henry Clay, Richard M. Johnson, Felix Grundy, John C. Calhoun, and others—who became known as War Hawks. Their influence was great but they did not drive Madison to war. Rather, they supplied the political nerve and muscle for the policy he had laid out, one which by measured steps led the nation to war on his own responsibility.

Unfortunately, the administration was deeply embarrassed by Napoleon, whose piratical acts against American commerce mocked the idea of repeal of his edicts. The country received nothing but outrages from France at the moment of arming for war on France's enemy. To clarify this anomalous situation, to obtain reparations and guarantees of respect in the future, Madison had sent Joel Barlow as Minister to France. Before the event of war with Britain, he desperately wished to be free of embarrassment with France, as was evident in his message to Barlow in November.

Shawnee chief Tecumseh

Washington Nov. 17. 1811

You will receive by this conveyance the proper communications from the Dept. of State. You will see in them, the ground now avowed for the B. Orders in Council. It must render them codurable with the war; for nothing but a termination of it will re-open the continental market to British products. Nor is it probable that peace will do it on its former extent. The Instruction which requires the U.S. as a neutral power to assert an obligation on one belligerent, to favor, by its internal reputations, the manufactures of another, is a fitter subject for ridicule than refutation. It accordingly has no countenance here even among the most devoted Champions of G.B. Whether some of them by arming themselves with simulated facts & sophisticated distinctions may not be embolded to turn out in her defence, will soon be seen. Nothing has yet passed in Congs. disclosing the sense of that Body, with respect to the moment &

manner of meeting the conduct of G.B. in its present hostile shape. A disposition appears to enter at once on preparations, which will probably be put in force or not, as the effect of them on the British Councils, shall be ascertained in the course of the session. In the mean time it is not improbable that the merchant vessels may be permitted to arm for self-Defence. This can scarcely fail to bring on maritime reprisals and to end in the full extent of war, unless a change in the British system should arrest the career of events. All proceedings however relating to G. Britain will be much influenced by the conduct of France not only as it relates to a violation of our neutral rights; but of our national ones and that too not only in cases strictly French, but in those in Naples & elsewhere indirectly also, and to justice for the past as well as for the future. Altho' in our discussions with G.B. we have been justified in viewing the repeal of the French decrees as sufficiently substantiated to require a fulfillment of the pledge to repeal the order in Council; yet the manner in which the F. Govt. has managed the repeal of the Decrees, and evaded a correction of other outrages, has mingled with the conciliatory tendency of the repeal, as much of irritation and disgust as possible. And these sentiments are not a little strengthened by the sarcastic comments on that management with which we are constantly pelted in our discussions with the B. Govt. and for which the F. Govt. ought to be ashamed to furnish the occasion. In fact without a systematic change from an appearance of crafty contrivance, and insatiate cupidity, to an open manly & upright dealing with a nation whose example demands it, it is impossible that good will can exist; and that the ill will which her policy aims in directing against her enemy, should not, by her folly and iniquity be drawn off against herself. The late licenciousness of the F. privateers in the Baltic, the ruinous transmission of their cases to Paris, and the countenance said to be there given to such abuses, are kindling a fresh flame here: And if a remedy be not applied, & our merchantmen should arm, hostile collisions will as readily take place with one nation as the other. Were it not that our frigates would be in danger of rencounters with British Ships of superior force in that quarter, there could be no scruple at sending thither some of them, with orders to suppress by

Madison's call to arms delivered
to Congress on November 5, 1811

Virginia, HOWE

*In December, 1811, a number of
the Madisons' friends were killed in
a fire in the Richmond Theatre.*

force the French and Danish depredations. I am aware
that a pretext for these has been sought in the practice
of our vessels in accepting British Convoy; but have they
not in many instances at least been driven to this irregular step by the greater irregularities practised agst.
them? We await the return of the [U.S.S.] Constitution
not without a hope of finding the good effect of your remonstrances in a radical change of the French policy
towards this Country.

Barlow got only a runaround in France. As late as April,
1812, Madison entertained the possibility of making war on both belligerents simultaneously. But Britain always loomed as the major enemy. During a tempestuous winter, when Washington was even visited by an earth-
quake, Madison fretted alternately over the glimmering hope of peace and
the nation's laggard preparations for war. Of the army voted by Congress,
he wrote sarcastically to Jefferson: "With a view to enable the Executive
to step at once into Canada they have provided after two months delay, for
a regular force requiring 12 to raise it; and after 3 months for a volunteer
force, on terms not likely to raise it at all." Instead of new ships for the
navy, Congress only reactivated old ones. Loans and higher tariffs were
voted but not new taxes. The Republicans were a leaderless herd. Anti-
Madisonian factions—Smith's Invisibles, Randolph's "Quids," the Clinton-
ians of New York—blunted the best efforts of the administration party. It
may have been some consolation to Madison that the government in London
stood in worse straits. George III was insane, Ireland rebellious, and economic distress widespread. Angry opposition to the orders in council further
jeopardized Spencer Perceval's government. Partly because of this situation,
Madison delayed the decision for war. Even on April 1, when he asked Congress for an embargo preparatory to war, he clung to the hope that it might
yet be an instrument of negotiating peace. He waited, too, to hear from
France. Dispatches from both foreign capitals were expected on the return
of the U.S.S. *Hornet,* which fixed the hour of decision. He wrote to Jefferson
at this time.

Washington April 3. 1812
A late arrival from G.B. brings dates subsequent to the
maturity of the Prince Regents Authority. It appears that
Percival, &c. are to retain their places, and that they
prefer war with us, to a repeal of their orders in Council.
We have nothing left therefore, but to make ready for it.
As a step to it an embargo for 60 days was recommended
to Congs. on Wednesday and agreed to in the H. of Reps.
by about 70 to 40. The Bill was before the Senate yes-

Joel Barlow

terday, who adjourned about 4 or 5 O Clock without a decision. . . . The temper of that body is known to be equivocal. Such a measure, even for a limited and short time, is always liable to adverse as well as favorable considerations; and its operation at this moment, will add fuel to party discontent, and interested clamor. But it is a rational & provident measure, and will be relished by a greater portion of the Nation, than an omission of it. If it could have been taken sooner and for a period of 3 or 4 months, it might have inlisted an alarm of the B. Cabinet. . . . Whether if adopted for 60 days, it may beget apprehensions of a protraction, & thence lead to admissible overtures, before the sword is stained with blood, cannot be foreknown with certainty. Such an effect is not to be counted upon. You will observe, that Liverpool was Secy. for the Foreign Dept. ad interim, & that Castlereah is the definitive successor of Wellesley [as Britain's Foreign Minister]. The resignation of this last, who has recd. no other appt is a little mysterious. There is some reason for believing that he is at variance with Percival; or that he distrusts the stability of the existing Cabinet, and courts an alliance with the Grenville party, as likely to overset it. If none of that party desert their colours, the calculation cannot be a very bad one; especially in case of war with the U.S: in addition to the distress of B. trade & manufactures, and the inflammation in Ireland: to say nothing of possible reverses in Spain & Portugal, which alone would cut up the Percival ascendency by the roots. From France we hear nothing. The delay of the Hornet is inexplicable, but on the reproachful supposition, that the F Govt. is waiting for the final turn of things at London, before it takes its course, which justice alone ought to prescribe, towards us. If this be found to be its game, it will impair the value of concessions if made, and give to her refusal of them, consequences it may little dream of.

The *Hornet* at last reached New York on May 19 and Madison read the fateful dispatches three days later. Castlereagh's letter to Foster confirmed what Madison thought he already knew: the British orders were "co-durable" with the war. He had, at least, hoped for some escape from the dilemma with France, but Napoleon, too, ran true to form. Madison relayed the sorry news to Jefferson.

Washington May 25. 1812

The inclosed letters came under cover to me, by the Hornet. France has done nothing towards adjusting our differences with her. It is understood that the B[erlin] & M[ilan] Decrees are not in force agst. the U.S. and no contravention of them can be established agst. her. On the contrary positive cases rebut the allegation. Still the manner of the F. Govt. betrays the design of leaving G.B. a pretext for enforcing her O[rders] in C[ouncil] And in all other respects the grounds of our complaints remain the same. The utmost address has been played off on Mr. Barlow's wishes & hopes; inasmuch that at the Departure of the Hornet which had been so long detained for a final answer, without its being obtained, he looked to the return of the Wasp which had just arrived, without despair of making her the Bearer of some satisfactory arrangement. Our calculations differ widely. In the mean time, the business is become more than ever puzzling. To go to war with Engd. and not with France arms the federalists with new matter, and divides the Republicans some of whom with the Quids make a display of impartiality. To go to war agst. both, presents a thousand difficulties; above all that of shutting all the ports of the Continent of Europe agst. our Cruisers who can do little without the use of them. It is pretty certain also, that it would not gain over the Federalists, who wd. turn all those difficulties agst. the Administration. The only consideration of weight in favor of this triangular war as it is called, is that it might hasten thro' a peace with G.B. or F: a termination, for a while at least, of the obstinate questions now depending with both. But even this advantage is not certain. For a prolongation of such a war might be viewed by both Belligts. as desireable with as little reason for the opinion, as has prevailed in the past conduct of both.

It only remained for the President to write his war message. He reviewed the long history of grievance with Britain, not omitting France from the tale, but as before excepting her from the wrath of American justice. Whatever the transgressions of France, they did not strike at the independence of the United States; besides, France could nowhere be attacked on the American continent, so the question of war with her was, in a sense, academic. The message went to Congress on the first day of June.

War Hawks included Richard M. Johnson (top) and Felix Grundy.

[June 1, 1812]

To the Senate and House of Representatives of the United States.

I communicate to Congress certain Documents, being a continuation of those heretofore laid before them, on the subject of our Affairs with Great Britain.

Without going back beyond the renewal in 1803, of the war in which Great Britain is engaged, and omitting unrepaired wrongs of inferior magnitude; the conduct of her Government presents a series of acts, hostile to the United States, as an Independent and neutral nation.

British cruisers have been in the continued practice of violating the American flag on the great high way of nations, and of seizing and carrying off persons sailing under it; not in the exercise of a Belligerent right founded on the Law of Nations against an Enemy; but of a municipal prerogative over British subjects. British jurisdiction is thus extended to neutral vessels in a situation where no laws can operate but the law of nations, and the laws of the Country to which the vessels belong; and a self-redress is assumed . . . which falls within the definition of War. . . .

The practice, hence, is so far from affecting British subjects alone, that under the pretext of searching for these, thousands of American Citizens, under the safeguard of public law, and of their national flag, have been torn from their country, and from every thing dear to them, have been dragged on board ships of war of a foreign nation; and exposed, under the severities of their discipline, to be exiled to the most distant and deadly climes, to risk their lives in the battles of their oppressors, and to be the melancholy instruments of taking away those of their own brethren.

Against this crying enormity, which Great Britain would be so prompt to avenge if committed against herself, the United States have, in vain, exhausted remonstrances and expostulations. And that no proof might be wanting of their conciliatory dispositions, and no pretext left for a continuance of the practice, the British Government was formally assured of the readiness of the United States to enter into arrangements, such as could not be rejected, if the recovery of British subjects were the real and sole object. The communication passed without effect.

British cruisers have been in the practice also of violat-

John C. Calhoun (top) and Henry Clay were also militant patriots.

ing the rights and the peace of our Coasts. They hover over and harass our entering and departing commerce. To the most insulting pretentions, they have added the most lawless proceedings in our very harbors; and have wantonly spilt American blood, within the sanctuary of our territorial jurisdiction. . . .

Under pretended blockades, without the presence of an adequate force, and sometimes without the practicability of applying one, our commerce has been plundered in every Sea; the great staples of our Country have been cut off, from their legitimate markets; and a destructive blow aimed at our agricultural and maritime interests. . . .

Not content with these occasional expedients for laying waste our neutral trade, the cabinet of Great Britain resorted, at length, to the sweeping system of Blockades, under the name of orders in Council; which has been moulded and managed, as might best suit its political views, its commercial jealouses, or the avidity of British cruisers.

To our remonstrances against the complicated and transcendent injustice of this innovation, the first reply was that the orders were reluctantly adopted by Great Britain, as a necessary retaliation on decrees of her Enemy proclaiming a general Blockade of the British Isles, at a time when the naval force of that Enemy dared not to issue from his own ports. She was reminded, without effect, that her own prior blockades, unsupported by an adequate naval force actually applied and continued, were a bar to this plea: that executed Edicts against millions of our property, could not be retaliation on Edicts, confessedly impossible to be executed: that retaliation to be just, should fall on the party setting the guilty example, not on an innocent party, which was not even chargeable with an acquiescence in it.

When deprived of this flimsy veil for a prohibition of our trade with her enemy, by the repeal of his prohibition of our trade with Great Britain; her Cabinet, instead of a corresponding repeal, or a practical discontinuance, of its orders, formally avowed a determination to persist in them against the United States, until the markets of her enemy should be laid open to British products: thus asserting an obligation on a neutral power to require one Belligerent to encourage, by its internal regulations, the trade of another Belligerent; contradicting her own practice towards all nations, in peace as well as in war....

It has become indeed sufficiently certain, that the commerce of the United States is to be sacrificed, not as interfering with the Belligerent rights of Great Britain; not as supplying the wants of her enemies, which she herself supplies; but as interfering with the monopoly which she covets for her own commerce and navigation. She carries on a war against the lawful commerce of a friend, that she may the better carry on a commerce with an enemy; a commerce polluted by the forgeries and perjuries, which are, for the most part, the only passports by which it can succeed.

Anxious to make every experiment, short of the last resort of injured nations, the United States have witheld from Great Britain, under successive modifications, the benefits of a free intercourse with their market.... To these appeals her Government has been equally inflexible; as if willing to make sacrifices of every sort, rather than yield to the claims of justice, or renounce the errors of a false pride....

In reviewing the conduct of Great Britain towards the United States, our attention is necessarily drawn to the warfare just renewed by the Savages, on one of our extensive frontiers; a warfare which is known to spare neither age nor sex, and to be distinguished by features peculiarly shocking to humanity. It is difficult to account for the activity, and combinations, which have for some time been developing themselves among tribes in constant intercourse with British traders and garrisons, without connecting their hostility with that influence; and without recollecting the authenticated examples of such interpositions, heretofore furnished by the officers and agents of that Government.

Such is the spectacle of injuries and indignities which have been heaped on our Country: and such the crisis which its unexampled forbearance and conciliatory efforts have not been able to avert....

...We behold our Seafaring Citizens still daily victims of lawless violence committed on the great common and high way of nations, even within sight of the Country which owes them protection. We behold our vessels, freighted with the products of our soil and industry, or

Broadside printed in Philadelphia of the official declaration of war by Congress, approved by the President

Lord Castlereagh

returning with the honest proceeds of them, wrested from their lawful destinations, confiscated by prize Courts, no longer the organs of public law, but the instruments of arbitrary Edicts; and their unfortunate crews dispersed and lost, or forced, or inveigled in British ports, into British fleets: whilst arguments are employed, in support of these aggressions, which have no foundation but in a principle equally supporting a claim, to regulate our external commerce, in all cases whatsoever.

We behold, in fine, on the side of Great Britain a state of War against the United States; and on the side of the United States, a state of peace towards Great Britain.

Whether the United States shall continue passive under these progressive usurpations, and these accumulating wrongs; or, opposing force to force in defence of their national rights, shall commit a just cause into the hands of the almighty disposer of events; avoiding all connections which might entangle it in the contests or views of other powers, and preserving a constant readiness to concur in an honorable reestablishment of peace and friendship, is a solemn question, which the Constitution wisely confides to the Legislative Department of the Government. In recommending it to their early deliberations, I am happy in the assurance, that the decision will be worthy the enlightened and patriotic councils, of a virtuous, a free and a powerful Nation.

The House voted to declare war, 79 to 49, on June 4; the Senate followed, 19 to 13, on June 17. Ironically, on June 23 Britain suspended the orders in council. Fifteen years later, recalling the coming of the war in a letter to Henry Wheaton, Madison indicated that had the *Hornet* brought this news instead of Castlereagh's epistle to Foster, there would have been no war, the rest of the budget of causes in the war message presumably being negotiable.

Montpellier, Feb 26, 1827.

In none of the Comments on the Declaration of the last war has the more immediate impulse to it been sufficiently brought into view. This was the letter from Castlereah to Foster, which, according to the authority given, the latter put into the hands of the Secretary of State, to be read by him, and by the President also. In that letter it was distinctly and emphatically stated that the Orders in Council, to which we had declared we would not submit, would not be repealed, without a repeal of internal measures of France, which, not violating any neutral right of the U. States, they had no right to call on France to repeal, and which, of course, could give to G. Britain no imaginable right against the U.S. With this formal notice, no choice remained but between War and Degradation; a degradation inviting fresh provocations, and rendering war sooner or later inevitable.

It is worthy of particular remark that, notwithstanding the peremptory declaration of the British Cabinet in the letter of Castlereah, such was the distress of the British manufacturers produced by our prohibitory and restrictive laws, as pressed on the House of Commons by Mr. Brougham and others, that the Orders were soon after repealed, but not in time to prevent the effect of the declaration that they would not be repealed. The cause of the war lay, therefore, entirely on the British side. Had the repeal of the Orders been substituted for the declaration that they would not be repealed, or had they been repealed but a few weeks sooner, our declaration of war as proceeding from that cause would have been stayed, and negociations on the subject of impressments, the other great cause, would have been pursued with fresh vigor and hopes, under the auspices of success in the case of the orders in Council.

DECLARATION OF WAR,
BY EXPRESS!!!

A Messenger has just arrived in town from Boston, by express, bearing the important intelligence of a Declaration of War with England. Having been favored with a copy of the Letter from General Dearbon, we hasten to lay the following extract before the Public.

Argus Office, Portland, *June 23, 1812,*

Head-Quarters—Boston, June 22, 1812.

" Lieut Col Ripley

Sir,

Having received Official information of the Declaration of War, against Great-Britain, you will take every measure in your power for preparation for defence—I have sent an express with this, & wish you to forward this dispatch by an express that can be relied on, to Passamaquoddy—The express will proceed with all possible dispatch, and deliver this letter to the Commanding Officer of the U. S. troops at that place."

HENRY DEARBORN:

Broadside of a message from General Dearborn in Boston alerting Colonel Ripley in Maine to prepare for war

The decision for war resulted fundamentally from the Anglo-American conflict over neutral rights, and whatever may be said of Madison's wisdom in this matter, it is impossible to question his logic or his consistency. The other causes mentioned in the war message were not fundamental. But the conflict over neutral rights was in itself a symbol of much more. It involved the sovereignty and independence and commercial power of the United States against the pretensions of the mother country. It involved the honor of a new nation committed to the ways of peace in a world where force had always been the rule. It involved the ability of a free republican government—the only one on the face of the earth—to defend itself and survive. For Madison, who had been fighting the British lion all his life, the War of 1812 was morally justified as the Second War for American Independence.

A Picture Portfolio

Mr. Madison's War

A CALL TO ARMS

During the first three years of his Presidency, James Madison tried every means at his disposal to avoid the conflict that finally erupted and became known among his opponents as "Mr. Madison's War." But a series of British actions "hostile to the United States" led him in June, 1812, to present a war message to Congress (first and last pages below) citing, among other things, the continuing and intolerable impressment of American seamen, harassment of United States ships "in every Sea," and intrigues to arouse Indians along the western frontier to warfare. Madison knew that, despite the backing of a group of young western congressmen called the War Hawks, there was far from unanimity of opinion on such a war. The country was short of money and the American army was woefully inadequate. Madison at first put his faith in volunteer militiamen, such as the resplendent Philadelphia group shown at right assembling for a muster. But during the grim days in 1814 when the British marched into Washington itself, Madison had the opportunity to view the armies in combat at Bladensburg, Maryland. "I could never have believed," he admitted after seeing the British army make a shambles of his forces, "that so great a difference existed between regular troops and a militia force, if I had not witnessed the scenes of this day."

NATIONAL ARCHIVES

To the Senate and House of Representatives of the United States.

I communicate to Congress certain Documents, being a continuation of those heretofore laid before them, on the subject of our affairs with Great Britain.

Without going back beyond the renewal in 1803, of the war in which Great Britain is engaged, and omitting unrepaired wrongs of inferior magnitude, the conduct of her Government presents a series of acts, hostile to the United States as an Independent and neutral nation.

British cruisers have been in the continued practice of violating the American flag on the great high way of nations, and of seizing and carrying off persons sailing under it; not in the exercise of a Belligerent right, founded on the Law of Nations against an Enemy, but of a municipal prerogative over British subjects. British jurisdiction is thus extended to neutral vessels, in a situation where no laws can operate but the law of nations, and the laws of the Country to which the ves-
-sels

by its privateers and public ships; and that other outrages have been practiced on our vessels and our citizens. It will have been seen also, that no indemnity had been provided, or satisfactorily pledged for the extensive spoliations, committed under the violent and retrospective orders of the French Government against the property of our citizens seized within the jurisdiction of France. I abstain at ~~this time~~, from recommending to the consideration of Congress definitive measures with respect to that nation, in the expectation, that the result of unclosed discussions between our Minister Plenipotentiary at Paris and the French Government, will speedily enable Congress to decide with greater advantage, on the course due to the rights, the interests, and the honor of our Country.

James Madison

Washington June 1st 1812

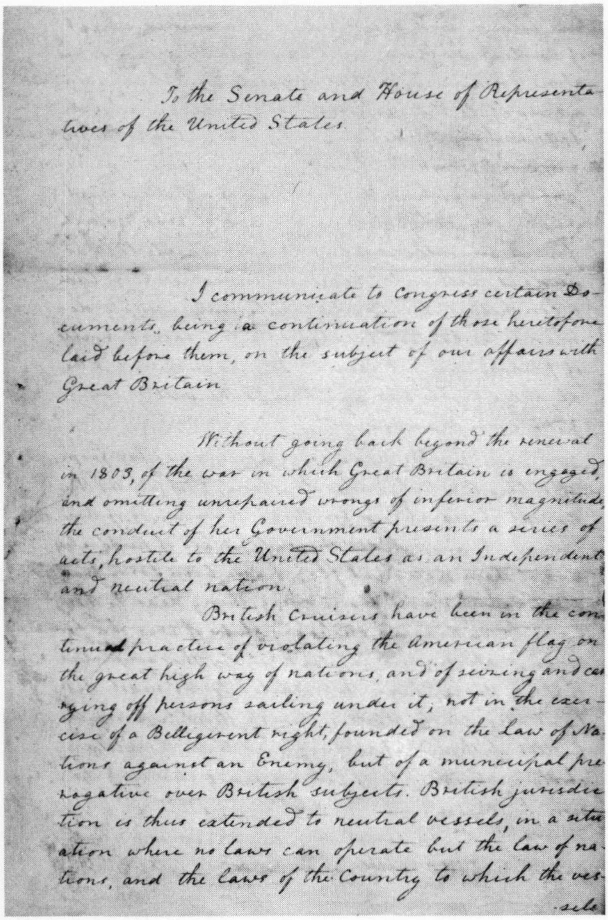

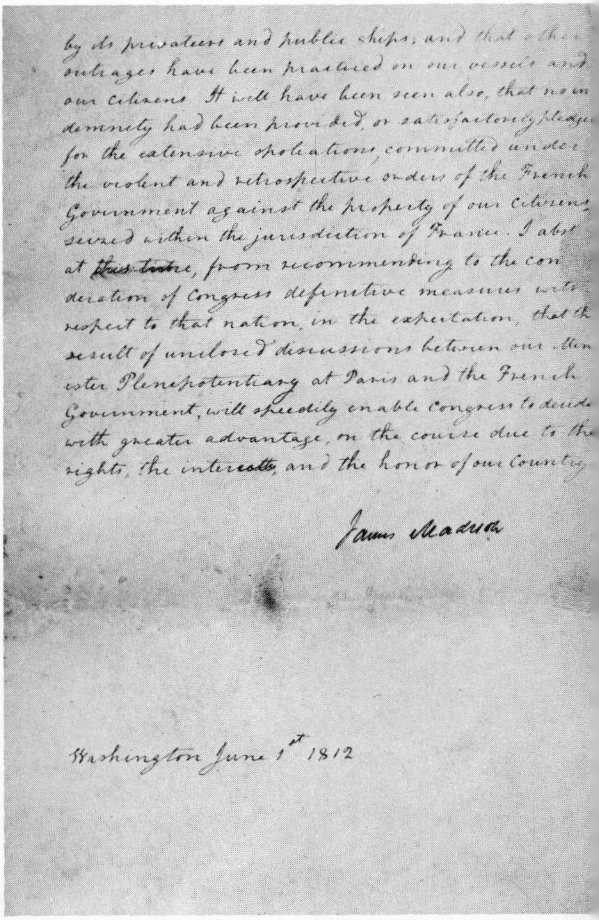

DESPAIR AND HOPE

Exactly three days after aging Brigadier General William Hull (above, left) plunged the country into despair by surrendering Detroit and losing twenty-five hundred American prisoners, his young nephew Isaac Hull (left) scored the war's first naval victory. On August 19, 1812, his frigate

NEW HAVEN COLONY HISTORICAL SOCIETY

Constitution, in a short and bloody battle, destroyed the *Guerrière* while the young American captain shouted in victory, "By Heaven, that ship is ours!" "Old Ironsides" is seen above firing broadsides after the mizzenmast of the *Guerrière* had snapped. Hull reported proudly: "From the smallest boy in the ship to the oldest seamen not a look of fear was seen."

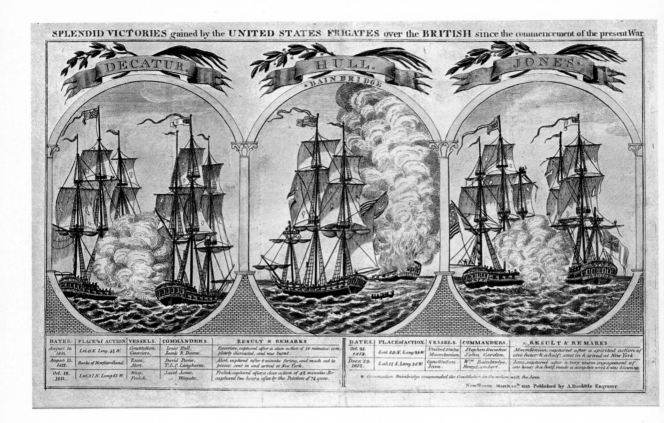

DECATUR. HULL. JONES.

BAINBRIDGE.

DATES.	PLACE of ACTION.	VESSELS.	COMMANDERS.	RESULT & REMARKS
August 10. 1812.	Lat. 41 N. Long. 55 W.	Constitution. Guerriere.	Isaac Hull. James R. Dacres.	Guerriere, captured after a close action of 30 minutes: completely dismantled, and was burnt.
August 13. 1812.	Banks of Newfoundland.	Essex. Alert.	David Porter. T.L.P. Laugharne.	Alert, captured after 8 minutes firing, and much cut to pieces: sent in and arrived at New York.
Oct. 18. 1812.	Lat. 37 N. Long. 65 W.	Wasp. Frolick.	Jacob Jones. — Wingates.	Frolick, captured after a close action of 42 minutes: Re-captured two hours after by the Poictiers of 74 guns.

DATES.	PLACE of ACTION.	VESSELS.	COMMANDERS.	RESULT & REMARKS
Oct. 25. 1812.	Lat. 29 N. Long. 29 W.	United States. Macedonian.	Stephen Decatur. John Carden.	Macedonian, captured after a spirited action of one hour & a half: sent in & arrived at New York.
Decr. 29. 1812.	Lat. 12 S. Long. 38 W.	Constitution. Java.	Wm. Bainbridge. Henry Lambert.	Java, captured after a very warm engagement of one hour & a half: made a complete wreck & was blown up.

* Commodore Bainbridge commanded the Constitution in the action with the Java.

New Haven March 20th 1813. Published by A. Doolittle Engraver.

DRAMA ON THE HIGH SEAS

Following the success of the *Constitution*, more "Splendid Victories" over the British were won by the infant American navy in the first year of the war. The print above commemorates not only the *Constitution*, but the capture of the frigate *Macedonian* by the *United States* under the young and dashing Commodore Stephen Decatur (above, right) and the capture of the sloop of war *Frolic* by the *Wasp* with Captain Jacob Jones (above, far right) in command. The men of the weak and unprepared American navy, which had only seventeen ships when the war began, displayed nerve and seamanship in daring single-ship combat and stirred their countrymen's pride. Even the defeat of the *Chesapeake* by the *Shannon*, seen in the print opposite as the British swarmed aboard her, became a lasting inspiration when her mortally wounded captain, James Lawrence (right), commanded as he was carried below: "Don't give up the ship. Fight her till she sinks."

DON'T GIVE UP THE SHIP.

☞ Most Glorious News !

Sept. 21, 1813.

Copy of a letter from Com. PERRY to the Secretary of the Navy.

U. S. Brig Niagara, off the Western Sister, Head of Lake Erie, Sept. 10, 1813 4 P. M

SIR—It has pleased the Almighty to give to the arms of the U. States a signal victory over their enemies on this Lake. The British squadron, consisting of two Ships, two Brigs, one Schooner and one Sloop, have this moment surrendered to the force under my command, after a sharp conflict — I have the honor to be, sir, very respectfully your obt servant,
O H PERRY.

Hon. Wm. Jones Secretary of the Navy.

SOME PARTICULARS.

Chilicothe, September 14.

Last evening an express arrived in town from General Harrison's head quarters, bringing the highly gratifying intelligence of the capture

the whole of the British fleet on Lake Erie by commodore Perry. The subjoined extracts of letters from two gentlemen at head quarters, contain the most essential particulars relative to that brilliant affair.

Camp Senca Sept. 12.

"An express has this moment arrived from Commodore Perry, dated the 10th inst. at 4 P. M. Head of Lake Erie, with the pleasing intelligence of the British fleet, consisting of two ships, two brigs and two schooners, being in our possession, with more prisoners on board than we had men to conquer them. A great many were killed on both sides."

Camp Senca Sept. 12.

"Victory perches on our Naval Standard! Commodore Perry has captured nearly if not all the enemy's fleet; two ships, two brigs one sloop, and one schooner and taken more prisoners than he had men on board."

310

SECURING THE NORTHWEST

The first fleet action of the War of 1812 was fought far from the ocean on Lake Erie, where in record time nine ships had been built to try to wrest control of that important lake from the British. Under the command of twenty-eight-year-old Commodore Oliver Hazard Perry—whose flagship was named the *Lawrence* and whose flag bore Lawrence's dying words—the small American fleet defeated an entire British squadron, even though Perry was forced to abandon the *Lawrence* and transfer to the *Niagara* in a rowboat in mid-battle (left). His report to the Secretary of the Navy was issued as a broadside on September 21, 1813, headlined "Most Glorious News!" (left, center). To General William Henry Harrison (left, bottom) he wrote: "We have met the enemy and they are ours," and he then transported Harrison's army to its rendezvous with British General Henry Proctor at Moraviantown on the Thames River in Ontario. Here the Americans won one of their few land victories over the British and their Indian allies (below).

Huzza for our Navy!

Another 15 minutes Job.

Being the 8th Naval Victory in which John Bull has been obliged to douce his flag, to the invincible skill of *American Tars.*

CHARLESTON, SUNDY MORNING, SEPT. 19th, 1813.

We have the satisfaction of announcing to the public that the United States sloop of war ARGUS is in the offing, with the British sloop of war BARBADOES her prize in company, taken after a desperate engagement of 15 minutes, carried by boarding.

Capt. Allen, of the Argus, has just come up, and we have conversed with a midshipman who states that she was taken off Halifax, but it was deemed expedient to proceed to this place for the purpose of escaping the British blockading squadrons. He also states that the captain, R. P. Davies, of the Barbadoes was killed, and the vessel was commanded the most part of the action by the 1st Lieut. Savage.

British loss, 97 killed and wounded. American loss, 12 killed and wounded. The Argus rates 16 and carries 20 guns, the Barbadoes rates 28 and carries 32 guns. She had previously captured, Aug. 22, the James Madison of 14 guns.

☞ *This is the second Engagement in which Captain ALLEN has signalised himself, as he was 1st Lieut. of the U. States, war in the Engagement with the Macedonian,* took Command of her and brought her into port.

Stop, Stop Stop Brother Jonathan, or I shall fall with the loss of blood— I thought to have been too heavy for you— But I must acknowledg your Superior skill —Two blows to my one! —And so well directed too! Mercy, mercy on me, how does this happen!!!

Ha—ah Johnny, you thought yourself a *Boxer* did you!—I'll let you know we are an *Enterprizing* Nation. and ready to meet you with equal force any day.

W. Charles del et Sculp

A BOXING MATCH, or, Another Bloody Nose for JOHN BULL.

IRVING S. OLDS COLLECTION, NEW-YORK HISTORICAL SOCIETY

"HUZZA FOR OUR NAVY!"

Naval victories abounded. The cartoon at left of a boxing match between King George III and President Madison was a play on the name of the British brig *Boxer* which had been captured by the American *Enterprize* in September, 1813. In the same month a broadside (left, above) was issued to celebrate the "8th Naval Victory" for the "American Tars"—the *Argus* over the British *Barbadoes*. But it was not until a year later that one of the most decisive naval actions of the war was fought, once again on a lake and once again between an American and a British fleet. The British plan was to invade from Canada along Lake Champlain with a large and well-trained army of veterans supported by their entire Lake Champlain fleet. Their defeat on September 11, 1814, by the American fleet under the command of Commodore Thomas McDonough near Plattsburg (above), aided by land forces under General Alexander Macomb, ended the threat of a northern invasion once and for all.

313

WASHINGTON AFLAME

While the British were still preparing their invasion in the North, attention was diverted by the landing of British troops on the Maryland shore in August, 1814. After defeating the inept Americans at Bladensburg, General Robert Ross and "that undaunted seaman" Rear Admiral George Cockburn (left) marched into Washington. "You may thank old Madison for this," Cockburn said to some citizens en route; "it is he who has got you into this scrape." The British then set fire to every public building in the capital (below), except the Patent Office. Meanwhile, intrepid Dolley Madison, who had spent an anxious day "turning my spy glass in every direction," fled the White House, having first assured the safety of the Stuart portrait of George Washington (right).

"THE STAR-SPANGLED BANNER"

Flushed with their easy success in Washington, the British forces next eyed Baltimore, the third largest city in the United States. It was protected on the water side by Fort McHenry, whose commander Major George Armistead had ordered its huge flag (above, right) to be made "so large that the British will have no difficulty seeing it at a distance." The night assault beginning on September 13 lasted for twenty-five hours, as the Royal Navy poured bombs, shells, and rockets on the fort (above). Far out in the harbor on a flag-of-truce boat, a young American lawyer and occasional poet named Francis Scott Key stood on deck and watched. He anxiously awaited the dawn to see if Fort McHenry had withstood the withering attack. Greatly moved to see the flag still "gallantly streaming," Key wrote the words (right) that stirred the hearts of Americans overnight and later became the national anthem.

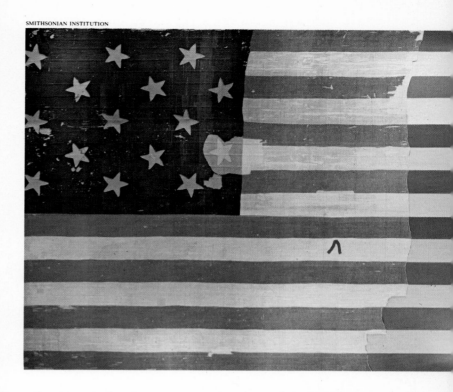

O say can you see through by the dawn's early light,
What so proudly we hail'd at the twilight's last gleaming,
Whose broad stripes & bright stars through the perilous fight
O'er the ramparts we watch'd, were so gallantly streaming?
And the rocket's red glare, the bomb bursting in air
Gave proof through the night that our flag was still there,
O say does that star spangled banner yet wave
O'er the land of the free & the home of the brave?

On the shore dimly seen through the mists of the deep,
Where the foe's haughty host in dread silence reposes,
What is that which the breeze, o'er the towering steep,
As it fitfully blows, half conceals, half discloses?
Now it catches the gleam of the morning's first beam,
In full glory reflected now shines in the stream,
'Tis the star-spangled banner — O long may it wave
O'er the land of the free & the home of the brave!

And where is that band who so vauntingly swore,
That the havoc of war & the battle's confusion
A home & a Country should leave us no more?
Their blood has wash'd out their foul footstep's pollution.
No refuge could save the hireling & slave
From the terror of flight or the gloom of the grave,
And the star-spangled banner in triumph doth wave
O'er the land of the free & the home of the brave.

O thus be it ever when freemen shall stand
Between their lov'd home & the war's desolation!
Blest with vict'ry & peace may the heav'n rescued land
Praise the power that hath made & preserv'd us a nation!
Then conquer we must when our cause it is just,
And this be our motto — "In God is our trust,"
And the star-spangled banner in triumph shall wave
O'er the land of the free & the home of the brave. —

317

ONE-SIDED VICTORY

Unaware that a peace treaty had been signed on Christmas Eve, the British attacked the American forces under General Andrew Jackson at New Orleans on January 8, 1815. Entrenched behind a wall of earth, the Americans mowed down the arrogant redcoats (above), killing or wounding twenty-six hundred to their own loss of fifty-two — an incredible, one-sided victory.

DISSENSION AND PEACE

In November, 1814, Madison had written to Governor Wilson Cary Nicholas of Virginia that he was "not mistaken in viewing the conduct of the Eastern States as the source of our greatest difficulties in carrying on the war...." That December, a group of New England Federalists actually met in convention at Hartford, Connecticut, to draft proposals for amendments to the Constitution that would challenge what they termed Madison's military despotism and force him to resign. In the cartoon below, George III is shown trying to lure Massachusetts, Connecticut, and Rhode Island back into the British fold. But when the delegation from Hartford arrived in Washington, the Treaty of Ghent had already been signed and endorsed by Madison with the old seal of the United States (right) and news of Jackson's victory at New Orleans had reached the excited capital. "Their position," according to a French diplomat, "was awkward, embarrassing, and lent itself to cruel ridicule," and they quickly withdrew. Madison completed his term and retired in triumph to Montpelier in 1817. A government official going through the State Department papers at that time, so many of which had been drawn by Madison, remarked admiringly: "What history, what anecdote, what genius, what industry!"

To all and singular to whom these presents shall come, greeting:

Be it known, That I, James Madison, president of the United States of America, having seen and considered the within treaty, do, by and with the advice and consent of the Senate thereof, accept, ratify, and confirm, the same, and every clause and article thereof.

In testimony whereof I have caused the seal of the said United States to be hereunto affixed, and signed the same with my hand.

Done at the city of Washington, this seventeenth day of February, in the year of our Lord one thousand eight hundred and fifteen, and of the sovereignty and independence of the United States the thirty-ninth.

James Madison

Chapter 9

Second War for Independence

An accounting of American assets and liabilities as the War of 1812 began would include, on one side, command of the principal theater of operations, the enemy's preoccupation with the war in Europe, and superiority of available manpower and resources; on the other side was a feeble war machine, widespread public apathy and outright opposition in one quarter of the Union, and a government that possessed neither the organization nor the leadership to conduct war. The navy boasted seventeen oceangoing ships against a potential armada of seven hundred. The regular army, then well below its authorized peacetime strength of ten thousand, was to be raised to thirty-five thousand, but only five thousand had been recruited by June. Any additional muscle must come from volunteers and militia. To raise such an army, equip it, and officer it would take many months. Madison had asked Congress for a smaller elite force, one that could be brought into the field instantly to exploit the American advantage of choosing the time of hostilities. The army he got could not be mobilized for the first strike. The War Department consisted of the Secretary and eight clerks; commissary and quartermaster services scarcely existed; and officers to command the army were either tired Revolutionary War veterans or young men inexperienced in combat.

The American target was Canada. Taking it would be, said Jefferson in a flight of fancy, "a mere matter of marching." Some enthusiasts looked upon the acquisition of Upper Canada, from Lake Huron to the St. Lawrence, as the great aim of the war. But for the administration the attack on Canada was a means of waging war declared for maritime objectives, and it was to be a hostage for securing those objectives. The strategy of the first summer's campaign called for a three-pronged invasion of Canada. In the east, General Henry Dearborn was to advance along Lake Champlain for an assault on Montreal. In the center, General Stephen van Rensselaer was to attack across the Niagara River in western New York. And in the west, General William Hull at Detroit was to cut British lines to their Indian allies, capture Fort Malden and other posts across the Detroit River, and wrest control of Lake Erie from the enemy.

The campaign ended in crushing defeat. Poor generalship and the unreliability of state militia contributed to the collapse on all fronts. Dearborn, in particular, was hampered by hostility to the war in the eastern states. Both Massachusetts and Connecticut refused the President's orders to furnish militia for the Montreal campaign. Madison temporized with them rather than risk open rebellion. But the crucial defeat was the first one, in the west, in August. General Hull with a vastly superior force surrendered Detroit without firing a shot. Madison recalled the disaster at Detroit and spoke to the often repeated charge of the nation's unpreparedness for war in his 1827 letter to Henry Wheaton, a distinguished jurist.

Montpellier, Feby. 26, 1827.

But the war was commenced without due preparation: this is another charge. Preparations in all such cases are comparative. The question to be decided is, whether the adversary was better prepared than we were; whether delay on our side, after the approach of war would be foreseen on the other, would have made the comparative preparations better for us. As the main theatre of the war was to be in our neighbourhood, and the augmented preparations of the enemy were to be beyond the Atlantic, promptitude of attack was the evident policy of the U.S. It was in fact not the suddenness of the war as an Executive policy, but the tardiness of the Legislative provisions, which gave whatever colour existed for the charge in question. The recommendation of Military preparations went from the Executive on the fifth day of November, and so impressed was that Department of the Government with the advantage of despach in the measures to be adopted by Congress, that the recommendation was known to contemplate a force, of a kind & extent which it was presumed might be made ready within the requisite period. Unfortunately this consideration had not its desired effect on the proceedings in Congress. The Laws passed on the subject were delayed, that for filling up the peace establishment until the twenty-fourth of December, and that for the new Army to be raised, until the fourteenth of January: and such were the extent & conditions prescribed for the latter, that it could scarcely, under any circumstances, and by no possibility under those existing, be forthcoming within the critical season....

General van Rensselaer established a toehold on Queenston Heights in Canada, but his army was dislodged by the British who crossed the Niagara River to retake the position.

Yet, with all the disadvantages under which hostilities were commenced, their progress would have been very different, under a proper conduct of the initiative expedition into Upper Canada. The individual at the head of it [Hull] had been pointed out for the service by very obvious considerations. He had acquired during the Revolutionary War the reputation of a brave & valuable officer. He was of course an experienced one. He had been long the Chief Magistrate in the quarter contiguous to the theatre of his projected operations, with the best opportunities of being acquainted with the population & localities on the hostile as well as his own side of the dividing straight. He had also been the Superintendent of our Affairs with the Indian Tribes holding intercourse with that district of Country, a trust which afforded him all the ordinary means of understanding, conciliating, and managing their dispositions. With such qualifications and advantages which seemed to give him a claim above all others to the station assigned to him, he sunk before obstacles at which not an officer near him would have paused, and threw away an entire army, in the moment of entering a career which would have made the war as prosperous in its early stages, and as promising in its subsequent course, as it was rendered by that disaster, oppressive to our resources, and flattering to the hopes of the Enemy. By the surrender of Gen. Hull, the people of Canada, not indisposed to favour us, were turned against us; the Indians were thrown into the service of the Enemy; the expence & delay of a new armament

The bad news of Hull's defeat at Detroit is trumpeted to Madison in this British cartoon by Cruikshank.

CULVER PICTURES, INC.

Surrender by General William Hull

were incurred, the Western Militia & volunteers were witheld from offensive co-operation with the troops elsewhere, by the necessity of defending their own frontiers & families against incursions of the Savages; and a general damp spread over the face of our Affairs. What a contrast would the success so easy at the outset of the war have presented? A triumphant army would have seized on Upper Canada, and hastened to join the armies at the points below; the important command of Lake Erie would have fallen to us of course; the Indians would have been neutral or submissive to our will; the general spirit of the Country would have been kindled into enthusiasm; enlistments would have been accelerated, volunteers would have stepped forward with redoubled confidence & alacrity; the Militia would have felt a like animation; and what is not of small moment, the intrigues of the disaffected would have been smothered in their embryo State.

Writing to Jefferson before learning of General Hull's defeat at Detroit in August, 1812, Madison touched on the frustrations and difficulties of the early months of the war.

Washington Aug. 17. 1812

The seditious opposition in Mass. & Cont. with the intrigues elsewhere insidiously co-operating with it, have so clogged the wheels of the war, that I fear the campaign will not accomplish the object of it. With the most united efforts in stimulating volunteers, they would have probably fallen much short of the number required by the deficiency of regular enlistments. But under the discouragements substituted, and the little attraction contained in the volunteer act, the two classes together, leave us dependent, for every primary operation, on Militia, either as volunteers or draughts for six months. We are nevertheless doing as well as we can, in securing the maritime frontier, and in providing for an effective penetration into upper Canada. It would probably have been best if it had been practicable in time, to have concentrated a force which could have seized on Montreal & thus at one stroke, have secured the upper Province, and cut off the sap that nourished Indian hostilities. But this could not be attempted, without sacrificing the Western & N. W. Frontier, threated with an

A PROCLAMATION

BY THE

PRESIDENT OF THE UNITED STATES.

WHEREAS, information has been received that a number of individuals, who have deserted from the Army of the United States, have become sensible of their offence, and are desirous of returning to their duty....

A full pardon is hereby granted and proclaimed to each and all such individuals as shall, within four months from the date hereof, surrender themselves to the Commanding Officer of any Military Post within the United States, or the territories thereof.

IN TESTIMONY WHEREOF, I have caused the seal of the United States to be affixed to these presents, and signed the same with my hand.

DONE at the City of Washington, the 7th day of February, in the year of our Lord, one thousand eight hundred and twelve, and of the Independence of the United States, the thirty-sixth.

JAMES MADISON.

By the President,

JAMES MONROE,

Secretary of State

Proclamation by President Madison granting pardon to deserters from army who surrendered themselves

War of 1812, LOSSING

Fort Mackinac (or Michilimachinac)

inundation of savages under the influence of the British establishment near Detroit. Another reason for the expedition of Hull was that the unanimity and ardor of Kentucky & Ohio, provided the requisite force at once for that service, whilst it was too distant from the other points to be assailed. We just learn, but from what cause remains to be known, that the important fort at Machilimackinac [on Mackinac Island in the straits joining lakes Huron, Michigan, and Superior] has fallen into the hands of the Enemy. If the re-enforcement of about 200 ordered from the Ohio, and on the way to Hull, should not enable him to take Malden, and awe the Savages emboldened by the British success, his situation will be very ineligible....

We have no information from England since the war was known there, or even, seriously suspected, by the public. I think it not improbable that the sudden change in relation to the Orders in Council, first in yielding to a qualified suspension, & then a repeal, was the effect of apprehensions in the Cabinet that the deliberations of Congs. would have that issue, and that the Ministry could not stand agst. the popular torrent agst. the Orders in Council, swelled as it would be by the addition of a war with the U.S. to the pressure of the non-importation Act. What course will be taken, when the declaration here, shall be known, is uncertain, both in reference to the American shipments instituted under the repeal of the Orders, and to the question between vindictive efforts for pushing the war agst. us, and early advances for terminating it. A very informal, & as it has turned out erronious communication of the intended change in the Orders, was hurried over, evidently with a view to prevent a declaration of war, if it should arrive in time. And the communication was accompanied by a proposal from the local authorities at Halifax sanctioned by Foster, to suspend hostilities both at sea & on land....The insuperable objections to a concurrence of the Executive in the project are obvious....As we do not apprehend invasion by land, and preparations on each side were to be unrestrained, nothing could be gained by us, whilst arrangements & re-enforcements adverse to Hull, might be decisive; and, on every supposition, the Indians wd. continue to be active agst. our frontiers, the more so in consequence of the fall of Machilimackinac. Nothing but triumphant operations on the Theatre which forms their connection with the Enemy, will controul their bloody inroads.

Indian chiefs had been beating a path to the national capital since Washington's time. Two delegations—forty chiefs in all— arrived opportunely in August, 1812. One of Sac, Fox, Osage, and other Missouri tribes had been sent by General William Clark; the other was of Sioux tribes from farther north. Both were dinner guests of the President, and of course they provided a colorful spectacle for the entire city. One enthralled spectator called their powwow at Greenleaf's Point "the most magnificent, imposing native human pagentry" ever seen outside the wilds. It was customary for the Great White Father to address visiting chiefs, and for this purpose a stylized rhetoric, naive and rich in metaphor, had long existed. Madison repeated the usual admonitions of peace, but also tried to explain the war to the Indians and wean them from the British.

Washington [August,] 1812

My red children,

You have come thro' a long path to see your father, but it is a straight and a clean path, kept open for my red children, who hate crooked walks. I thank the great spirit that he has brought you in health through the long journey; and that he gives us a clear sky & bright sun, for our meeting. I had heard from General Clarke of the good dispositions of several of the nations on & West of the Mississippi: and that they shut their ears to the bad birds hovering about them for sometime past. This made me wish to see the principal chiefs of those bands. I love to shake hands with hearts in them.

The red people who live on the same great Island with the White people of the 18 fires [the eighteen states], are made by the great spirit out of the same earth, from parts of it differing in colour only. My regard for all my red children, has made me desirous that the bloody tomahawk should be buried between the Osages, the Cherokees, & the Choctaws. I wish also that the hands of the Shawenee, & the Osage, should be joined in my presence, as a pledge to cherish & observe the peace made at St. Louis. This was a good peace for both. It is a chain that ought to hold them fast in friendship. Neither blood nor rust should ever be upon it....

A father ought to give good advice to his children, and it is the duty of his children to harken to it. The

ional Instruction to the public and private armed vessels of the United States.

HE public and private armed vessels of the United States to interrupt any vessels belonging to citizens of the United coming from British ports to the United States laden with merchandize, in consequence of the alledged repeal of the Orders in Council, but are on the contrary to give aid and ce to the same; in order that such vessels and their cargoes dealt with on their arrival as may be decided by the compehorities.

y command of the President of the United States of America,

Secretary of State.

ASHINGTON CITY, AUGUST 28, 1812.

A broadside signed by James Monroe, Secretary of State, after repeal of the British orders in council people composing the 18 fires, are a great people. You have travelled thro' their Country; you see they cover the land, as the stars fill the sky, and are thick as the Trees in your forests. Notwithstanding their great power, the British King has attacked them on the great water beyond which he lives. He robbed their ships, and carried away the people belonging to them. Some of them he murdered. He has an old grudge against the 18 fires, because when he tried to make them dig and plant for his people beyond the great water, not for themselves, they sent out warriors who beat his warriors, they drove off the bad chiefs he had sent among them, and set up good chiefs of their own. The 18 fires did this when they had not the strength they now have. Their blows will now be much heavier, and will soon make him do them justice. It happened when the 13 fires, now increased to 18, forced the British King, to treat them as an independent nation, one little fire [Canada] did not join them. This he has held ever since. It is there that his Agents and traders plot quarrels and wars between the 18 fires and their red brethren, and between one red tribe and another. Malden is the place where all the bad birds have their nests. There they are fed with false tales agst. the 18 fires, and sent out with bloody belts in their bills, to drop among the red people, who would otherwise remain at peace. It is for the good of all the red people, as well as the people of the 18 fires, that a stop should be put to this mischief. Their warriors can do it. They are gone & going to Canada for this purpose. They want no help from their red brethren. They are strong enough without it. The British, who are weak, are doing all they can by their bad birds, to decoy the red people into the war on their side. I warn all the red people to avoid the ruin this must bring upon them. And I say to you my children, your father does not ask you to join his warriors. Sit still on your seats: and be witnesses that they are able to beat their enemies and protect their red friends. This is the fatherly advice I give you.

I have a further advice for my red children. You see how the Country of the 18 fires is filled with people. They increase like the corn they put into the ground. They all have good houses to shelter them from all weathers, good clothes suitable to all seasons: and as

Fort Malden remained in British hands until October, 1813.

328

War of 1812, LOSSING

Victories such as that of the Wasp over the Frolic (above) led to an expansion of the navy; its successes helped Madison win reelection.

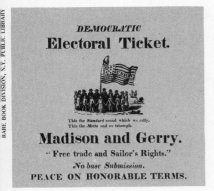

for food of all sorts, you see they have enough & to spare. No man woman or child of the 18 fires ever perished of hunger. Compare all this with the condition of the red people. They are scattered here & there in handfuls. Their lodges are cold, leaky, and smokey. They have hard fare, and often not eno' of it. Why this mighty difference? The reason, my red children, is plain. The white people breed cattle and sheep. They plow the earth and make it give them every thing they want. They spin and weave. Their heads and their hands make all the elements & the productions of nature useful to them. Above all; the people of the 18 fires live in constant peace & friendship. No Tomahawk has ever been raised by one agst. another. Not a drop of blood has ever touched the Chain that holds them together as one family. All their belts are white belts. It is in your power to be like them. The Ground that feeds one, by hunting, would feed a great band, by the plow and the hoe. The great spirit has given you, like your white brethren, good heads to contrive: strong arms, and active bodies. Use them like your white brethren; not all at once, which is difficult, but by little & little, which is easy. Especially live in peace with one another, like your white brethren of the 18 fires: and like them, your little sparks will grow into great fires.

Madison learned of Hull's ignominious surrender on the road to Montpelier. He turned around and, back in the capital, called an emergency meeting of the Cabinet. It was decided to retake Detroit, under a commander with blood in his veins, and also to build a naval force on Lake Erie. After all, 1812 was an election year. Victory somewhere would help revive flagging confidence in the administration and make the war popular. The West, where it was already popular, offered the best hope. But for the next several months Madison would hear of nothing but failure and defeat on land. The infant navy, on the other hand, scored impressive victories, beginning with the *Constitution*'s capture of the *Guerrière* in August. The President, who had shared the Republican prejudice against the navy, became its ardent champion.

The election of 1812 turned on the issue of war or peace. DeWitt Clinton was the candidate of the "peace party." In addition to being the leader of the New York Republicans, some of whom opposed the war and had long been at odds with the Republican leadership in Washington, Clinton was also taken up by the Federalists. An opposition broadside stated the issue.

Madison & War!
or,
Clinton and Peace.

Arise! ye Patriot Spirits! rise!
    The all-important hour's at hand
When, by your Votes, you must decide
    If War shall longer scourge our land! . . .
Do you hate War — vote *not* for him
    Who's plung'd you *unprepar'd* in War, —
A War which was, no doubt, designed
    To lash you fast to Bona[parte]'s *Car!*
Think, think, upon those *blissful days*
    When Commerce spread her flowing sails,
And wafted to our *then* bless'd shore
    The choicest fruits of India's vales!
'Twas then the *"Golden Age"* of Peace, —
    The age when Patriots reign'd —
When Washington stood at the helm,
    And *Democratic power restrain'd!*

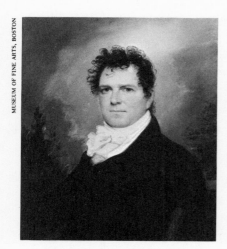

DeWitt Clinton by John W. Jarvis

The electoral vote, 128 to 89, gave Madison a clear-cut victory. But Clinton won three of the five New England states, plus New York, New Jersey, and Delaware; and the Federalists doubled their numbers in Congress. Persistent opposition to the war divided the country against itself and encouraged the enemy to exploit New England disaffection and thus draw that region into "common interest" with Old England. Trade was the bait. Early in the new year Britain threw a blockade around Delaware Bay and Chesapeake Bay. In May it was extended to the mouth of the Mississippi and some months later easterly to Long Island Sound. But New England ports were open until near the end of the war. Yankee merchants reaped handsome profits either in the disguise of neutrals or in trading with the enemy. To supply her colonies Britain issued special licenses for American imports, confined, however, to those from New England ports. Outraged by this "insidious discrimination," Madison sent a special message to Congress.

February 24th 1813

The policy [of Great Britain] now proclaimed to the world, introduces into her modes of warfare, a system equally distinguished by the deformity of its features, and the depravity of its character; having for its object to dissolve the ties of allegiance and the sentiments of loyalty in the adversary nation, and to seduce and seperate its componant parts, the one from the other.

The general tendency of these demoralizing and disorganizing contrivances, will be reprobated by the civilized and Christian world; and the insulting attempt on the virtue, the honor, the patriotism, and the fidelity of our brethren of the Eastern States, will not fail to call forth all their indignation and resentment; and to attach more and more all the States, to that happy union and constitution, against which such insidious and malignant artifices are directed.

The better to guard, nevertheless, against the effect of individual cupidity and treachery, and to turn the corrupt projects of the Enemy against himself, I recommend to the consideration of Congress, the expediency of an effectual prohibition of any trade whatever, by Citizens or inhabitants of the United States, under special licences, whether relating to persons or ports; and in aid thereof a prohibition of all exportations from the United States in foreign bottoms; few of which are actually employed; whilst multiplying counterfeits of their flags and papers are covering and encouraging the navigation of the Enemy.

Brown's Indian Queen Hotel, site of Madison's second inaugural ball

A bill based on President Madison's recommendation passed the House but failed in the Senate. His call for a full-fledged embargo met the same fate in July. Finally, in December, Congress legislated the embargo and stiffened the nonimportation law. Whether in war or in peace Madison believed the British vulnerable to American commercial coercion. The embargo completed the alienation of affections in New England. But the President coolly let sedition run its course, fully confident that the good sense and republicanism of the mass of citizens would eventually assert itself. A letter to Federalist David Humphreys, the Connecticut manufacturer of Madison's suit of homespun, shows his forbearance.

Washington Mar. 23. 1813

Altho' it is neither usual, nor often eligible, to enter into political explanations on such an occasion, as the present, I am induced by the frank & friendly tenor of your remarks, to express (under the reserves which you will infer) my regret that you should be able to cite a prevailing opinion that "an alliance with France, and a systematic exclusion of Commerce" were within the views of the Administration.

To say nothing of the extreme improbability of such a

David Humphreys

policy on the first point, it is not easy to conceive a more formal disavowal, of it, than has been repeatedly made & published both by my predecessor & myself, particularly in the Messages relating to the war, which emphatically impugn political alliances or connections with any foreign power. In full conformity with these disavowals, is the letter from Mr. Barlow to Mr. Monroe lately published, from which it must be necessarily inferred that he was forbidden to enter into any arrangements with France beyond the subjects of indemnity & commerce. With such strong presumptions & decisive proofs before the public, it is impossible that a purpose in this Government of allying itself with that of France, can be seriously believed by any intelligent individual not in a temper to reject a Witness even from the dead. [Barlow had died.]

As to a systematic exclusion of commerce, a belief of it, is still more incomprehensible. Temporary abridgments or suspensions of it, must have for their object, its permanent freedom, as interruptions of peace, have for their object, a re-establishment of peace on improved foundations. In such a light only can the restrictive measures applied to our commerce be rationally viewed. The avowed object of them, in fact, was to liberate our commerce from restrictions equally obnoxious to all parties. Whether the means were well applied or not, may be made a question. The object itself never can. . . .

Viewing the topics which have so much agitated the public mind, in the light here presented, I have never allowed myself to believe that the Union was in danger, or that a dissolution of it could be desired, unless by a few individuals, if such there be, in desperate situations or of unbridled passions. In addition to the thousand affinities belonging to every part of the Nation, every part has an interest as deep as it is obvious, in maintaining the bond which keeps the whole together; and the Eastern part certainly not less than any other. Looking to the immediate & *commercial* effect of a dissolution, it is clear that the Eastern part would be the greatest loser, by such an event; and not likely therefore deliberately to rush into it; especially when it takes into view the groundlessness of the suspicions which alone could suggest so dreadful an alternative; and the turn which would probably grow out of it, to the relations with Europe. The great road of profitable intercourse for New England, even with Old England, lies through the Wheat, the Cotton & the Tobacco fields of her Southern & Western confederates. On what basis cd. N. E. & O. E. form commercial stipulations, on all the great articles, they would be in direct rivalship. The real source of our revolution was the commercial jealousy of G.B. towards that part of her then Colonies. If there be links of common interest between the two Countries, they wd. connect the S. & not the N. States, with that part of Europe.

The President's second inaugural address had underscored the administration's efforts to arrange a negotiated peace. "The sword was scarcely out of the scabbard," he had said, "before the enemy was apprized of the reasonable terms on which it would be resheathed." These terms included the abandonment of impressment, the protection of neutral commerce from illegal blockades and seizures, and indemnification for maritime losses. Britain spurned the overture. However, Emperor Alexander of Russia, hard pressed by Napoleon's armies, offered to mediate the Anglo-American war. Alexander's Armageddon was at hand, and he hoped to free Britain from the sideshow in America for the main event in Europe. By the time Madison learned of the emperor's offer, in March, 1813, the main event had occurred and Napoleon was in retreat from Russia. Madison promptly communicated the news to Jefferson.

Washington Mar. 10. 1813

Emperor Alexander I of Russia

If you do not receive the N.Y. Mercantile advertiser, the inclosed will give you the Russian acct. of the Catastrophe of the French Army. It is doubtless much exaggerated; but there is no doubt that the losses are beyond example. Whether they can be replaced so as to prevent the defection of allies, and to present another formidible countenance to the North, is uncertain. It does not appear that any thing like despondence is felt in Paris, and so many interests on the Continent have become associated with the ascendancy of Napoleon, that it will not be surprizing if with the terrors of his name, he should surmount his difficulties. In England the usual exultation is indulged, on the recent events: and united with the rage & jealousy produced by our little naval triumphs, account for the gigantic force she is bringing agst. us on the water. In the mean time Russia as you will observe is tendering her mediatory friendship; with the collateral view there is reason to believe, of deriving advantage from our neutral interference with British monopoly in the trade with her.

We shall endeavor to turn the good will of Russia to the proper acct. Whether England will accede to the mediation, or do so with evasive purposes remains to be seen.

Madison nominated two peace commissioners, Albert Gallatin and James A. Bayard, a Delaware Federalist, and dispatched them at once to St. Petersburg. They arrived there in July, just as Madison learned of Castlereagh's rebuff of Russian mediation. The Senate, meanwhile, turned down Gallatin because Madison declined to consider the Treasury office vacant. The obstructionism of the Senate had become chronic, but the rejection of Gallatin was more than an ordinary defeat. It stabbed at the President himself. He was, in fact, gravely ill at the time. Dolley wrote to Mrs. Gallatin via John Jacob Astor.

[Washington,] 29th. July [18]13

I cannot allow Mr Astor to leave us without his bearing a few lines, from me, to you, my beloved friend: You to whom my heart has often addressed itself, since our seperation and constantly sympathised with, on the subject of our dear Voyagers. You have heard no doubt, of the illness of my Husband but can have no idea of its extent, and the dispair, in which I attended his bed for nearly five weeks! Even now, I watch over him, as I would an infant, so precarious is his convalessence. Added to this, the disappointments & vexations, heaped upon him by party spirit. Nothing however has borne so hard, as the conduct of the Senate in regard to Mr Gallatin. Mr A will tell you many particulars, that *I aught not* to *write*, of the desertion of some whose support we had a right to expect; & of the *maneauvering* of others, allways hostile to superior merit. We console ourselves with the hope of its terminating both in the Public good, and Mr. Gallatins honorable triumph.

Just before setting out for Montpelier to recuperate from his illness, Madison reported to Gallatin on the Senate proceedings.

Washington, Aug 2, 1813

You will learn from the Secy. of State the painful manner in which the Senate have mutilated the Mission to St Petersburg. But the course & circumstances of the proceeding require more of explanation than may fall within his scope, and more indeed, than can well be conveyed on paper.

Albert Gallatin (above) and James A. Bayard (below) were sent to St. Petersburg as peace commissioners.

Previously to sending in the nomination of the Envoys, there was no indication, that, if the popularity of the object did not prevent opposition, it would extend beyond a portion of the Senate essentially short of a majority. And there is reason to believe that if a preliminary attempt to embarrass the subject had been decided on at the proper time, and before out-door means could be interposed, the desired & expected result would have been secured. Liberality however yielded to an adjournment of the question, and the opportunity afforded by it was industriously improved. The first step was, after formally ascertaining the arrangement under which you were included in the Mission, to obtain a vote declaring an incompatibility (without specifying whether Constitutional or otherwise) between the domestic & diplomatic appts. The tendency of this proposition to comprehend as many and to commit as much as possible, is obvious. It would seem notwithstanding that the vote of incompatibility was concurred in by some who regarded it not as an obstacle to an ultimate concurrence in the nomination, but rather as a protest throwing the whole responsibility upon the Executive. The next step was to communicate this opinion of the Senate to me, with a view either to extort a compliance, or to unite against the nomination all, or as many as possible, who had concurred in the vote of incompatibility. In this stage of the business it was the confident opinion of the supporters of the nomination that inflexibility on the part of the Ex would ensure a majority for it and their unanimous & urgent advice as well on general grounds, as on that particular calculation, not to yield to the irregular views of the adverse party. The event proved that the final purposes of certain individuals on whom the turning of the scale depended, had been miscounted. It is not easy to express the mixed feelings produced by the disappointment, or the painfulness of my own in particular. It was at first suggested from some friendly sources, as most advisable in such a posture of things to send in a renomination founded on a vacancy in the Secretaryship of the Treasury; and under certain points of view this expedient had its recommendations. They were met however by difficulties & considerations not to be got over. . . . It was apprehended by some of the best disposed & best informed of the Senate that a renomination would not secure the object. As it had become certain that the open & secret adversaries together amounted to a formidable number who would be doubly gratified by a double triumph, it was suspected that after succeeding in getting the Treasury vacated, it would be a prerequisite to a confirmation of the other appt. that the vacancy should be actually filled in order to prevent its being kept open for your return, which might be looked for within the term of six months; and that with this view a resolution might be obtained declaring the inconsistency of a protracted vacancy with the public service. . . . It is certain that some who had intimated an intended change of their votes, in case the Treasury Dept. should be vacated, had in view that the vacancy should be forthwith filled & even that a nomination to it should go in with the renomination. Whether a majority would have gone such lengths is uncertain; but strong symptoms existed of a temper in the Body capable of going very great lengths. And apart from all other considerations it would have been impossible even if it had been intended to make & fill a vacancy in the Treasy Dept that the consent of the Senate in the other case could be purchased by a pledge to that effect. Besides the degradation of the Ex., it would have introduced a species of barter of the most fatal tendency.

I have given you this summary that you may understand the true character of a proceeding which has given us so much concern. I will add to it two observations only, 1. that the Senate by resting their negative on the opin-

John Bull makes a new batch of ships (left) to send to the Great Lakes, and the Governor of Ohio invites more enlistments (above). Perry won on Lake Erie (right).

ion of official incompatibility tacitly acknowledge a personal fitness & so far defeat their own hostility: 2. that the whole proceeding according to every friendly opinion, will have the effect of giving you a stronger hold on the confidence & support of the Nation. Judging from the effect as already known this cannot fail to be the case.

I have just recovered strength eno', after a severe & tedious attack of bilious fever, to bear a journey to the Mountains whither I am about setting out. The Physicians prescribe it as essential to my thorough recovery, & security agst. a relapse at the present season.

The war went somewhat better for the Americans in 1813. In part this may be credited to long overdue changes in the War and Navy departments. The incompetence of Secretaries William Eustis and Paul Hamilton had made them public scandals. Executive duty finally overcame personal loyalty and Madison replaced them with John Armstrong and William Jones. In the case of Armstrong, the former Minister to France, Madison traded one problem for another. Ambitious, abrasive, and headstrong, the new Secretary of War created friction within the Cabinet and between himself and the commander in chief. On the wide Canadian front, a second campaign against Montreal failed; American forces made a strong bid to control Lake Ontario, raiding towns all along the northern shore, including York (Toronto), capital of Upper Canada; and Captain Oliver Perry's momentous victory on Lake Erie opened that region to American arms. General William Henry Harrison seized the opportunity, regained Detroit, drove the British back, and in the Battle of the Thames, where

This British cartoon dedicated to Madison shows Indians handing over a captured American general, daubed with paint, to a British officer.

Tecumseh was killed, virtually eliminated the Indian menace on the northwestern frontier. On the southern frontier, a bloody Indian war pitted General Andrew Jackson and his volunteer army against the unruly Creeks, who finally capitulated the following summer.

Glory had sufficiently vanquished shame for Madison to offer a generally cheerful report on the state of the Union in December. He dwelled at length on British "barbarities" and "enormities," glossed over serious problems of finance and disaffection, and accented the redeeming features of the war.

Washington December 7th 1813

NEW-YORK HISTORICAL SOCIETY

It would be improper to close this communication without expressing a thankfulness, in which all ought to unite, for the numerous blessings with which our beloved Country, continues to be favored; for the abundance which overspreads our land, and the prevailing health of its inhabitants; for the preservation of our internal tranquility, and the stability of our free institutions; and above all for the light of divine truth, and the protection of every man's conscience in the enjoyment of it. And although among our blessings we cannot number an exemption from the evils of war; yet these will never be regarded as the greatest of evils by the friends of liberty and the rights of Nations. Our Country has before preferred them to the degraded condition which was the alternative, when the sword was drawn in the cause which gave birth to our national Independence; and none who contemplate the magnitude; and feel the value of that glorious event, will shrink from a struggle to maintain the high and happy ground, on which it placed the American people.

With all good Citizens, the justice and necessity of

Battle of the Thames, October 5, 1813, in which Tecumseh was killed resisting wrongs and usurpations no longer to be borne; will sufficiently outweigh the privations and sacrifices inseparable from a State of war. But it is a reflection, moreover, peculiarly consoling, that whilst wars are generally aggravated by their baneful effects on the internal improvements and permanent prosperity of the nations engaged in them, such is the favored situation of the United States, that the calamities of the contest into which they have been compelled to enter, are mitigated by improvements and advantages of which the contest itself is the source.

If the war has increased the interruptions of our Commerce, it has at the same time cherished and multiplied our manufactures; so as to make us independent of all other Countries for the more essential branches, for which we aught to be dependent on none; and is even rapidly giving them an extent which will create additional staples in our future intercourse with foreign markets.

If much treasure has been expended, no inconsiderable portion of it has been applied to objects durable in their value, and necessary to our permanent safety.

If the war has exposed us to increased spoliations on the Ocean, and to predatory incursions on the land, it has developed the national means of retaliating the former, and of providing protection against the latter; demonstrating to all that every blow aimed at our maritime independence, is an impulse accelerating the growth of our maritime power.

By diffusing through the mass of the nation the

Above: John Bull offers his terms of capitulation in detail from 1814 cartoon. Below: Cruikshank's satire of "British Valour and Yankee Boasting" after British Shannon *defeated the* Chesapeake

*America's naval heroes surround
scene of the Battle of Lake Erie.*

elements of military discipline and instruction, by augmenting and distributing warlike preparations applicable to future use; by evincing the zeal and valour with which they will be employed, and the cheerfulness with which every necessary burden will be borne; a greater respect for our rights, and a longer duration of our future peace, are promised than could be expected, without these proofs of the national character and resources.

The war has proved, moreover, that our free Government, like other free Governments, though slow in its early movements, acquires, in its progress, a force proportioned to its freedom; and that the Union of these States, the guardian of the freedom and safety of all and of each, is strengthened by every occasion that puts it to the test.

In fine, the war, with all its vicissitudes, is illustrating the capacity and the destiny of the United States to be a great, a flourishing, and a powerful nation; worthy of the friendship which it is disposed to cultivate with all others; and authorized, by its own example, to require from all, an observance of the laws of justice and reciprocity. Beyond these, their claims have never extended; and in contending for these, we behold a subject for our Congratulations, in the daily testimonies of increasing harmony throughout the nation, and may humbly repose our trust in the smiles of heaven, on so righteous a cause.

At the beginning of 1814, Madison accepted Castlereagh's sudden offer of direct negotiations. Congress approved a new commission consisting of Gallatin, who was released from the Treasury, Bayard, John Quincy Adams, then Minister to Russia, Henry Clay, and Jonathan Russell. Again Madison shuffled his Cabinet, always a painful political operation, and at the same time elevated a corps of vigorous young officers — Andrew Jackson, Winfield Scott, Jacob Brown, and several others — to command of armies in the field. Instant acceptance of the British overture stemmed less from confidence in the American position at the bargaining table than from realistic assessment of the French collapse and Allied ascendancy in Europe. Castlereagh was doubtless tired of the annoying little war in America, but he gave no sign of yielding on impressment and other matters, and if peace came to Europe, Britain could turn all her might to America. With the end of the Continental System, European ports were open to trade. Suddenly embargo and nonimportation were no longer in season. Madison recommended their repeal on March 31. A few days later, in Paris, Napoleon abdicated and retired to Elba. Britain at once reinforced her blockade and extended it from Maine to Louisiana. Admiral Sir Alexander Cochrane, in command, audaciously invited southern slaves to rebel. Madison's reaction to these fast-moving events may be gauged from letters to Jefferson and Monroe during a brief respite at Montpelier.

Montpelier May 10. 1814

We have recd. no information from our Envoys to the [neutral countries along the] Baltic for a very long time. From those last appointed there has not been time to hear after their arrival at Gothenburg. Neither have we any accts. from England, other than the newspaper paragraphs which you have seen. The B. Govt. can not do less than send negociators to meet ours; but whether in the spirit of ours is the important question. The turn of recent events in Europe, if truly represented, must strengthen the motives to get rid of the war with us; and their hopes by a continuance of it, to break down our Govt. must be more & more damped, by occurrences here as they become known there. The election in N. York alone crushed the project of the [Essex] Junto faction [to form a confederacy of northern states] so long fostered by and flattering the expectations of the B. cabinet. Still it is possible that new fallacies may suffice for a willingness to be deceived. Our difficulties in promising money without heavy taxes, and the supposed odium of these, will probably be made the most of by our internal enemies, to recommend the experiment of prolonged hostilities.

Montpelier May 21. 1814

The aggregate intelligence from Europe, with Cochrane's Procln. to the Blacks, warn us to be prepared for the worst measures of the Enemy and in their worst forms. They suggest the earliest attention to the wants of the Treasury, and the policy of securing them, with less scruple as to the terms. As it appears that Mr. Gallatin was in Holland, I hope he may have done something then, provisionally at least. We may count however on the influence of Engd. there as a collateral obstacle that may be fatal. It is not improbable that the intention of the Dutch Govt. to send a Minister here, is delayed, if not abandoned, in consequence of that interposition. . . .

But the strongest evidence of B. influence on the Continent, in opposition to our views, is seen in the unkind and even uncivil treatment of our Envoy in Russia. It is painful to see such a blot on the character of [Emperor] Alexander, as it is ominous to our expectations from his friendship & importance. Whilst the tide of B. ascendancy continues to direct the movements of that and probably the other sovereign having a common interest with us, we must be patient, in the hope that it will not be of long duration, and must endeavor to shorten it by all honorable means of conciliation.

Back in the capital in June, Madison met repeatedly with the Cabinet. Final plans were made for the summer campaign on the northern frontier—a campaign that tended to vindicate American arms but left the British in full possession of Canada. Convinced of an enemy buildup during the summer, and receiving nothing but discouragement from the commissioners in Europe, he proposed to the Cabinet a revision of peace terms. His own memoranda of these meetings explain the result.

submitted to Cabinet
June 23 & 24, 1814

1. Shall the surrender by G.B. of the practice of impressment, in a treaty, limited to a certain period be an ultimatum? Monroe, [the new Secretary of the Treasury George] Campbell, Armstrong, Jones—no. [Attorney General Richard] Rush inclining but not insisting otherwise.

2. Shall a treaty of peace, silent on the subject of Impressment be authorized? All no: but Armstrong & Jones, who were aye.

*By the President of the United
States of America.
A Proclamation*

*Whereas it is manifest that the
blockade, which has been proclaimed by the
enemy, of the whole Atlantic coast of the United
States, nearly two thousand miles in extent,
and abounding in ports harbours and navigable inlets, cannot be carried into effect, by
any adequate force, actually stationed for the
purpose; and it is rendered a matter of certainty and notoriety, by the multiplied and
daily arrivals and departures of the public
and private armed vessels of the United States,
and of other vessels, that no such adequate
force has been so stationed; And whereas
Blockade thus destitute of the character
of regular and legal blockade as defined
and recognised by the established law of
nations, whatever other purposes it may be
made to answer, forms no lawful prohibition...*

*Proclamation issued by Madison on
June 29, 1814, offering aid to all
vessels running the enemy blockade*

3. Shall a treaty be authorized comprising an article, referring the subject of impressment along with that of Commerce to a seperate negotiation? Monroe, Campbell Armstrong & Jones aye—Rush for awaiting further information from Europe.

June 27. 1814.

in consequence of the letter from Messrs. Bayard & Gallatin of May 6 or 7. and of other accts from Europe, as to the ascendency & views of G. B. and the dispositions of the Great Contl. powers, the pending Question No. 2 was put to the Cabinet, and agreed to by Monroe, Campbell, Armstrong & Jones; Rush being absent: our Ministers to be instructed, besides trying the other conditions to make a previous trial, to insert or to annex some declaration or protest, agst. any inference from the silence of the Treaty on the subject of impressment, that the British claim was admitted or that of the U.S. abandoned.

The time had come to look to the defense of Washington. During the past year a British squadron had freely raided and pillaged in Chesapeake Bay, even into the Potomac. Rumors of invasion had often circulated in the capital. The First Lady heard tales of enemy plans to descend upon the city at night and set fire to the Capitol and President's House; and she confessed that, although she was a Quaker, "the old Tunesian Sabre" was always within her reach. Only after Napoleon's collapse, however, did the administration act on these fears. Madison perceived correctly that thousands of British troops in Europe would be transported to the bay with the capital a likely target. On July 1, over the dissent of the Secretary of War, Madison established a military district in the Potomac area, placed General William Winder in command, and directed him to carry out plans for its defense. Winder was hampered by Armstrong, who pooh-poohed danger to the capital and thought local militia sufficient for its defense. Armstrong had repeatedly presumed to act as commander in chief. Madison blew the whistle on him in early August, but by then it was too late. Panic descended on the city ahead of the invading army. Madison seemed unperturbed; not so his wife, who wrote to Mrs. Gallatin.

[Washington,] July 28. [18]14.

We have been in a state of purturbation here, for a long time. The depredations of the Enemy approaching within 20 miles of the City & the disaffected, makeing incessant difficulties for the Government. Such a place as this has

An ink and watercolor sketch of the Capitol made by Benjamin H. Latrobe, showing the building's appearance before a fire destroyed wooden corridor connecting wings

become I can not describe it. I wish (for my own part) *we were* at Phila. The people here do not deserve that *I* should prefer it & among other exclamations & threats they say if Mr. M. attempts to move from *this House*, in case of an attack, they will *stop him*, & that he shall *fall with it*. I am not the least alarmed at these things, but entirely disgusted, & determined to stay with him. Our preperations for defence by some means or other, is constantly retarded but the small force the British have on the Bay will never venture nearer than at the present 23 miles. I desired Mr. Astor to tell you the strange story they made, about your haveing recd. a letter from Mr. G. full of alarming information, such, as his having no prospect of making peace & urgeing you for your personal safety to quit N. York & reside in Phila. It had a distressing effect on our Loan & threw many in to consternation for a while but we were able to contradict & soften consequences. I was rejoiced at your last letter containing the acct. of my precious Payne's going to France from England.

A British fleet sailed up Chesapeake Bay in mid-August, dropped anchor at the mouth of the Patuxent River, discharged an army of four thousand veteran troops at Benedict on the west bank of the Maryland river, and this force at once advanced on the capital. There, as the populace fled, Armstrong calmly insisted the army's destination was Baltimore. The President, with Monroe and Winder, took charge of military operations while Armstrong sulked. On the twenty-second Madison rode a dozen miles or so east of the city to reconnoiter the enemy at Marlboro. Winder had assembled a motley force of seven thousand men, mostly raw militia, and taken his position at Old Fields halfway between Marlboro and Bladensburg, the gateway to the capital. Madison sent a confident report to Dolley the next day.

Mt. Williams about 6 or 7 miles from Washington. Tuesday Aug. 23.
We reached our quarters last evening at the Camp between 8 & 9 o'c. and made out very well. I have passed the forenoon among the troops, who are in high spirits & make a good appearance. The reports as to the enemy have varied every hour. The last & probably truest information is that they are not very strong, and are without cavilry and artillery, and of course that they are not in a condition to strike at Washington. It is be-

General William Winder

lieved also that they are not about to move from Marlbro unless it be from an apprehension of our gathering force, and on a retreat to their ships. It is possible, however they may have a greater force or expect one, than has been represented or that their timerity may be greater than their strength. I sent you a message last night by Col. M. and one today by messenger of Genl. Winder who set out at a moment when it was impossible to write. I have detained Shorter, that I might give you by him some final & certain information. We expect every hour to have something further from the camp concerning the Enemy.

That evening Madison returned to the capital and slept in the President's House for what was to be the last time. The next morning, August 24, as the British advanced on Bladensburg, he and most of the Cabinet officers rushed to the field to counsel with poor Winder. Soon they were fleeing in all directions. The Battle of Bladensburg passed quickly as the militia were routed. The Redcoats marched unopposed to Washington. Preceding them by several hours, Madison discovered that Dolley had fled the deserted city. Her last two days in the executive mansion are recorded in a breathless letter to her sister.

[Washington,] Tuesday Augt. 23d. 1814

Dear Sister

My husband left me yesterday morng. to join Gen. Winder. He enquired anxiously whether I had courage, or firmness to remain in the President's house until his return, on the morrow, or succeeding day, and on my assurance that I had no fear but for him and the success of our army, he left me, beseeching me to take care of myself, and of the cabinet papers, public and private. I have since recd. two dispatches from him, written with a pencil; the last is alarming, because he desires I should be ready at a moment's warning to enter my carriage and leave the city; that the enemy seemed stronger than had been reported and that it might happen that they would reach the city, with intention to destroy it.... I am accordingly ready; I have pressed as many cabinet papers into trunks as to fill one carriage; our private property must be sacrificed, as it is impossible to procure wagons for its transportation. I am determined not to go myself until I see Mr Madison safe, and he can accompany me, as I hear of much hostility towards him....

Countryside near Bladensburg

My friends and acquaintances are all gone; Even Col. C [Charles Carroll] with his hundred men, who were stationed as a guard in the enclosure. French John [Sioussat, the majordomo], with his usual activity and resolution, offers to spike the cannon at the gate, and to lay a train of powder which would blow up the British, should they enter the house. To the last proposition I positively object, without being able, however, to make him understand why all advantages in war may not be taken.

Wednesday morng., twelve o'clock. Since sunrise I have been turning my spyglass in every direction and watching with unwearied anxiety, hoping to discern the approach of my dear husband and his friends, but, alas, I can descry only groups of military wandering in all directions, as if there was a lack of arms, or of spirit to fight for their own firesides!

Three O'clock. Will you believe it, my sister? We have had a battle or skirmish near Bladensburg, and I am still here within sound of the cannon! Mr. Madison comes not; may God protect him! Two messengers covered with dust, come to bid me fly; but I wait for him.... At this late hour a wagon has been procured, I have had it filled with the plate and most valuable portable articles belonging to the house; whether it will reach its destination, the Bank of Maryland, or fall into the hands of British soldiery, events must determine.

Watercolors by George Heriot, 1815, portray the Capitol and White House after destruction by the British.

Our kind friend, Mr. Carroll, has come to hasten my departure, and is in a very bad humor with me because I insist on waiting until the large picture of Gen. Washington is secured, and it requires to be unscrewed from the wall. This process was found too tedious for these perilous moments; I have ordered the frame to be broken, and the canvass taken out it is done, and the precious portrait placed in the hands of two gentlemen of New York, for safe keeping. And now, dear sister, I must leave this house, or t[he] retreating army will make me a prisoner in it, by filling up the road I am direc[ted] to take. When I shall again write you, or where I shall be tomorrow, I cannot tell!!

Madison too beat a fast retreat, alone on horseback, first to Georgetown, then from place to place on both sides of the Potomac. The enemy entered Washington that night, fired the Capitol, burned the President's House, put a torch to every public building except the ramshackle Patent Office, and after twenty-four hours retired unscathed from destruction estimated at one and a half million dollars. From his last refuge Madison sent off a dispatch to Dolley who had found shelter with her sister Anna Cutts.

Brookville Aug. 27. 10 OC. [1814]

My dearest

Finding that our army had left Montgomery Court House we pushed on to this place, with a view to join it, or proceed to the City as further information might prescribe. I have just recd. a line from Col. Monroe, saying that the Enemy were out of Washington, & on the retreat to their Ships & advising our immediate return to Washington. We shall accordingly set out thither immediately. You will all of course take the same resolution. I know not where we are in the first instance to hide our heads; but shall look for a place on my arrival. Mr Rush offers his house in the six buildings, and the offer claims attention. Perhaps I may fall in with Mr. Cutts, and have the aid of his advice. I saw Mr. Bradley at Montgomery Ct. H. who told me that Mrs Cutts was well. *Jamey will give you some particulars wch. I have not time to write.

Truly yours

J. MADISON

*Since the above it is found necessary to detain Jamey, & send a Trooper

347

Madison, followed by his wife, returned to the ravaged city on the same day. The danger was not over. Enemy troops were still in the neighborhood. Madison gathered the Cabinet on the twenty-ninth to concert new defense measures. On September 1 he issued a proclamation denouncing Britain's act of "barbarism" against the capital and exhorting the people to unite to expel the invader. The humiliating disaster produced a torrent of accusation and recrimination. Madison did not escape blame, nor was he blameless. He had been indecisive, overly tolerant of weak or unreliable subordinates, courageous in his own person but timid in driving others, more intent on quieting than arousing the populace, and hopelessly naive about the fighting power of raw militia. Yet Monroe was probably right in later insisting that the capital could have been saved had the President's July orders been carried out. This put the onus on Armstrong. The city was enraged against him. He would have to go, though even in this extremity Madison was anxious to provide a dignified exit. He filed a memorandum of his last interview with Armstrong.

[after August 29, 1814]

In the evening of the 29th, of Augst. 1814 Being on Horseback I stopped at General Armstrong's lodgings for the purpose of communicating with him on the state of things in the District, then under apprehensions of an immediate visit from the force of the Enemy at Alexandria.

I observed to him that he could not be unaware of the great excitement in the District produced by the unfortunate event which had taken place in the City; that violent prejudices were known to exist against the Ad-

English woodcut (left) of burning of Washington illustrates massive destruction of public buildings; Octagon House (above) was saved because the French minister moved in, giving it diplomatic immunity, and the Madisons lived there while the gutted White House was restored.

The Octagon BY GLENN BROWN, 1917

ministration, as having failed in its duty to protect it, particularly agst. me & himself as head of the War Department; that threats of personal violence had, it was said, been thrown out agst us both, but more especially agst. him; that it had been sufficiently known for several days & before his return to the City (which was about one OClock P. M. of the 29th.) that the temper of the troops was such as made it expedient, if possible, that he should have nothing to do with them; that I had within a few hours recd. a message from the commanding General of the Militia informing me that every Officer would tear off his epaulets, if Genl. Armstrong was to have any thing to do with them; that before his arrival there was less difficulty, as Mr. Monroe who was very acceptable to them, had, as on preceding occasions of his absence, though very reluctantly on this, been the medium for the functions of Secretary of war, but that since his return & presence the expedient could not be continued, and the question was, what was best to be done. Any convulsion at so critical a moment could not but have the worst consequences.

He said he had been aware of the excitement agst. him; that it was altogether artificial, and that he knew the sources of it, and the intrigues by which it had been effected, which this was not the proper time for examining, that the excitement was founded on the most palpable falsehoods, and was limited to this spot; that it was evident he could not remain here . . ., he was ready to give up his appointment; or he could, with my permission, retire from the scene, by setting out immediately on a visit to his family in the State of N. York.

I observed that a resignation was an extent which had not been contemplated that if made under such circumstances, it might receive constructions which could not be desirable, either in a public or a personal view, that a temporary retirement, as he suggested, tho' also subject to be viewed in some lights not agreeable, was on the whole less objectionable, and would avoid the existing embarrassment, without precluding any future course which might be deemed most fit. . . .

He returned to an exculpation of himself, and remarked that he had omitted no preparations or steps whatever for the safety of the place which had been enjoined on him.

Death of British General Robert
Ross during the battle of Baltimore

I replied that as the conversation was a frank one, I could not admit this justification; that it was the duty of the Secretary of war not only to execute plans or orders committed to him, but to devise and propose such as would in his opinion be necessary & proper; that this was an obvious and essential part of his charge, and that in which related to military plans & proceedings elsewhere, he had never been scrupulous or backward in taking this course; that on the contrary he well knew from what on another occasion had passed between us, he had taken a latitude in this respect which I was not satisfied with; that it was due to truth & to myself, to say, that he had never appeared to enter into a just view either of the danger to the City wch. was to be apprehended; or of the consequences of its falling into the hands of the Enemy; that he had never himself proposed or suggested a single precaution or arrangement for its safety, every thing done on that subject having been brought forward by myself, and that the apparent difference of his views on that subject from mine had naturally induced a reduction of my arrangements to the minimum, in order to obtrude the less on a reluctant execution. I reminded him also that he had fallen short of the preparations even decided on in the Cabinet, in some respects, particularly in not having arms & equipments brought to convenient depots from distant ones, some of the Militia whom called on for the defence of the City, being obliged to get arms first at Harper's ferry.

I remarked that it was not agreeable thus to speak, nor on an occasion less urgent would it be done; that I had selected him for the office he filled from a respect to his talents, and a confidence that he would exert them for the public good, that I had always treated him with friendliness & confidence, and that as there was but a short distance before me to the end of my public career, my great wish, next to leaving my Country in a state of peace & prosperity, was to have preserved harmony and avoid changes, and that I had accordingly as he well knew acquiesed in many things, to which no other consideration would have reconciled me.... We parted as usual in a friendly manner; on the next morning he sent word by Mr. Parker that he should proceed immediately to visit his family; and on his arrival at Baltimore, transmitted his resignation....

The government, though inconvenienced by the devastation, was little hampered in its functions. Madison had already called Congress into session September 19, two months earlier than usual, in order to deal with urgent fiscal and military needs. Fortunately, at this moment, the humiliation of the capital was offset by news of American victory in the Battle of Lake Champlain and of the gallant defense of Fort McHenry which, besides inspiring "The Star-Spangled Banner," saved Baltimore and led to a British withdrawal from the Chesapeake. Congress, however, was no more cooperative with the administration than before. On the Treasury's recommendation, Congress approved the establishment of a national bank but because it omitted the provision most wanted, that of bank loans to the government, Madison vetoed the bill. The army was as depleted as the treasury, standing at about one-half the authorized strength of sixty-two thousand men. Monroe, Armstrong's successor in the War Department, proposed conscription to raise the army to one hundred thousand. The House rejected the measure with cries of tyranny.

Meanwhile, the Americans negotiated at Ghent. On the basis of Gallatin's pessimistic assessment in June, the administration threw away the remaining war aims and called for peace on the status quo antebellum. Almost at once, on October 8, new dispatches arrived detailing British demands to treat the United States as a conquered nation. Letters more than two months apart to two former presidents, Jefferson and John Adams, suggest Madison's response to this development.

Monument built to commemorate the Battle of Baltimore and the gallant defense of Fort McHenry

Washington Oct. 10. 1814

We have just recd. despatches from Ghent which I shall lay before Congs. today. The British sine qua non. excluded us from fishing within the sovereignty attached to her shores, and from using these in curing fish—required a Cession of as much of Maine as wd. remove the obstruction to a direct communication between Quebec & Halifax, confirmed to her the Passamaquoddy Islands as always hers of right—included in the pacification the Indian Allies, with a boundary for them, (such as that of the Treaty of Greenville [with the Northwest Indians in 1795]) agst. the U.S. mutually guaranteed, and the Indians restrained from selling their lands to either party, but free to sell them to a *third* party—prohibited the U.S. from having an armed force on the Lakes or forts on their shores, the British prohibited as to neither—and substituted for the present N. W. limit of the U. S. a line running direct from the W. end of L. Superior to the Mississippi, with a right of G. B. to the navigation of this river. Our ministers were all present & in perfect harmony of opinion on the arrogance of such demands.

They wd. probably leave Ghent shortly after the sailing of the vessels just arrived. Nothing can prevent it, but a sudden change in the B. Cabinet not likely to happen, tho' it might be somewhat favored by indignant rupture of the negociation, as well as by the intelligence from this Country, and the fermentations taking place in Europe.

Washington Dcr. 17. 1814

The view of the discussions at Ghent presented by the private letters of all our Ministers there, as well as by their official dispatches leaves no doubt of the policy of the B. Cabinet. . . . Our Enemy knowing that he has peace in his own hands, speculates on the fortune of events. Should these be unfavorable he can at any moment, as he supposes, come to our terms. Should they correspond with his hopes, his demands may be insisted on, or even extended. The point to be decided by our Ministers is whether during the uncertainty of events, a categorical alternative of immediate peace or a rupture of the negociation would not be preferable to a longer acquiescence in the gambling procrastinations of the other party. It may be presumed that they will before this have pushed the negociations to this point.

It is very agreeable to find that the superior ability which distinguishes the notes of our Envoys extorts commendation from the most obdurate of their politi-

The Americans were victorious at the Battle of Plattsburgh (below) largely due to the naval triumph of Captain Macdonough's fleet on Lake Champlain, seen in background.

BOTH: *War of 1812*, LOSSING

View of the city of Ghent

cal Enemies. And we have the satisfaction to learn that the cause they are pleading is beginning to overcome the prejudice which misrepresentations had spread over the Continent of Europe agst. it. The B. Govt. is neither inattentive to this approaching revolution in the public opinion there, nor blind to its tendency. If it does not find in it a motive to immediate peace, it will infer the necessity of shortening the war by bringing upon us [in] the ensuing Campain, what it will consider, as a force not to be resisted by us.

It were to be wished that this consideration had more effect in quickening the preparatory measures of Congress. I am unwilling to say how much distress in every branch of our affairs is the fruit of their tardiness. . . .

His hopes for an early peace blasted, Madison prayed for more victories like Captain Thomas Macdonough's at Champlain to bring the British government to its senses. As an aid to this he prepared a propaganda paper on the causes and character of the war. With the return of peace to Europe, he argued, the original causes of the conflict, and hence the American demands, had been removed, but Britain kept up the fight with the view to "strangling the maritime power of the United States in its cradle and cutting off their commerce with other nations." Two extreme points on the compass, New Orleans and New England, drew Madison's fears. An attack on New Orleans had been expected since May, when General Jackson had been placed in command there. Subversion and disunion were the dangers in New England. But for the "traitors" in that quarter, Gallatin had said, a just peace would have already been signed. A young Virginian who called on the President in the fall described him as "miserably shattered and woe-begone" because of disunionism in the East. Madison did not disguise his anger on the subject in a letter to Wilson Cary Nicholas, Governor of Virginia.

Washington Novr. 26. 1814

You are not mistaken in viewing the conduct of the Eastern States as the source of our greatest difficulties in carrying on the war; as it certainly is the greatest, if not the sole inducement with the Enemy to persevere in it. The greater part of the people in that quarter have been brought by their leaders, aided by their priests, under a delusion scarcely exceeded by that recorded in the period of Witchcraft, and the leaders are becoming daily more desperate in the case they make of it. Their object is power. If they could obtain it by menaces,

Cartoon of Hartford Convention

their efforts would stop there. These failing, they are ready to go every length for which they can train their followers. Without foreign cooperation, revolts & separation will hardly be risked; and what the effect of so profligate an experiment may be first on deluded partizans, and next on those remaining faithful to the nation who are respectable for their consistency and even for their numbers, is for conjecture only. The best may be hoped, but the worst ought to be kept in view. In the meantime the Course to be taken by the Govt. is full of delicacy & perplexity; and the more so under the pinch which exists in our fiscal affairs, & the lamentable tardiness of the Legislature in applying some relief.

All the while, of course, Britain, her treasury empty and her attentions focused on the reconstruction of Europe, was backing away from the war in America. At the end of November her negotiators accepted the American formula and the treaty of peace was signed on Christmas Eve. As the good tidings crossed the Atlantic, the Battle of New Orleans was fought and won. Thus the American victory had no bearing on the outcome of the war, but that was not known at the time, and as the news spread across the country—it reached Washington on February 4—there was great rejoicing at this vindication of American pride and power. The commissioners of the Hartford Convention, a group of New England Federalists who had long been restive under Jeffersonian Republicanism and had met to protest "Mr. Madison's War," arrived in the capital to present their demands in the midst of the rejoicing. They sheepishly retired. The Treaty of Ghent was in Madison's hands on February 14. Four days later he sent it to Congress with the following felicitations.

Washington February 18th 1815
The late war although reluctantly declared by congress, had become a necessary resort, to assert the rights and independence of the Nation. It has been waged with a success, which is the natural result of the wisdom of the Legislative Councils, of the patriotism of the people, of the public spirit of the Militia, and of the valor of the Military and Naval forces of the Country. Peace, at all times a blessing, is peculiarly welcome therefore, at a period, when the causes for the war have ceased to operate; when the Government had demonstrated the efficiency of its powers of defence; and when the Nation can review its conduct, without regret, and without reproach.

The Battle of New Orleans (above) was fought two weeks after Treaty of Ghent had been signed abroad. Madison later signed the treaty in this house at 21 Lafayette Square.

I recommend to your care and beneficences, the gallant men, whose achievements, in every department of the military service, on the land, and on the water, have so essentially contributed to the honor of the American name, and to the restoration of peace. The feelings of conscious patriotism and worth, will animate such men under every change of fortune and pursuit; but their Country performs a duty to itself, when it bestows those testimonials of approbation and applause which are, at once, the reward, and the incentive, to great actions.

The reduction of the public expenditures, to the demands of a peace establishment will doubtless engage the immediate attention of Congress. There are, however, important considerations, which forbid a sudden and general revocation of the measures, that have been produced by the war. Experience has taught us, that neither the pacific dispositions of the American people, nor the pacific character of their political institutions, can altogether exempt them from that strife, which appears, beyond the ordinary lot of Nations, to be incident to the actual period of the World; and the same faithful monitor demonstrates, that a certain degree of preparation for war, is not only indispensable to avert disasters in the onset; but affords also the best security, for the continuance of peace. The wisdom of Congress will, therefore, I am confident, provide for the maintenance of an adequate regular force; for the gradual advancement of the naval establishment; for improving all the means of harbour defence, for adding discipline, to the distinguished bravery of the Militia; and for cultivating the Military art, in its essential branches, under the liberal patronage of the Government.

The resources of our Country were, at all times, competent to the attainment of every national object; but they will now be enriched and invigorated by the activity, which peace will introduce, into all the scenes of domestic enterprize and labour....

The termination of the Legislative Sessions will soon separate you, Fellow-Citizens, from each other, and restore you to your Constituents. I pray you to bear with you, the expressions of my sanguine hope, that the Peace, which has been just declared, will not only be the foundation of the most friendly intercourse between the United

States and Great Britain; but that it will, also be productive of happiness and harmony in every section of our beloved Country. The influence of your precepts and example, must be, every where, powerful: And while we accord in grateful acknowledgements, for the protection, which Providence has bestowed upon us, let us never cease to inculcate obedience to the laws, and fidelity to the Union, as constituting the palladium of the National independence and prosperity.

The American people, following their President, erased all the shame from the war and put upon it the face of glory. If the peace resolved none of the issues on which the war began, it nevertheless placed American independence on impregnable foundations and proved the strength of republican government and national character. The war, as Madison suggested, had been a great teacher—of patriotism, of union, of the firmness and energy that not even the most favored nation on God's footstool could ignore but at its peril. The war had ended gloriously precisely because it had been such an ordeal. To emerge stronger from trials of adversity, division, and disgrace was to emerge victoriously.

For the first time in six years the country was calm. Madison hastened to Montpelier in March and remained there except for one brief interlude in the capital until some weeks before Congress convened in December. His State of the Union message was a landmark in the history of the Republican party. In the opinion of doctrinaire Old Republicans, some of whom, like John Randolph, had never been convinced of Madison's political purity, the message "out-Federalized" Federalism. Politically, it seemed, Madison had traveled a circle back to the nationalism of his youth. And so he had. Yet this nationalism was different because it rested on the achievement of democracy and independence. It was nearly one hundred and eighty degrees to the left of Federalist nationalism, with its vitiating British connection, its narrow sectional views, and its distrust of democracy. In 1815, filled with the patriotic *élan* that followed the Peace of Ghent, Madison believed that the American political experiment had proved itself and that the Union could sustain a program of national improvement and consolidation. He therefore called upon Congress to establish a national bank and uniform currency, build a national defense, nurture manufactures, plan a system of roads and canals, and create a national university within the new "district of Columbia."

[December 5, 1815]

The arrangements of the finances, with a view to the receipts and expenditures of a permanent peace establishment, will necessarily enter into the deliberations

Madison's message of December 4, 1815, communicating "successful termination of the war" to Congress

of Congress, during the present Session. It is true that the improved condition of the public revenue will not only afford, the means of maintaining the faith of the Government with its Creditors, inviolate, and of prosecuting Successfully the measures of the Most liberal policy, but will also, justify an immediate alleviation of the burthens imposed by the necessities of the war. It is, however, essential, to every modification of the finances, that the benefits of an uniform national currency should be restored to the community.... If the operation of the State Banks cannot produce this result, the probable operation of a National Bank will merit consideration; and if neither of these expedients be deemed effectual, it may become necessary to ascertain the terms, upon which the notes of the Government (no longer required as an instrument of credit) shall be issued, upon motives of general policy, as a common medium of circulation.

Notwithstanding the security for future repose, which the United States ought to find in their love of peace, and their constant respect for the rights of other nations, the character of the times, particularly inculcates the lesson, that whether to prevent or repel danger, we ought not to be unprepared for it. This consideration will sufficiently recommend to Congress, a liberal provision for the immediate extension and gradual completion of the works of defence, both fixed and floating, on our maritime frontier; and an adequate provision for guarding our inland frontier, against dangers to which certain portions of it may continue to be exposed.

As an improvement in our military establishment, it will deserve the consideration of Congress, whether a corps of Invalids might not be so organized & employed.... I recommend also an enlargement of the military Academy already established, and the establishment of others in other sections of the Union. And I cannot press too much on the attention of Congress, such a classification and organization of the militia as will most effectually render it the safeguard of a free State....

The signal services which have been rendered by our navy, and the capacities it has developed for successful co-operation in the national defense, will give to that portion of the public force, its full value in the eyes of congress, at an epoch which calls for the constant vigilance of all Governments. To preserve the ships now in sound State; to compleat those already contemplated; to provide amply the imperishable materials for prompt augmentations; and to improve the existing arrangements, into more advantageous establishments, for the construction, the repairs, and the security, of vessels of war, is dictated by the soundest policy.

In adjusting the duties on imports, to the object of revenue, the influence of the Tariff on manufactures, will necessarily present itself for consideration. However wise the theory may be, which leaves to the Sagacity and interest of individuals, the application of their industry and resources, there are in this, as in other cases, exceptions to the general rule.... Under circumstances giving a powerful impulse to manufacturing industry, it has made among us a progress, and exhibited an efficiency, which justify the belief, that with a protection not more than is due to the enterprizing citizens whose interests are now at stake, it will become, at an early day, not only Safe against occasional competitions from abroad, but a source of Domestic Wealth, and even of external commerce.... It will be an additional recommendation of particular manufactures, where the materials for them are extensively drawn from our agriculture, and consequently impart and ensure to that great fund of national prosperity and independence, an encouragement which cannot fail to be rewarded.

Among the means of advancing the public interest, the occasion is a proper one for recalling the attention of Congress, to the great importance of establishing, throughout our Country, the roads and canals which can best be executed, under the National authority. No objects within the circle of political economy, so richly repay the expence bestowed on them; there are none, the utility of which is more universally ascertained and acknowledged; none that do more honor to the Governments, whose wise and & enlarged patriotism duly appreciates them. Nor is there any Country which presents a field, where nature invites more the art of man, to compleat her own work for his accomodation and benefit. These Considerations are strengthened moreover by the political effect of these facilities for intercommunication, in bringing and binding more closely together, the various parts of our extended confederacy....

The present is a favorable season also, for bringing

Certificate of membership in the Berkshire Agricultural Society of Massachusetts issued to Madison

*French army taking flight in the
Battle of Waterloo, June 18, 1815*

again into view, the establishment of a national seminary
of learning within the district of Columbia, and with
means drawn from the property therein subject to the
authority of the General government. Such an institution claims the patronage of Congress, as a monument of
their solicitude for the advancement of Knowledge, without which the blessings of liberty cannot be fully enjoyed,
or long preserved; as a model instructive in the formation
of other Seminaries; as a nursery of enlightened precep-
tors; and as a central resort of youth and genius from
every part of their Country, diffusing, on their return,
examples of those national feelings, those liberal sentiments, and those congenial manners, which contribute
cement to our union, and strength to the great political
fabric, of which that is the foundation.

Congress made a beginning on this program by charter-
ing the Second Bank of the United States and adopting the first peacetime
protective tariff. Meanwhile, events in Europe had given Madison some
anxious moments in 1815. With the return of Napoleon, the peace looked
more like an armistice, and if Europe again became a slaughterhouse America could not escape the carnage. Britain's hostility must again be felt — and
indeed, actuated by zeal "to recover her lost reputation," more potently
than before. Waterloo ended the immediate danger. Although Madison shed
no tears for Napoleon, he could not help but regret the loss of France in
the scales of power and the utter collapse of European liberty twenty-five
years after its rise. An Anglo-American commercial treaty was signed in
July, 1815. An important step forward, it nonetheless kept the Americans
from the West Indies trade; and other serious matters — the Newfoundland
fisheries and armament on the Great Lakes — remained in dispute between
the two countries. Madison wrote of these problems to John Quincy Adams,
now Minister to Great Britain, in the following year.

Washington May 10. 1816.
You will receive from the Secretary of State the communications relating to the topics in discussion with the B Govt.
Being sincerely desirous of maintaining peace and friendship between the two Countries, we wish every fair
experiment to be made for guarding against causes which
may interrupt them. On questions such as impressments
and blockades, on which we consider ourselves as standing on the ground of right and of public law, and consequently connect a defence of them with our honor &
independence, collisions must be unavoidable in the

John Quincy Adams

event of wars in Europe, unless amicable adjustments precede them, or G B should be more yeilding than we are authorized to expect. It is much to be desired also that on questions not of right, but of prudence & reciprocity, as a discontinuance of armaments on the lakes, and the commerce with the West Indies, an understanding or stipulations satisfactory to both parties, should not be delayed. You will learn that with respect to the lakes Congs. declined to make appropriations for keeping pace with British armaments on them. But it is not to be inferred that if these should be actually carried on, they will not lead at another Session to a different policy. The effect of a display of British superiority on the upper lakes on the spirit of the Savages will be decisive. In this view only the question of naval superiority in that quarter is important to the U.S. whilst it is not so to Canada which has no apprehensions from Savage inroads. In any other view the extention of British armaments on the lakes would have nothing in them to be dreaded. In time of peace they are harmless and in the event of a future war, the object of the U. S. would be to take the lakes themselves, which the inducement would be strengthened by so rich a prize on them. This was the first object in the late war, and wd. have succeeded in any hands but those of Genl. Hulls. On future occasions, should they unfortunately not be precluded, the U. S. will have greater comparative means, with an application of them enlightened by experience. As to the commerce with the West Indies, there can be but one sentiment. What passed on that subject in Congs. is a proof that if intermediate negociation be not successful, it will be taken up at the next session, with a determination to put an end to the existing inequality. If G B will not admit American vessels into the W. India ports, American ports will be shut agst. B vessels coming from those ports. The consequence must be either that the intercourse will cease, which tho' disadvantageous to the U. S. will be not less so to G B: or that neutral ports will be interposed, which will furnish a greater proportion of the navigation employed, to the Amn than to the B tonnage. The present monopoly will be the less submitted to, as it is found to destroy the equality which was the object of the Commercial Convention in the branches of trade embraced by it.

The Rush-Bagot Convention of 1817 disarmed the Lakes and secured American rights to the fisheries. Free trade would take a little longer, but in time Britain would come to that policy as well. Meanwhile, Madison's term as President was coming to an end; in his last annual message he offered his own "farewell address" to the American people.

[December 3, 1816]

The period of my retiring from the public service being at little distance, I shall find no occasion more proper than the present, for expressing to my fellow Citizens, my deep sense of the continued confidence, and kind support which I have received from them. My grateful recollection of these distinguished marks of their favorable regard, can never cease; and with the consciousness, that if I have not served my Country with greater ability, I have served it with sincere devotion, will accompany me as a source of unfailing gratification.

Happily, I shall carry with me from the public Theatre, other sources, which those who love their country most, will best appreciate. I shall behold it blessed with tranquility and prosperity at home; and with peace and respect abroad. I can indulge the proud reflection, that the American people have reached in safety and success their fortieth year, as an independent nation; that for nearly an entire generation, they have had experience of their present constitution, the offspring of their undisturbed deliberations and of their free choice; that they have found it to bear the trials of adverse as well as prosperous circumstances; to contain in its combination of the federate and elective principles, a reconcilement of public strength with individual liberty, of national power for the defence of national rights, with a security against wars of injustice, of ambition or of vain glory, in the fundamental provision which subjects all questions of war to the will of the nation itself, which is to pay its costs, and feel its calamities. Nor is it less a peculiar felicity of this constitution, so dear to us all, that it is found to be capable, without losing its vital energies, of expanding itself over a spacious territory, with the increase and expansion of the community for whose benefit it was established.

And may I not be allowed to add to this gratifying spectacle, that I shall read in the character of the American people, in their devotion to true liberty, and to the constitution which is its palladium, sure presages, that

Above and at right, the first and last pages of Madison's "farewell address," given December 3, 1816

the destined career of my country will exhibit a Government, pursuing the public good as its sole object, and regulating its means by the great principles consecrated in its charter, & by those moral principles, to which they are so well allied: a Government, which watches over the purity of elections, the freedom of speech and of the press, the trial by Jury, and the equal interdict against encroachments and compacts, between religion and the State; which maintains inviolably the maxims of public faith, the security of persons and property, and encourages, in every authorised mode, that general diffusion of knowledge which guarantees to public liberty its permanency, and to those who possess the blessing, the true enjoyment of it: a Government, which avoids intrusions on the internal repose of other nations, and repels them from its own; which does justice to all nations with a readiness, equal to the firmness with which it requires justice from them; and which, whilst it refines its domestic code from every ingredient not congenial with the precepts of an enlightened age, and the sentiments of a virtuous people, seeks, by appeals to reason, and by its liberal examples, to infuse into the law which governs the civilised world, a Spirit which may diminish the frequency or circumscribe the calamities of war, and meliorate the social and beneficent relations of peace: a Government, in a word, whose conduct within and without, may bespeak the most noble of all ambitions, that of promoting peace on Earth, and good will to man.

These contemplations, sweetening the remnant of my days, will animate my prayers for the happiness of my beloved Country, and a perpetuity of the Institutions, under which it is enjoyed.

Having helped to set the government on the course of power and responsibility for the national welfare, Madison retreated to the safety of Republican dogma in the last act of his Presidency. His veto of the bonus bill, which created a permanent fund for internal improvements from the charter price and the dividends to be paid by the Bank, came as a jolt to national-minded Republicans who had been the mainstay of Madison's support in Congress since 1811. Although the President had not blinked at the Bank, he could not approve federally financed internal improvements without the sanction of a constitutional amendment, as he told Congress.

*...ons on the internal repose of other nations, and
them from its own; which does justice to all
...ns with a readiness equal to the firmness with
it requires justice from them; and which,
...t it refines its domestic code from every
...dient not congenial with the precepts of
...lightened age, and the sentiments of a
...ous people, seeks, by appeals to reason,
...by its liberal examples, to infuse into
...w which governs the civilized world,
...nt which may diminish the frequency
...cumscribe the calamities of war, and
...orate the social and beneficent relations
...ace: A Government, in a word, whose
...ct, within and without, may bespeak
...ost noble of all ambitions, that of promo
...eace on Earth and good will to man.
These contemplations, sweetening
...mnant of my days, will animate
...rayers for the happiness of my beloved
...try, and a perpetuity of the institutions
...r which it is enjoyed.*

*James Madison
December 3ᵈ 1815.*

March 3, 1817.

The legislative powers vested in Congress are specified and enumerated in the eighth section of the first article of the Constitution, and it does not appear that the power proposed to be exercised by the bill is among the enumerated powers, or that it falls by any just interpretation within the power to make laws necessary and proper for carrying into execution those or other powers vested by the Constitution in the Government of the United States.

"The power to regulate commerce among the several States" can not include a power to construct roads and canals, and to improve the navigation of water courses in order to facilitate, promote, and secure such a commerce without a latitude of construction departing from the ordinary import of the terms strengthened by the known inconveniences which doubtless led to the grant of this remedial power to Congress.

To refer the power in question to the clause "to provide for the common defense and general welfare" would be contrary to the established and consistent rules of interpretation, as rendering the special and careful enumeration of powers which follow the clause nugatory and improper. Such a view of the Constitution would have the effect of giving to Congress a general power of legislation instead of the defined and limited one hitherto understood to belong to them, the terms "common defense and general welfare" embracing every object and act within the purview of a legislative trust. It would have the effect of subjecting both the Constitution and laws of the several States in all cases not specifically exempted to be superseded by laws of Congress.... Such a view of the Constitution, finally, would have the effect of excluding the judicial authority of the United States from its participation in guarding the boundary between the legislative powers of the General and the State Governments....

A restriction of the power "to provide for the common defense and general welfare" to cases which are to be provided for by the expenditure of money would still leave within the legislative power of Congress all the great and most important measures of Government, money being the ordinary and necessary means of carrying them into execution.

If a general power to construct roads and canals, and to improve the navigation of water courses, with the

Festive election scene outside Independence Hall ushered in the Presidency of James Monroe.

train of powers incident thereto, be not possessed by Congress, the assent of the States in the mode provided in the bill cannot confer the power. The only cases in which the consent and cession of particular States can extend the power of Congress are those specified and provided for in the Constitution.

I am not unaware of the great importance of roads and canals and the improved navigation of water courses, and that a power in the National Legislature to provide for them might be exercised with signal advantage to the general prosperity. But seeing that such a power is not expressly given by the Constitution, and believing that it can not be deduced from any part of it without an inadmissible latitude of construction and a reliance on insufficient precedents; believing also that the permanent success of the Constitution depends on a definite partition of powers between the General and the State Governments, and that no adequate landmarks would be left by the constructive extension of the powers of Congress as proposed in the bill, I have no option but to withhold my signature from it, and to cherishing the hope that its beneficial objects may be attained by a resort for the necessary powers to the same wisdom and virtue in the nation which established the Constitution in its actual form and providently marked out in the instrument itself a safe and practicable mode of improving it as experience might suggest.

Thus ended, on a somewhat ambiguous note, the Presidency of James Madison. No President since Washington retired from the office with greater public esteem. "Never was a country left in a more flourishing situation," Gallatin wrote in a personal tribute, or its people "more united at home and respected abroad." Madison was even fortunate in his successor, James Monroe, whose politics were virtually indistinguishable from his own. He lingered in Washington several days after the inauguration. "I am in the midst of preparations to get to my farm, where I shall make myself a fixture," he told Gallatin, "and where I anticipate many enjoyments, which if not fully realized, will be a welcome change from the labors and solicitudes of public life."

Chapter 10

Last of the Fathers

Sixty-six years of age when he retired to Montpelier, James Madison still had many years of happiness before him. He enjoyed good health, benign temperament, a fine estate, a loving family and many friends, the pleasures of his books and of farming, and the veneration of his countrymen. The mansion had been enlarged, with wings on either side, and the grounds much improved. Its central feature, a large drawing room, opened to the entire house and the luxuriant landscape beyond. "The drawing-room walls are covered with pictures," wrote one visitor, "some very fine, from the ancient masters, but most of them portraits of our most distinguished men, six or eight by Stewart [Gilbert Stuart]. The mantelpiece, tables in each corner and in fact wherever one could be fixed, were filled with busts, and groups of figures in plaster, so that the apartment had more the appearance of a museum of the arts than of a drawing-room." In the immediate house-hold were Dolley and Madison's aged mother, who would live to the ripe age of ninety-eight. But the house was often filled with his wife's relatives and his own, as well as guests from far and near. Lacking children of his own, Madison doted on his nieces and nephews. Perhaps his favorite was young Richard Cutts, in his twelfth year when he received this patriarchal letter from "Uncle Madison."

> Montpellier. Jany. 4. 1829
>
> Your letter, my dear Richard, gave me much pleasure, as it shews that you love your studies, which you would not do if you did not profit by them. Go on, my good boy, as you have begun; and you will find that you have chosen the best road to a happy life, because a useful one; the more happy because it will add to the happiness of your parents, and of all who love you and are anxious to see you deserving to be loved.
>
> When I was at an age which will soon be yours, a book

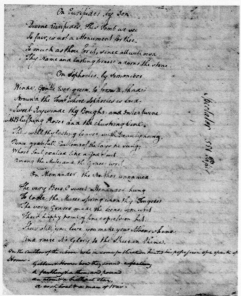

Excerpts from the Spectator, *which Madison recommended to his nephew Richard in 1829, appear on this page from his commonplace book, written when he was a young boy.*

fell into my hands which I read, as I believe, with particular advantage. I have always thought it the best that had been written, for cherishing in young minds a desire of improvement, a taste for Learning, and a lively sense of the duties, the virtues, and the proprieties of life. The work I speak of is the "Spectator" well known by that title. It had several Authors, at the head of them Mr. Addison, whose papers are marked at the bottom of each, by one of the letters in the name of the Muse, C.L.I.O. They will reward you for a second reading, after reading them along with the others.

Addison was of the first rank among the fine writers of the Age, and has given a definition of what he shewed himself to be an example. "Fine writing" he says "consists of sentiments that are natural, without being obvious"; to which adding the remark of Swift, another celebrated author of the same period, making a good style to "consist of proper words in their proper places," a definition is formed, which will merit your recollection, when you become qualified, as I hope you will one day be, to employ your pen for the benefit of others and for your own reputation.

I send you a copy of the "Spectator" that it may be at hand when the time arrives for making use of it; and as a token, also, of all the good wishes of your affectionate Uncle.

Montpelier, like Monticello only thirty miles away, was a republican mecca. Citizens great and ordinary and many distinguished foreign visitors beat a path to Madison's door. During the summer months the normal flow was swelled by the tide of tourists journeying to the Virginia springs. Under the arbor on the lawn, "Queen" Dolley spread dinner for as many as ninety guests at one time. The world came to Madison; and although he made the round of the plantations in the neighborhood,

only once in nineteen years did he venture more than a day's ride from home. A young Harvard professor, George Ticknor, accompanied by his wife and Daniel Webster, visited Montpelier in 1824. Ticknor wrote of the visit to a friend in Boston.

Album of Virginia BY ED. BEYER, 1858

On his return to America in 1824 (left), Lafayette visited Madison; George Ticknor (below) was also a guest at Montpelier. Others stopped en route to Warm Springs (above).

Monticello, December 16, 1824.

On Saturday morning we reached Mr. Madison's, at Montpellier, on the west side of what is called the Southwest Mountain; a very fine, commanding situation, with the magnificant range of the Blue Ridge stretching along the whole horizon in front, at the distance of from twenty to thirty miles....

We were received with a good deal of dignity and much cordiality, by Mr. and Mrs. Madison, in the portico, and immediately placed at ease; for they were apprised of our coming an hour or two before we arrived, and were therefore all in order, to show a little of that ceremony in which Mrs. Madison still delights.

Mr. Madison is a younger-looking man—he is now seventy-four—than he was when I saw him ten years ago, with an unsuccessful war grinding him to the earth; and he is one of the most pleasant men I have met, both from the variety and vivacity of his conversation. He lives, apparently, with great regularity. We breakfasted at nine, dined about four, drank tea at seven, and went to bed at ten; that is, we went to our rooms, where we were furnished with everything we wanted, and where Mrs. Madison sent us a nice supper every night and a nice luncheon every forenoon. From ten o'clock in the morning till three we rode, walked, or remained in our rooms, Mr. and Mrs. Madison being then occupied. The table is very ample and elegant, and somewhat luxurious; it is evidently a serious item in the account of Mr. M.'s happiness, and it seems to be his habit to pass about an hour, after the cloth is removed, with a variety of wines of no mean quality.

On politics he is a little reserved, as he seems determined not to be again involved in them; but about everything else he talked with great freedom, and told an interminable series of capital stories, most of which have some historical value. His language, though not very rich or picturesque, was chosen with much skill, and combined into very elegant and finished sentences; and both Mr. Webster and myself were struck with a degree of good-sense in his conversation which we had

Robert Walsh

not anticipated from his school of politics and course of life. We passed our time, therefore, very pleasantly, and feel indebted to him for a hospitality which becomes one who has been at the head of the nation.

On Sunday forenoon we took a ride of a dozen miles across different plantations, to see the country and the people. Mr. Madison's farm—as he calls it—consists of about three thousand acres, with an hundred and eighty slaves, and is among the best managed in Virginia. We saw also one or two others that looked very well, but in general things had a very squalid appearance.

Madison maintained a lively interest in public affairs, but his principal business was farming. With little practical experience in this calling, he weathered the severe economic depression in Virginia agriculture after 1818 better and longer than most of his neighbors. Jefferson, who was broken by it, called Madison "the best farmer in the world." Within a year of his return, the prominent planters of the region named him president of the newly formed Agricultural Society of Albemarle. His address to the society in 1818 combined enlarged philosophical views of the place of agriculture in the advance of civilization with a detailed "catalogue of errors" in Virginia husbandry. Most of these errors were well known to scientific agriculturists, as were most of the correctives proposed—deep plowing, crop rotation, the use of manures, improvement of livestock, reforestation, contour plowing—but they were still novel in the common practice of American agriculture and would remain so for decades to come. The address was printed in the *American Farmer* and circulated widely in the United States and abroad.

After nearly forty years on the national scene, Madison was impressed by the changes in the manners and morals of his native state. In 1819 the Philadelphia journalist Robert Walsh solicited his aid in the defense of American character and institutions against the verbal onslaught of carping English critics after the war. In all areas—slavery, religion, property, education—Madison wrote, he saw striking progress since the Revolution.

Montpellier Mar 2. 1819

In reference to the actual condition of slaves in Virga. it may be confidently stated, as better beyond comparison, than it was before the Revolution. The improvement strikes every one who witnessed their former condition, and attends to their present. They are better fed, better clad, better lodged, and better treated in every respect; insomuch that what was formerly deemed a moderate treatment wd. now be a rigid one, and what formerly a rigid one would now be denounced by the public feeling. With respect to the great article of food particularly it is a common remark among those who have visited Europe, that it includes a much greater proportion of the animal ingredient, than is attainable by the free labourers even in that quarter of the Globe. As the two great causes of the general melioration in the lot of the slaves since the establishment of our Independence, I should set down 1. the sensibility to human rights, and sympathy with human sufferings excited and cherished by the discussions preceding, & the spirit of the Institutions growing out of that event. 2. the decreasing proportions which the slaves bear to the individual holders of them: a consequence of the abolition of entails, & the rule of primogeniture, and of the equalizing tendency of parental affection unfettered from old prejudices, as well as from the restrictions of law.

With respect to the moral features of Virga. it may be observed, that the pictures which have been given of them are, to say the least, outrageous caracatures, even when taken from the state of Society previous to the Revolution; and that so far as there was any ground or colour for them, the same cannot be found for them now.

Omitting more minute or less obvious causes tainting the habits and manners of the people under the Colonial Govt. the following offer themselves. 1. the negro slavery chargeable in so great a degree on the very quarter which has furnished most of the libellers. It is well known that during the Colonial dependence of Virga. repeated attempts were made to stop the importations of slaves each of which attempts, was successively defeated by the foreign negative on the laws, and that one of the first offsprings of independent & republican legislation was an Act of perpetual prohibition 2. the too unequal distribution of property favored by laws derived from the British code, which generated examples in the opulent class, inauspicious to the habits of the other classes. 3. the indolence of most & the irregular lives of many of the established Clergy consisting, of in a very large proportion of foreigners, and these in no inconsiderable proportion, of men willing to leave their homes in the parent Country when their demerit was an obstacle to a provision for them, and whose

Certificate of membership that Madison received from the New-York Horticultural Society in 1824

View of Richmond in 1819

degeneracy here was promoted by their distance from the controuling eyes of their kindred & friends, by the want of Ecclesiastical superiors in the Colony, or efficient ones in G.B. who might maintain a salutary discipline among them, and finally by their independence both of their congregations and of the Civil authority for their stipends.   4. A source of contageous dissipation might be traced in the British Factors, chiefly from Scotland, who carried on the general trade external & internal of the Colony. These being interdicted by their principals from marrying in the Country, being little prone to apply their leisure to intellectual [pursuits] and living in knots scattered in small towns or detached spots affording few substitutes of social amusements easily fell into irregularities of different sorts, and of evil example....

With the exception of slavery these demoralizing causes have ceased or are wearing out; and even that as already noticed, has lost no small share of its former character. On the whole the moral aspect of the State may at present be fairly said to bear no unfavorable comparison with the average standard of the other States. It certainly gives the lie to the foreign Calumniators whom you propose to arraign.

That there has been an increase of religious instruction since the revolution can admit of no question. The English Church was originally the established religion: the character of the clergy that above described. Of other sects there were but few adherents, except the Presbyterians who predominated on the W. side of the Blue ridge Mountains. A little time previous to the Revolutionary struggle the Baptists sprang up, and made a very rapid progress. Among the early acts of the Republican Legislature were those abolishing the Religious establishment and putting all Sects at full liberty and on a perfect level. At present the population is divided, with small exceptions, among the Protest[ant]: Episcopalians, the Presbyterians the Baptists & the Methodists.... On a general comparison of the present & former times, the balance is certainly & vastly on the side of the present, as to the number of religious teachers the zeal which actuates them, the purity of their lives, and the attendance of the people on their instructions. It was the universal opinion of the Century preceding the last,

Drawing of a slave auction from the sketchbook of artist Lewis Miller

Portraiture of Domestic Slavery BY JESSE TORREY, JR., 1817

Although Madison felt the living conditions of slaves had improved, whippings such as the one portrayed in this illustration from a book published in 1817 still occurred.

that civil Govt. could not stand without the prop of a religious establishment, & that the Christian religion itself, would perish if not supported by a legal provision for its Clergy. The experience of Virginia conspicuously corroborates the disproof of both opinions. The Civil Govt. tho' bereft of everything like an anointed hierarchy possesses the requisite Stability and performs its functions with complete success: Whilst the number, the industry, and the morality of the priesthood & the devotion of the people have been manifestly increased by the total separation of the Church from the State.

On the subject of education I am not eno' informed to give a view of its increase.... Those who are best able to compare the present intelligence of the mass of the people, with that antecedent to the revolution, will all agree I believe on the great superiority of the present.

However much the condition of Virginia's blacks may have improved, Madison could not rest until slavery was abolished. Slavery was a moral crime, a curse to the society, and a menace to the Union. In his youth he had hoped to rid himself of dependence on slave labor and he had expected with most revolutionary Virginians that the system would fall before the advance of liberty and enlightenment. Instead, the monster had fastened its hold on Virginia and the states to the south. Simply to free the slaves was no solution, in Madison's opinion. The system must be eradicated and its benighted victims removed from society. To Madison, the coexistence of the two races in a state of freedom and equality was inconceivable. With the birth of the idea of colonization, he came to believe that the problem could be solved. He was one of the founders of the American Colonization Society in 1817, and until the end of his life he clung desperately to its program. In a letter to an acquaintance, Robert J. Evans, he sketched his own more ambitious version of that program.

Montpellier June 15. 1819

A general emancipation of slaves ought to be   1. gradual. 2. equitable & satisfactory to the individuals immediately concerned. 3. consistent with the existing & durable prejudices of the nation.

That it ought, like remedies for other deep rooted, and wide spread evils, be gradual, is so obvious that there seems to be no difference of opinion on that point.

To be equitable & satisfactory, the consent of both the Master & the slave should be obtained. That of the Master will require a provision in the plan for compensating a loss of what he has held as property guaranteed by the laws, and recognized by the constitution. That of the slave requires that his condition in a state of freedom, be preferable in his own estimation, to his actual one in a state of bondage.

To be consistent with existing and probably unalterable prejudices in the U.S. the freed blacks ought to be permanently removed beyond the region occupied by or allotted to a white population. The objections to a thorough incorporation of the two people, are with most of the Whites insuperable, and are admitted by all of them to be very powerful. If the blacks, strongly marked as they are by physical & lasting peculiarities, be retained amid the whites, under the degrading privation of equal rights political or social, they must be always dissatisfied with their condition as a change only from one to another species of oppression; always secretly confederated agst. the ruling & privileged class; and always uncontroulled by some of the most cogent motives to moral and respectable conduct. The character of the freed blacks, even where their legal condition is least affected by their colour, seems to put these truths beyond question. It is material also that the removal of the blacks be to a distance precluding the jealousies & hostilities to be apprehended from a neighboring people stimulated by the contempt known to be entertained for their peculiar features; to say nothing of their vindictive recollections, or the predatory propensities which their State of Society might foster. Nor is it fair, in estimating the danger of Collusions with the Whites, to charge it wholly on the side of the Blacks. There would be reciprocal antipathies doubling the danger.

The colonizing plan on foot, has as far as it extends a due regard to these requisites; with the additional object of bestowing new blessings civil & relegious on the quarter of the Globe most in need of them. The Society proposes to transport to the African Coast, all free & freed blacks who may be willing to remove thither; to provide by fair means, & it is understood with a prospect of success, a suitable territory for their reception; and to initiate them into such an establishment as may gradually, and indefinitely expand itself.

The experiment under this view of it, merits encouragement from all who regard slavery as an evil, who wish

Madison's letter of June 15, 1819, giving his views on colonization

to see it diminished and abolished by peaceable & just means; and who have themselves no better mode to propose. Those who have most doubted the success of the experiment must at least have wished to find themselves in an error.

But the views of the Society are limited to the case of blacks already free, or who may be *gratuitously* emancipated. To provide a commensurate remedy for the evil, the plan must be extended to the great mass of blacks, must embrace a fund sufficient to induce the Master as well as the slave to concur in it. Without the concurrence of the Master, the benefit will be very limited as it relates to the Negroes; and essentially defective, as it relates to the U. States; And the concurrence of Masters, must for the most part, be obtained by purchase....

Happily... if slavery as a national evil is to be abolished, and it be just that it be done at the national expence, the amount of the expence is not a paramount consideration. It is the peculiar fortune, or rather a providential blessing of the U.S. to possess a resource commensurate to this great object, without taxes on the people, or even an increase of the Public debt.

I allude to the vacant territory the extent of which is so vast, and the vendible value of which is so well ascertained.

Supposing the number of slaves to be 1,500,000. and the price to average 400. d[ollar]rs the cost of the whole would be 600 millions of dollrs....

This will require 200 Mils. of acres at 3 dolrs. per acre; or 300 Mills. at 2 dollrs. per acre a quantity, which tho' great in itself, is perhaps not a third part of the disposable territory belonging to the U.S. And to what object so good so great & so glorious, could that peculiar fund of wealth be appropriated? Whilst the sale of territory would on one hand be planting one desert with a free & civilized people, it would on the other, be giving freedom to another people, and filling with them another desert. And, if in any instances, wrong has been done by our forefathers to people of one colour in dispossessing them of their soil, what better atonement is now in our power than that of making what is rightfully acquired a source of justice & of blessings to a people of another colour?...

It is evident however that in effectuating a general

emancipation of slaves in the mode which has been hinted, difficulties of other sorts would be encountered. The provision for ascertaining the joint consent of the masters & slaves; for guarding agst. unreasonable valuations of the latter; and for the discrimination of those not proper to be conveyed to a foreign residence, or who ought to remain a charge on Masters in whose service they had been disabled or worn out and for the annual transportation of such numbers, would require the mature deliberations of the National Councils. The measure implies also the practicability of procuring in Africa, an enlargement of the district or districts, for receiving the exiles, sufficient for so great an augmentation of their numbers.

Perhaps the Legislative provision best adapted to the case would be an incorporation of the Colonizing Society or the establishment of a similar one, with proper powers under the appointment & superintendence of the national Executive....

One difficulty presents itself which will probably attend every plan which is to go into effect under the Legislative provisions of the National Govt. But whatever may be the defect of the existing powers of Congress, the Constitution has pointed out the way in which it can be supplied, And it can hardly be doubted that the requisite powers might readily be procured for attaining the great object in question, in any mode whatever approved by the nation.

If these thoughts can be of any aid in your search of a remedy for the great evil under which the nation labors, you are very welcome to them. You will allow me however to add that it will be most agreeable to me, not to be publickly referred to in any use you may make of them.

Principally because of slavery, Madison feared for the duration of the Union. The Missouri question raised a mighty storm in 1820. Madison disapproved of the Missouri Compromise's prohibition of slavery above the latitudinal line 36°30′ in the Louisiana Purchase lands. Whatever its motives, the effect of the restriction, Madison thought, was to cause a division of parties along a geographical line and hence to weaken, perhaps eventually to destroy, national political consensus. And whatever the value of restricting slavery above the Ohio in 1787 when the door to the African trade was open, Madison believed that gradual emancipation would be more readily accomplished now by diffusion of the slaves over a vast area, thereby lightening the burden in the South and bringing more shoulders under it. Finally, he felt that since slavery was a local institution, Congress could not control its destiny in any new or old state. Madison expressed these views of the Missouri Compromise and its sequel, the so-called Second Missouri Compromise, in letters to President Monroe and his old friend Lafayette.

Speaker of the House Henry Clay supported Missouri Compromise.

Montpellier Feby. 10. 1820

I find the idea is fast spreading that the zeal with which the extension, so called, of slavery is opposed, has with the coalesced *leaders,* an object very different from the welfare of slaves, or the check to their increase; and that the real object is, as you intimate, to form a new State of parties founded on local instead of political distinctions; thereby dividing the republicans of the North from those of the South, and making the former instrumental in giving the opponents of both an ascendancy over the whole. If this be the view of the subject at Washington, it furnishes an additional reason for a conciliatory proceeding in relation to Maine.

I have been truly astonished at some of the doctrines & declarations to which the Missouri question has led....

I have observed as *yet,* in none of the views taken of the ordinance of 1787 interdicting slavery N.W. of the Ohio, an allusion to the circumstances, that when it passed, the Congs. had no authority to prohibit the importation of slaves from abroad; that all the States had, and some were in the full exercise of, the right to import them; and consequently, that there was no mode in which Congress could check the evil, but the indirect one of narrowing the space open for the reception of slaves. Had the federal authority then existed to prohibit directly & totally the importation from abroad, can it be doubted that it would have been exerted, and that a regulation having merely the effect of preventing an interior dispersion of slaves actually in the U.S. and creating a distinction among the States in the degrees of their sovereignty, would not have been adopted? or perhaps thought of?

Montpellier Novr. 25. 1820

Here, we are, on the whole, doing well, and giving an example of a free system, which I trust will be more of a pilot to a good port, than a Beacon, warning from a bad one. We have, it is true, occasional fevers; but they are of the transient kind, flying off through the surface, without preying on the vitals. A Government like ours has so many safety-valves, giving vent to overheated passions, that it carries within itself a relief against the infirmities from which the best of human Institutions can not be exempt. The subject which ruffles the surface of public affairs most at present, is furnished by the transition of the "Territory" of Missouri, from a state of nonage, to a maturity for self-Government, and for a membership in the Union. Among the questions involved in it, the one most immediately interesting to humanity, is the question whether a toleration or prohibition of slavery westward of the Mississippi, would most extend its evils. The humane part of the argument agst. the prohibition turns on the position, that whilst the importation of slaves from abroad is precluded, a diffusion of those in the Country, tends at once to meliorate their actual condition, and to facilitate their eventual emancipation. Unfortunately the subject which was settled at the last session of Congress by a mutual concession of the parties, is reproduced on the arena, by a clause in the Constitution of Missouri; distinguishing between free persons of colour, and white persons, and providing that the Legislature of the new State shall exclude from it the former. What will be the issue of the revived discussion is yet to be seen. The Case opens the wider field, as the Constitutions and laws of the different States are at variance in the civic character given to free people of colour; those of most of the States, not excepting such as have abolished slavery, imposing various disqualifications which degrade them from the rank & rights of white persons. All these perplexities develope more & more, the dreadful fruitfulness of the original sin of the African trade.

Nineteenth-century illustration of the capture of rebel Nat Turner

The best hope for slavery reform in Virginia came in the wake of the hideous Nat Turner insurrection of 1831 in Southampton County, Virginia, in which fifty-seven whites were slain before the rebels were hunted down and captured or killed. But the state legislature, meeting after the massacre, slammed the door once and for all on emancipation in any form. Only the most slender thread of hope remained, but Madison clung to it. While northern abolitionists discredited colonization as a cheat and a sham and Southerners united on the theory of African slavery as the norm of history, the injunction of the Bible, and the bulwark of southern civilization, Madison stared down despair. The English author and reformer, Harriet Martineau, visited him in 1835, only a year before his death. Crippled by rheumatism, deaf in one ear, losing his sight, "his little person wrapped in a black silk gown, a warm gray and white cap upon his head, which his lady took care should always sit becomingly," Madison had lost none of his talent for spirited conversation. He talked of many things, from the diminutive size of Roman farms to the absurdities of geology, but most of all he talked of slavery.

Madison as Harriet Martineau saw him: "his little person wrapped in a black silk gown, a warm gray and white cap upon his head...."

Retrospect of Western Travel [1838]

With regard to slavery he owned himself almost to be in despair. He had been quite so till the institution of the Colonization Society. How such a mind as his could derive any alleviation to its anxiety from that source is surprising. I think it must have been from his overflowing faith; for the facts were before him that in eighteen years the Colonization Society had removed only between two and three thousand persons, while the annual increase of the slave population in the United States was upward of sixty thousand.

He talked more on the subject of slavery than on any other, acknowledging, without limitation or hesitation, all the evils with which it has ever been charged. He told me that the black population in Virginia increases far faster than the white; and that the licentiousness only stops short of the destruction of the race; every slave girl being expected to be a mother by the time she is fifteen. He assumed from this, I could not make out why, that the negroes must go somewhere, and pointed out how the free states discourage the settlements of blacks; how Canada disagrees with them; how Hayti shuts them out; so that Africa is their only refuge. He did not assign any reason why they should not remain where they are when freed. He found, by the last returns from his estates, that one third of his own slaves were under five years of age. He had parted with some of his best land to feed the increasing numbers, and had yet been obliged to sell a dozen of his slaves the preceding week. He observed that the whole Bible is against negro slavery; but that the clergy do not preach this, and the people do not see it. He became animated in describing ... the eagerness of the clergy of the four denominations to catch converts among the slaves, and the effect of

Harriet Martineau

religious teaching of this kind upon those who, having no rights, can have no duties. He thought the condition of slaves much improved in his time, and, of course, their intellects. This remark was, I think, intended to apply to Virginia alone, for it is certainly not applicable to the southwestern states. He accounted for his selling his slaves by mentioning their horror of going to Liberia, a horror which he admitted to be prevalent among the blacks, and which appears to me decisive as to the unnaturalness of the scheme. The willing mind is the first requisite to the emigrant's success. Mr. Madison complained of the difficulty and risk of throwing an additional population into the colony, at the rate of two or three cargoes a year; complained of it because he believed it was the fault of the residents, who were bent upon trading with the interior for luxuries, instead of raising food for the new comers.... Mr. Madison admitted the great and various difficulties attending the scheme, and recurred to the expression that he was only "less in despair than formerly about slavery." He spoke with deep feeling of the sufferings of ladies under the system, declaring that he pitied them even more than their negroes, and that the saddest slavery of all was that of conscientious Southern women. They cannot trust their slaves in the smallest particulars, and have to superintend the execution of all their own orders; and they know that their estates are surrounded by vicious free blacks, who induce thievery among the negroes, and keep the minds of the owners in a state of perpetual suspicion, fear, and anger.

Mr. Madison spoke strongly of the helplessness of all countries cursed with a servile population in a conflict with a people wholly free; ridiculed the idea of the Southern States being able to maintain a rising against the North; and wondered that all thinkers were not agreed in a thing so plain. He believed that Congress has power to prohibit the internal slave trade. He mentioned the astonishment of some strangers, who had an idea that slaves were always whipped all day long, at seeing his negroes go to church one Sunday. They were gayly dressed, the women in bright-coloured calicoes; and, when a sprinkling of rain came, up went a dozen umbrellas. The astonished strangers veered round to the conclusion that slaves were very happy; but were told of the degradation of their minds; of their carelessness of each other in their nearest relations, and their cruelty to brutes.

If slavery headed Madison's agenda of unfinished business from the Revolution, the conquest of ignorance stood not far behind. In 1785 he had tried and failed to win legislative approval of Jefferson's comprehensive plan of public education. Jefferson, always the captain of this cause, revived his plan in 1814. This time the Virginia assembly eliminated the provisions for elementary and secondary schools but gave Jefferson his dream of a state university. Madison must have wondered, as Jefferson did, at the folly of the legislature in thus choosing to raise the apex without laying the foundations in the schools. Since knowledge will ever govern ignorance, Madison observed, a popular government without popular education "is but a prologue to a Farce or a Tragedy, or perhaps both." His essentially civic conception of education, as an ally of republican government, is developed in a letter to William T. Barry of Kentucky.

[Montpelier,] Aug. 4 1822

Learned Institutions ought to be favorite objects with every free people. They throw that light over the public mind which is the best security against crafty & dangerous encroachments on the public liberty. They are nurseries of skilful Teachers for the schools distributed throughout the Community. They are themselves Schools for the particular talents required for some of the public Trusts, on the able execution of which the welfare of the people depends. They multiply the educated individuals from among whom the people may elect a due portion of their public agents of every description more especially of those who are to frame the laws; by the perspicuity, the consistency, and the stability, as well as by the just & equal spirit of which the great social purposes are to be answered.

Without such Institutions, the more costly of which can scarcely be provided by individual means, none but the few whose wealth enables them to support their sons abroad, can give them the fullest education; and in proportion as this is done, the influence is monopolized which superior information everywhere possesses. At cheaper & nearer seats of Learning parents with slender incomes may place their sons in a course of Education putting them on a level with the sons of the richest. Whilst those who are without property, or with but little,

In 1818 Madison had been appointed a commissioner "to aid the Legislature in ascertaining a permanent scite for a University."

379

must be peculiarly interested in a System which unites with the more Learned Institutions, a provision for diffusing through the entire Society the education needed for the common purposes of life....

But why should it be necessary in this case, to distinguish the Society into classes according to their property? When it is considered that the establishment and endowment of Academies, Colleges, and Universities are a provision not merely for the existing generation, but for succeeding ones also; that in Governments like ours a constant rotation of property results from the free scope to industry, and from the laws of inheritance, and when it is considered moreover, how much of the exertions and privations of all are meant not for themselves, but for there posterity, there can be little ground for objections from any class, to plans of which when contributing to a permanent plan for the education of the poor, ought to reflect that he is providing for that of his own descendants; and the poor man who concurs in a provision for those who are not poor that at no distant day it may be enjoyed by descendants from himself. It does not require a long life to witness these vicisitudes of fortune.

It is among the happy peculiarities of our Union, that the States composing it derive from their relations to each other and to the whole, a salutary emulation, without the enmity involved in competitions among States alien to each other. This emulation, we may perceive, is not without its influence in several important respects; and in none ought it to be more felt than in the merit of diffusing the light and the advantages of public Instruction....

Throughout the Civilized World, nations are courting the praise of fostering Science and the useful arts, and are opening their eyes to the principles and the blessings of Representative Government. The American people owe it to themselves, and to the cause of free Government to prove by their establishments for the advancement and diffusion of Knowlege, that their political Institutions, which are attracting observation from every quarter, and are respected as Models, by the newborn States in our own Hemisphere, are as favorable to the intellectual and moral improvement of man, as they are conformable to his individual & social Rights. What spectacle can be more edifying or more seasonable, than that of Liberty & Learning, each leaning on the other for their mutual & surest support?

Madison was closely associated with Jefferson in founding the University of Virginia. It was to be, among other things, a secular institution in strict conformity to the principle of separation of Church and State. The idea of a "godless university" was novel, threatening to Virginia's evangelical leadership, and the university rose over its opposition. For Madison, freedom of religion was involved with freedom of mind and therefore with what would later be called academic freedom. It was the one principle upon which there could be no compromise. He stated his views in a letter to Edward Everett, then a professor and later president of Harvard—a university that still labored under the constraints of its Puritan founding.

Edward Everett of Harvard

Montpellier Mar. 19. 1823

I am not suprised at the dilemma produced at your University, by making Theological Professorships an integral part of the System. The anticipation of such an one, led to the omission in ours; the Visitors being merely authorized to open a public Hall for religious occasion, under *impartial* regulations; with the opportunity to different Sects to establish their Theological Schools, so near that the Students of the University may respectively attend the religious exercises in them. The Village of Charlottesville, where different Religious Worships will be held, is also so near that resort may be conveniently had to them.

A University with Sectarian professorships, becomes of course, a Sectarian Monopoly: with professorships of rival sects, it would be an arena of Theological Gladiators: without any such professorship, it must incur for a time at least, the imputation of irreligious tendencies if not designs. The last difficulty was thought more manageable, than either of the others.

On this view of the subject, there seems to be no alternative but between a public University without a Theological professorship, or Sectarian Seminaries without a University.

I recollect to have seen a great many years ago, a project of a paper by Govr [of New Jersey William] Livingston, father of the present Judge [Henry Brockholst Livingston on the Supreme Court], intended to comprehend & conciliate College Students of every denomination, by a Form composed wholly of texts & phrases of Scripture. If a trial of the expedient was ever made, it must have failed, notwithstanding its winning aspect, from the single cause that many sects reject all set forms of worship.

The difficulty of reconciling the Christian mind to the absence of religious Tuition from a University, established by Law & at the common expense, is probably less with us than with you. The settled opinion here is that religion is essentially distinct from Civil Govt. and exempt from its cognizance; that a connexion between them is injurious to both; that there are causes in the human breast which ensure the perpetuity of religion without the aid of the law; that rival sects with equal rights, exercise mutual censorships in favor of good morals; that if new sects arise with absurd opinions or overheated imaginations, the proper remedies lie in time, forbearance, and example: that a legal establishment of Religion without a toleration, could not be thought of, and with a toleration, is no security for public quiet & harmony, but rather a source itself of discord & animosity: and finally, that these opinions are supported by experience, which has shewn that every relaxation of the Alliance between Law & Religion, from the partial example of Holland, to its consumation in Pennsylvania, N. Jersey &c. has been found as safe in practice as it is sound in Theory.

Jefferson dedicated the university to "the illimitable freedom of the human mind." Still, his anxiety for the political purity of the School of Law and Government—one of the ten schools envisioned—led him to propose that the Board of Visitors prescribe correct texts. These ranged from Algernon Sydney's *Discourses* and Locke on civil government to Madison's Virginia Report on the Alien and Sedition Laws. If one reads between the lines of Madison's letter in response, it seems clear that he disliked the proposition—though in this, as in all things connected with the university, he had not the heart to quarrel with Jefferson. He confined himself to suggesting an amendment that softened the resolution.

Montpellier Feby. 8. 1825

I have looked with attention over your intended proposal of a textbook for the Law School. It is certainly very material that the true doctrines of Liberty, as exemplified in our Political System, should be inculcated on those who are to sustain and may administer it. It is at the same time, not easy to find Standard books that will be

Virginia, HOWE

The University of Virginia

both guides & guards for the purpose. Sydney & Locke are admirably calculated to impress on young minds the right of Nations to establish their own Governments, and to inspire a love of free ones, but afford no aid in guarding our Republican Charters against constructive violations. The Declaration of Independence tho' rich in fundamental principles, and saying everything that could be said in the same number of words, falls nearly under a like observation. The "Federalist" may fairly enough be regarded as the most authentic exposition of the text of the federal Constitution as understood by the Body which prepared & the Authorities which accepted it. Yet it did not foresee all the misconstructions which have occurred; nor prevent some that it did foresee. And what equally deserves remark, neither of the great rival parties have acquiesced in all its Comments. It may nevertheless be admissible as a Schoolbook, if any will be that goes so much into detail. It has been actually admitted into two Universities if not more, those of Harvard & Rh. Island; but probably at the choice of the Professors, without an injunction from the superior authority. With respect to the Virginia Document of 1799 there may be more room for hesitation.... In framing a political creed, a like difficulty occurs as in the case of religion tho the public right be very different in the two cases. If the Articles be in very general terms, they do not answer the purpose: if in very particular terms, they divide & exclude where meant to unite & fortify. The best that can be done in our case seems to be, to avoid the two extremes, by referring to selected Standards without requiring an unqualified conformity to them, which indeed might not in every instance be possible. The selection would give them authority with the Students, and might controul or counteract deviations of the Professor. I have for your consideration, sketched a modification of the operative passage in your draught, with a view to relax the absoluteness of its injunction, and added to your list of Documents, the Inaugural Speech and the Farewell Address of President Washington. They may help down what might be less readily swallowed, and contain nothing which is not good; unless it be the laudatory reference in the Address to the [Jay] Treaty of 1795 with G.B. which ought not to weigh against the sound sentiments characterizing it.

After all, the most effectual safeguard against heretical intrusions into the School of politics, will be an Able & Orthodox Professor, whose course of instruction will be an example to his Successors, and may carry with it a Sanction from the Visitors.

Madison saw Jefferson for the last time, at Monticello, in September, 1825. The collaboration of these two philosophical statesmen over half a century was one of the wonders of the world. The pilgrims who took in Montpelier as well as Monticello usually found Madison the more inviting figure. He seemed happier, friendlier, better informed on current affairs, and more resilient to change than the Sage of Monticello. "He appears less studied, brilliant, and frank, but more natural, candid and profound than Mr. Jefferson," one observer noted. "Mr. Jefferson has more imagination and passion, quicker and richer conceptions. Mr. Madison has a sound judgment, tranquil temper and logical mind." At eighty-two, as he labored to put the university into operation, Jefferson struggled against death and bankruptcy. In January, 1826, he appealed to the legislature for permission to dispose of the bulk of his property by lottery—a favor granted but to no avail. A month later, in his last letter to Madison, he explained his plight and closed with a moving farewell.

> Monticello. February 17, 1826
>
> The friendship which has subsisted between us, now half a century, and the harmony of our political principles and pursuits, have been sources of constant happiness to me through that long period. And if I remove beyond the reach of attentions to the University, or beyond the bourne of life itself, as I soon must, it is a comfort to leave that institution under your care, and an assurance that it will not be wanting. It has also been a great solace to me, to believe that you are engaged in vindicating to posterity the course we have pursued for preserving to them, in all their purity, the blessings of self-government, which we had assisted too in acquiring for them. If ever the earth has beheld a system of administration conducted with a single and steadfast eye to the general interest and happiness of those committed to it, one which, protected by truth, can never know reproach, it is that to which our lives have been devoted. To myself you have been a pillar of support through life. Take care of me when dead, and be assured that I shall leave with you my last affections.
>
> TH: JEFFERSON

Madison replied to his old friend a short time later.

Montpellier Feby. 24. 1826.

I had noticed the disclosures at Richmond with feelings which I am sure I need not express: any more than the alleviation of them by the sequel. I had not been without fears that the causes you enumerate were undermining your estate. But they did not reach the extent of the evil. Some of these causes were indeed forced on my attention by my own experience. Since my return to private life (and the case was worse during my absence in public) such have been the unkind seasons, & the ravages of insects, that I have made but one tolerable crop of Tobacco, and but one of Wheat; the proceeds of both of which were greatly curtailed by mishaps in the sale of them. And having no resources but in the earth I cultivate, I have been living very much throughout on borrowed means. As a necessary consequence, my debts have swelled to an amount, which if called for at the present conjuncture, would give to my situation a degree of analogy to yours. Fortunately I am not threatened with any rigid pressure, and have the chance of better crops & prices, with the prospect of a more leisurely disposal of the property which must be a final resort.

You do not overrate the interest I feel in the University as the Temple thro' which alone lies the road to that of Liberty. But you entirely do my aptitude to be your successor in watching over its prosperity. It would be the pretension of a mere worshipper "remplacer" the Tutelary Genius of the Sanctuary. The best hope is, in the continuance of your cares, till they can be replaced by the stability and self growth of the Institution. Little reliance can be put even on the fellowship of my services. The past year has given me sufficient intimation of the infirmities in wait for me. In calculating the probabilities of survivorship, the inferiority of my constitution forms an equation at least with the seniority of yours. . . .

You cannot look back to the long period of our private friendship & political harmony, with more affecting recollections than I do. If they are a source of pleasure to you, what ought they not to be to me? We can not be deprived of the happy consciousness of the pure devotion to the public good, with which we discharged the trusts committed to us. And I indulge a confidence that sufficient evidence will find its way to another generation, to

Harper's New Monthly Magazine, JULY, 1863

Monticello, where Madison saw his friend Jefferson for the last time

ensure, after we are gone, whatever of justice may be witheld whilst we are here. The political horizon is already yielding in your case at least, the surest auguries of it. Wishing & hoping that you may yet live to increase the debt which our Country owes you, and to witness the increasing gratitude, which alone can pay it, I offer you the fullest return of affectionate assurances.

Jefferson died on July 4, 1826, the fiftieth anniversary of American independence. Nicholas P. Trist, one of the Monticello family, informed Madison, who replied at once.

Montpellier July 6. 1826

I have just recd. yours of the 4th. A few lines from Doctr Dunglison had prepared me for such a communication; and I never doubted that the last scene of our illustrious friend would be worthy of the life which it closed. Long as this has been spared to his country and to those who loved him, a few years more were to have been desired for the sake of both. But we are more than consoled for the loss, by the gain to him; and by the assurance that he lives and will live in the memory and gratitude of the wise and good, as a luminary of science, as a votary of liberty, as a model of patriotism, and as a benefactor of human kind. In these characters I have known him, and not less in the virtues and charms of social life for a period of fifty years, during which there was not an interruption or diminution of mutual confidence and cordial friendship for a single moment in a single instance. What I feel therefore now need not, I should say, can not be expressed. If there be any possible way in which I can *usefully* give evidence of it do not fail to afford me the opportunity.

Jefferson and John Adams both died on July 4, 1826, fifty years after the Declaration of Independence. A friend sent Madison this dirge.

As Jefferson had wished, Madison succeeded him as rector of the university, a position that combined the duties of a president with those of a chairman of the board. Most of the business was transacted through young Trist stationed at Monticello. In one of his many letters to him, Madison departed from the business at hand to write a little essay on the Utopian experiment of Robert Owen, who had called at Montpelier in 1825 while en route to the new paradise, New Harmony, Indiana. For all his faith in man's capacity for justice, improvement, and self-government, Madison could not indulge Owen's dream of an egalitarian socialist society.

The streak of Calvinism in his thought, crossed now with the Malthusian teachings of the classical economists, caused him to look skeptically on Owen's scheme, though he wished to see it tried for the good it might hold for mankind.

Montpellier Apl. 1827

The Harmony Gazette has been regularly sent me; but in the crowd of printed things I receive, I had not attended to the Essays to which you refer me. The present situation of G. Britain which gave rise to them is full of instruction and Mr. Owen avails himself of it with address, in favour of his panacea. Such diseases are however too deeply rooted in human society to admit of more than great palliatives.

Every populous country is liable to contingenc[i]es that must distress a portion of its inhabitants. The chief of them are 1. unfruitful seasons, increasing the price of subsistence without increasing that of labour; and even reducing the price of labour, by abridging the demand of those whose income depends on the fruits of the Earth.

2. The sudden introduction of labour-saving machinery, taking employment from those whose labour is the only source of their subsistence.

3. The caprice of fashion, on which the many depend, who supply the wants of fancy. Take for a sufficient illustration a single fact. When the present King of England was Prince of Wales, he introduced the use of Shoe strings instead of Shoe buckles. The effect on the condition of the Bucklemakers was such that he received addresses from many thousands of them, praying him as the Arbiter of fashion, to save them from starving, by restoring the taste for buckles in preference to strings.

4. To the preceding occurrences to which an insulated community would be liable, must be added a loss of foreign markets to a manufacturing and commercial community from whatever of the various causes it may happen. Among these causes may be named even the changeableness of foreign fashion. The substitutions of shoe strings for shoe-buckles in the U.S., had a like effect with that in England, on her bucklemakers.

Mr. Owen's remedy for these vicissitudes, implies that labour will be relished without the ordinary impulses to it; that the love of equality will supercede the desire of distinction; and that the increasing leisure from the improvements of machinery will promote intellectual

Robert Owen

387

A circular announcing the Western Volunteer, *a newspaper in Frankfort, Kentucky; the publisher, Henry Banks, asked Madison to subscribe.*

cultivation, moral enjoyment, and innocent amusements, without any of the vicious resorts for the ennui of idleness....

The state of things promising most exemption from the distress exhibited in G. Britain, would be a freedom of commerce among all nations, and especially with the addition of universal peace. The aggregate fruits of the Earth, which are little varied by the Seasons, would then be accessible to all: The improvements of machinery, not being adopted every where at once, would have a diminished effect where first introduced: and there being no interruptions to foreign Commerce, the vicissitudes of fashion, would be limited in their sudden offset in one country by the numerous markets abroad for the same or similar articles.

After all there is one indelible cause remaining, of pressure on the condition of the laboring part of mankind: and that is, the constant tendency to an increase of their numbers, after the increase of food has reached its term. The competition for employment then reduces wages to their minimum, and privation to its maximum: and whether the evil proceeding from this tendency be checked, as it must be by either physical or moral causes, the checks are themselves but so many evils. With this knowledge of the impossibility of banishing evil altogether from human society, we must console ourselves with the belief that it is overbalanced by the good mixed with it, and direct our efforts to an increase of the good proportion of the mixture.

Republicanism for Madison was fundamentally a matter of balancing the will of the majority with the rights of minorities through a properly constituted government. The principal unfinished business in this regard was the Virginia Constitution of 1776, which he, though unhappily not Jefferson, would at last have an opportunity to reform. In 1829 the freeholders of Orange elected him a delegate to the convention to revise the constitution. The assemblage in Richmond was dazzling. Two former presidents, Madison and Monroe, Chief Justice John Marshall, Speaker of the House of Representatives Philip P. Barbour, vintage Jeffersonians John Randolph and William B. Giles, and even a President-to-be, John Tyler, were among its members. Representation was the great issue, and it divided Virginia geographically along the line of the Blue Ridge. The existing system took no account of population. New Virginia—the rapidly growing West—

was unfairly dominated by old Virginia. Western reformers, taking up the half-century-long Jeffersonian attack on the constitution, advocated a "one man, one vote" system on the basis of white population only. But the power and the wealth of Virginia, particularly the property in slaves who could not vote but were counted in apportioning the legislature, were concentrated in the East, and easterners demanded protection for these interests against the will of a hostile majority. Suffrage was a related issue. Somewhere between one-third and one-half of Virginia's adult white males were disfranchised under the freehold suffrage qualification, an intolerable vestige of the past in this new age of democracy. Both these matters were referred to a committee chaired by Madison, the lone survivor of the revolutionary convention. He cast the decisive vote in the committee for the white basis in the lower house of the assembly. This was unacceptable to the eastern majority in the convention, however, and Madison himself yielded his convictions to the eastern bloc. Early in December, the old gentleman, his small frame draped in a threadbare "snuff-colored" coat, his hair powdered, his voice low and weak, addressed the convention.

[December 2, 1829]

Having been for a very long period withdrawn from any participation in proceedings of deliberative bodies, and under other disqualifications now, of which I am deeply sensible, though, perhaps less sensible than others may perceive that I ought to be, I shall not attempt more than a few observations which may suggest the views I have

This painting by George Catlin shows Madison addressing the Virginia Convention at Richmond in 1829.

taken of the subject and which will consume but little of the time of the Committee, now become precious.

It is sufficiently obvious, that persons and property, are the objects on which Governments are to act: and that the rights of persons, and the rights of property are the objects for the protection of which Government was instituted. These rights cannot well be separated. The personal right to acquire property, which is a natural right, gives to property when acquired a right to protection as a social right. The essence of Government is power, and power lodged as it must be in human hands, will ever be liable to abuse. In Monarchies the interests and happiness of all may be sacrificed to the caprice and passion of a despot. In Aristocracies, the rights and welfare of the many may be sacrificed to the pride and cupidity of a few. In Republics, the great danger is that the majority may not sufficiently respect the rights of the minority. Some gentlemen, consulting the purity and generosity of their own minds, without adverting to the lessons of experience, would find a security against that danger in our social feelings; in a respect for character: in the dictates of the monitor within; in the interests of individuals: in the aggregate interests of the community.

But Man is known to be a selfish as well as a social being. Respect for character though often a salutary restraint, is but too often overruled by other motives. When numbers of men act in a body respect for character is often lost, just in proportion as it is necessary to control what is not right. We all know that conscience is not a sufficient safeguard, besides that conscience itself may be deluded; many being misled by an unconscious bias into acts which an enlightened conscience would forbid. As to the permanent interest of individuals in the aggregate interests of the community, & in the proverbial maxim that honesty is the best policy; present temptation is too often found to be an over match for those considerations. These favourable attributes of the human character are all valuable as auxiliaries, but they will not serve as a substitute for the coercive provisions belonging to government and law. They will always, in proportion as they prevail, be favourable to a mild administration of both; but they can never be relied on as a guaranty of the rights of the minority against a Majority disposed to take unjust advantage of its power. The only effectual

Among the impressive delegates to the convention was Philip P. Barbour, Speaker of the House.

safeguard to the rights of the minority must be laid in such a basis & structure of the Government itself as may afford, in a certain degree, directly or indirectly, a defensive authority in behalf of a minority having right on its side.

To come more nearly to the subject before the Committee, viz: that peculiar feature in our community which calls for a peculiar division in the basis of our Government, I mean the coloured part of our population. It is apprehended, if the power of the Commonwealth shall be in the hands of a majority, who have no interest in this species of property, that, from the facility with which it may be oppressed by excessive taxation, injustice may be done to its owners. It would seem therefore, if we can incorporate that interest into the basis of our system, it will be the most apposite and effectual security that can be devised. Such an arrangement is recommended to me by many very important considerations. It is due to justice: due to humanity: due to truth; to the sympathies of our nature: in fine, to our character as a people, both abroad and at home, that they should be considered, as much as possible, in the light of human beings; and not as mere property. As such they are acted upon by our laws; and have an interest in our laws. They may be considered as making a part, tho a degraded part of the families to which they belong. If they had the complexion of the Serfs in the north of Europe, or of the Villeins, formerly in England; in other terms, if they were of our own complexion, much of the difficulty would be removed. But the mere circumstance of complexion cannot deprive them of the character of men. The Federal number, as it is called [the three-fifths clause of the Constitution (Article I, Section 3) apportioning representation and direct taxes according to the number of free persons and three-fifths of the slaves of each state], is particularly recommended to attention in forming a basis of representation, by its simplicity, its certainty, its stability, and its permanency . . .

Should the federal number be made to enter into the basis in one branch of the Legislature and not into the other, such an arrangement might prove favourable to the slaves themselves. It may be, and I think it has been suggested, that those who have themselves no interest in this species of property, are apt to sympathize with

John Randolph of Roanoke was a long-time antagonist of Madison's.

the slaves more than may be the case with their masters; and would, therefore, be disposed, when they had the ascendency to protect them from laws of an oppressive character; whilst the masters, who have a common interest with the slaves, against undue taxation, which must be paid out of their labour, will be their protectors when they have the ascendency.

The Convention is now arrived at a point where we must agree on some common ground, all sides relaxing in their opinions, not changing, but mutually surrendering a part of them. In framing a Constitution, great difficulties are necessarily to be overcome; and nothing can ever overcome them but a spirit of compromise. Other nations are surprised at nothing so much as our having been able to form Constitutions in the manner which has been exemplified in this country. Even the Union of so many States is, in the eyes of the world, a wonder; the harmonious establishment of a common Government over them all, a miracle. I cannot but flatter myself, that, without a miracle, we shall be able to arrange all difficulties. I never have despaired, notwithstanding all the threatening appearances we have passed through. I have now more than a hope—a consoling confidence that we shall at last find that our labours have not been in vain.

Here was the last reprise of an old theme, and the dissonance of "interests" finally drowned the melody of democracy. What Madison was saying, though he seemed not to recognize it, was that slavery and democracy—even the democracy of the white community—were irreconcilable. Suffrage reform was finally compromised by the convention with Madison's support. He opposed going to universal white male suffrage but advocated admitting householders and taxpaying heads of families. Although he did not speak on this question, he developed his thoughts in a personal memorandum that focused his fears of the coming challenge to democracy from the massive growth of population on the Malthusian law.

[1829]

It is a law of nature, now well understood, that the earth under a civilized cultivation is capable of yielding subsistence for a large surplus of consumers, beyond those having an immediate interest in the soil; a surplus which must increase with the increasing improvements in agriculture, and the labor-saving arts applied to it. And it is a lot of humanity that of this surplus a large proportion is necessarily reduced by a competition for employment to wages which afford them the bare necessaries of life. That proportion being without property, or the hope of acquiring it, can not be expected to sympathize sufficiently with its rights, to be safe depositories of power over them.

What is to be done with this unfavored class of the community? If it be, on one hand, unsafe to admit them to a full share of political power, it must be recollected, on the other, that it cannot be expedient to rest a Republican Gov. on a portion of the society having a numerical & physical force excluded from, and liable to be turned against it; and which would lead to a standing military force, dangerous to all parties & to liberty itself.

This view of the subject makes it proper to embrace in the partnership of power, every description of citizens having a sufficient stake in the public order, and the stable administration of the laws; and particularly the House keepers & Heads of families; most of whom "having given hostages to fortune," will have given them to their Country also. . . .

It would be happy if a State of Society could be found or framed, in which an equal voice in making the laws might be allowed to every individual bound to obey them. But this is a Theory, which like most Theories, confessedly requires limitations & modifications, and the only question to be decided in this as in other cases, turns on the particular degree of departure, in practice, required by the essence & object of the Theory itself.

It must not be supposed that a crowded state of population, of which we have no example here, and which we know only by the image reflected from examples elsewhere, is too remote to claim attention.

The ratio of increase in the U.S. shows that the present

12 Millions will in	25 years be	24 Mils.
24 " " "	50 "	" 48 "
48 " " "	75 "	" 96 "
96 " " "	100 "	" 192 "

There may be a gradual decrease of the rate of increase; but it will be small as long as agriculture shall yield its abundance. G. Britain has doubled her population in the last 50 years; notwithstanding its amount in proportion to its territory at the commencement of that period, and Ireland is a much stronger proof of the effect of an increasing product of food, in multiplying the consumers.

How far this view of the subject will be affected by the Republican laws of descent and distribution, in equalizing the property of the citizens and in reducing to the minimum mutual surplusses for mutual supplies, cannot be inferred from any direct and adequate experiment. One result would seem to be a deficiency of the capital for the expensive establishments which facilitate labour and cheapens its products on one hand, and, on the other, of the capacity to purchase the costly and ornamental articles consumed by the wealthy alone, who must cease to be idlers and become labourers. Another the increased mass of labourers added to the production of necessaries by the withdrawal for this object, of a part of those now employed in producing luxuries, and the addition to the labourers from the class of present consumers of luxuries. To the effect of these changes, intellectual, moral, and social, the institutions and laws of the Country must be adapted, and it will require for the task all the wisdom of the wisest patriots.

Supposing the estimate of the growing population of the U.S. to be nearly correct, and the extent of their territory to be 8 or 9 hundred Mil of acres, and one fourth of it to consist of inarable surfaces, there will in a century or a little more, be nearly as crowded a population in the U.S. as in G. Britain or France, and if the present Constitution (of Virginia) with all its flaws, lasted more than half a century, it is not an unreasonable hope that an amended one will last more than a century.

If these observations be just, every mind will be able to develop & apply them.

Lafayette by Charles Willson Peale

After the convention adjourned, Madison reflected on its work in a letter to Lafayette. The old hero, long a friend of the black man, had hoped Madison would take up the cause of emancipation in Richmond. He explained why he did not, and could not, and speculated on the chances of ratification of the revised constitution. (It was approved in April on a straight sectional vote, the East for, the West against.)

Montpellier Feby 1. 1830

The Convention which called forth your interesting remarks & generous solicitudes, was pregnant with difficulties of various sorts, and at times, of ominous aspects. Besides the ordinary conflicts of opinion concerning the structure of Government, the peculiarity of local interests real or supposed, and above all, the case of our coloured population which happens to be confined to a geographical half of the State, and to have been a disproportionate object of taxation, were sources of jealousies & collisions which infected the proceedings throughout, and were finally overcome by a small majority only. Every concession of private opinion, not morally inadmissable, became necessary in order to prevent an abortion.... On the whole, the probability is, that the Constitution as amended will be sanctioned by the popular votes, and that by a considerable majority. Should this prove to be the case, the *peculiar* difficulties which will have been overcome, ought to render the experiment a new evidence of the capacity of men for Self-Government, instead of an argument in the hands of those who deny & calumniate it. The Convention was composed of the Elite of the Community, and exhibited great talents in the discussions belonging to the subject. Mr. Monroe, and still more myself, were too mindful of the years over our heads, to take an active part in them. The same consideration was felt by Mr. Marshall. I may add that each of us was somewhat fettered by the known & in some important instances, by the expressed will of our *immediate* Constituents.

Your anticipations with regard to the slavery among us, were the natural offspring of your just principles & Laudable sympathies. But I am sorry to say that the occasion which led to them, proved to be little fitted for the slightest interposition on that subject. A sensibility, morbid in its degree, was never more awakened among those who have the largest stake in that interest, and are most violent against any Governmental movement in relation to it. The excitability at the moment, happened also to be augmented by party questions between the South & the North, and the efforts used to make the circumstance common to the former, a sympathetic bond of co-operation. I scarcely express myself too strongly in saying, that an allusion in the Convention to the subject you have so much at heart, would have been a spark to a mass of Gunpowder. It is certain nevertheless, that Time "the great Innovator" is not idle in its salutary preparations. The Colonization Societies are becoming more and more one of its agents. Outlets for the freed blacks are alone wanted for a rapid erasure of that blot from our Republican character.

I observe in the foreign Journals the continued struggle between the Good & Evil principles on your side of the atlantic.

The cause that lay heaviest on Madison's heart and mind in these declining years was the cause of the Union and the Constitution. As the last of the founders, whose career surveyed the entire history of the nation, Madison became an acknowledged authority, almost an oracle, to historians, statesmen, and patriots seeking to light America's troubled course with the torch of the past. He thus came into public possession of his chief title to fame, Father of the Constitution. Men often inquired of him about some detail presumably buried in his voluminous record of the debates of the Federal Convention. He consistently refused disclosure even after the veil of secrecy was lifted by the publication in 1821 of the fragmentary record kept by Robert Yates, the New York Antifederalist. At that time Thomas Ritchie, editor of the Richmond *Enquirer,* tried to negotiate the publication of Madison's notes. Madison declined, as he continued to do as long as he lived.

Montpelr. Sep 15 1821

It is true as the public has been led to understand, that I possess materials for a pretty ample view of what passed in that Assembly. It is true also that it has not been my intention that they should for ever remain under the veil of secrecy. Of the time when it might be not improper for them to see the light, I had formed no particular determination: In general it had appeared to me that it might be best to let the work be a posthumous one, or at least that its publication should be delayed till the Constitution should be well settled by practice, & till a knowlege of the controversial part of the proceedings of its framers could be turned to no improper account. Delicacy also seemed to require some respect to the rule by which the Convention prohibited a promulgation without leave of what was spoken in it, so long as the policy of that rule could be regarded as in any degree unexpired. As guide in expounding and applying the provisions of the Constitution the debates and incidental decisions of the Convention can have no authoritative character. However desirable it be that they should be preserved as a gratification to the laudable curiosity felt by every people to trace the origin and progress of their political institutions, & as a source perhaps of some lights on the Science of Govt. the legitimate meaning of the Instrument must be derived from the text itself; or if a key is to be sought elsewhere, it must be not in the opinions or intentions of the Body which planned & proposed the Constitution, but in the sense attached to it by the people in their respective State Conventions where it recd. all the authority which it possesses.

Such being the course of my reflections I have suffered a concurrence & continuance of particular inconveniences for the time past, to prevent me from giving to my notes the fair & full preparations due to the subject of them. Of late, being aware of the growing hazards of postponements, I have taken the incipient steps for executing the task; and the expediency of not risking an ultimate failure is suggested by the Albany publication from the notes of a N. York member of the Convention. I have not seen more of the volume than has been extracted into the newspapers. But it may be inferred from these samples, that it is not only a very mutilated but a very erroneous edition of the matter to which it relates. There must be an entire omission also of the proceedings of the latter period of the Session from which Mr. Yates & Mr. Lansing [also a New York delegate] withdrew in the temper manifested by their report to their Constituents: the period during which the variant & variable opinions, converged & centered in the modifications seen in the final act of the Body.

It is my purpose now to devote a portion of my time to an exact digest of the voluminous materials in my hands. How long a time it will require under the interruptions & avocations which are probable I can not easily conjecture.

Published notes by Robert Yates of debates of 1787 Federal Convention

A jealous guardian of his reputation, especially as it touched the Constitution, Madison spent much paper and ink defending himself from charges of inconsistency. In the process he sometimes ran into new inconsistencies. Thus he repeatedly insisted that the Constitution should be construed in the sense given to it by the ratification conventions, since it was they who made the compact. Yet he held that *The Federalist*, a partisan work, was the most "authentic exposition" and that, in the instance of the national bank, a power deemed unconstitutional in 1791, or 1788, or 1798, might become valid through "the construction put on the Constitution, by the nation, which having made it had the supreme right to declare its meanings."

But Madison's most vexatious problem arose from the apparent discrepancy, if not contradiction, between the celebrated Resolutions of 1798 and the fervent unionism of his twilight years. During the 1820s the Virginia and Kentucky Resolutions were resurrected and mustered into the service of a revival of states' rights in Virginia politics. On the high authority of Jefferson and Madison, the movement assailed the tendency toward "consolidation" in the central government. Federal internal improvements and the protective tariff were the main targets, though the judicial nationalism of Chief Justice John Marshall was also condemned. Madison disapproved of Marshall's "latitudinarian" constructions of the Constitution; even more, however, he disapproved of the campaign mounted by Virginia's Old Republicans against the federal judiciary, which he believed essential to the preservation of the Union. Similarly, while he thought protectionism had gone far enough, he did not consider it responsible for Virginia's economic ills (slavery and the open door to the West were of first importance) nor an unconstitutional exercise of power by Congress.

By the end of the decade the states' rights doctrine employed by Jefferson and Madison to combat the Alien and Sedition Acts had been transformed under the hand of John C. Calhoun into the South Carolina doctrine of nullification. For the next several years Madison kept his pen working overtime to expose the heresy of that doctrine. From the celebrated Webster-Hayne debate of 1830 until the end of the great controversy in 1833, he found himself in the unenviable position of being quoted on both sides of the question and, even worse, on neither side correctly. Daniel Webster of Massachusetts associated him with the theory of unitary national sovereignty, while Robert Hayne of South Carolina associated him with the theory of state sovereignty. Both were in error, Madison said. The true theory was that of divided sovereignty. The Union originated in a compact of the people of the states, who divided the powers of government between two spheres, each government supreme in its sphere, and made the judiciary of the whole nation the final arbiter in cases requiring adjudication of the compact. The idea that a single state could nullify an act of the central government was an absurdity. To Hayne, who had sent him his famous Senate speech on the subject, Madison returned a four-thousand-word rebuttal, a copy of which went to a young admirer, Edward Everett of Massachusetts. When Everett expressed the wish to publish it, Madison recast the essay and it appeared in the *North American Review* in October, 1830.

Montpellier August 28th. 1830.

In order to understand the true character of the Consti-

*Painting by G.P.A. Healy depicts
Daniel Webster replying to Hayne.*

John Marshall

tution of the United States, the error, not uncommon, must be avoided, of viewing it through the medium, either of a Consolidated Government, or of a Confederated Government, whilst it is neither the one nor the other; but a mixture of both. And having in no model, the similitudes and analogies applicable to other systems of Government, it must more than any other, be its own interpreter according to its text and *the facts of the case.*

From these it will be seen, that the characteristic peculiarities of the Constitution are   1. the mode of its formation.   2. the division of the supreme powers of Government between the States in their united capacity, and the States in their Individual capacities.

1. It was formed not by the Governments of the component States, as the Federal Government for which it was substituted was formed: Nor was it formed by a majority of the people of the United States, as a single community, in the manner of a consolidated government.

It was formed by the States, that is by the people in each of the States, acting in their highest sovereign capacity; and formed consequently by the same authority which formed the State Constitutions.

Being thus derived from the same source as the Constitutions of the States, it has, within each State, the same authority as the Constitution of the State; and is as much a Constitution, in the strict sense of the term within its prescribed sphere, as the Constitutions of the States are, within their respective spheres: But with this obvious and essential difference, that being a compact among the States in their highest sovereign capacity, and constituting the people thereof one people for certain purposes, it cannot be altered or annulled at the will of the States individually, as the Constitution of a State may be at its individual will.

2. And that it divides the Supreme powers of Government, between the Government of the United States, and the Governments of the Individual States, is stamped on the face of the Instrument; the powers of war and of taxation, of commerce and of treaties, and other enumerated powers vested in the government of the United States. . . .

Between these different Constitutional governments, the one operating in all the States, the others operating separately in each, with the aggregate powers of government divided between them, it could not escape attention, that controversies would arise concerning the boundaries of jurisdiction; and that some provision ought to be made for such occurrences. A political system that does not provide for a peaceable and authoritative termination of occurring controversies, would not be more than the shadow of a Government; the object and end of a real government being, the substitution of law and order, for uncertainty confusion and violence. . . .

The Constitution . . . for its safe and successful operation, has expressly declared, on one hand 1. "that the Constitution and the laws made in pursuance thereof and all treaties made under the authority of the United States, shall be the Supreme law of the land; 2. that the Judges of every State shall be bound thereby, anything in the Constitution and laws of any State, to the contrary notwithstanding; 3. that the Judicial power of the United States shall extend to all cases in law and equity arising under the Constitution, the laws of the United States, and treaties made under their authority &c."

On the other hand, as a security of the rights and powers of the States, in their individual capacities, against an undue preponderance of the powers granted to the Government over them in their united capacity, the Constitution has relied on 1. the responsibility of the Senators and Representatives in the Legislature of the United States to the Legislatures and people of the States 2. the responsibility of the President to the people of the United States; and 3. the liability of the Executive and judiciary functionaries of the United States to impeachment. . . .

War of 1812, LOSSING

John C. Calhoun

How far this structure of the Government of the United States be adequate and safe for its objects, time alone can absolutely determine. Experience seems to have shewn that whatever may grow out of future stages of our national career, there is, as yet a sufficient controul, in the popular will, over the Executive and Legislative Departments of the Government. When the alien and sedition laws were passed in contravention of the opinions and feelings of the community, the first elections that ensued, put an end to them. And whatever may have been the character of other acts, in the judgment of many of us, it is but true, that they have generally accorded with the views of a majority of the States and of the people. At the present day it seems well understood, that the laws which have created most dissatisfaction, have had a like sanction without doors; and that whether continued varied or repealed—a like proof will be given of the sympathy and responsibility of the Representative body, to the Constituent body. Indeed the great complaint now is, against the results of this sympathy and responsibility in the Legislative policy of the nation....

Those who have denied or doubted the supremacy of the Judicial power of the United States and denounce at the same time a nullifying power in a State, seem not to have sufficiently adverted to the utter inefficiency of a supremacy in a law of the Land, without a supremacy in the exposition and execution of the law; nor to the destruction of all equipoise between the Federal Government and the State Governments if ... no constitutional controul of any sort belonged to the United States over the States. Under such an organization, it is evident that it would be in the power of the States, individually, to pass unauthorised laws, and to carry them into compleat effect, anything in the Constitution and laws of the United States to the contrary notwithstanding. This would be a nullifying power in its plenary character; and ... would be equally fatal to the constituted relation between the two Governments.

Should the provisions of the Constitution as here reviewed, be found not to secure the Government and rights of the States, against usurpations and abuses on the part of the United States, the final resort within the purview of the Constitution, lies in an amendment

*Portrait of the aged James Madison
painted by Asher B. Durand in 1833*

of the Constitution according to a process applicable by the States.

And in the event of a failure of every Constitutional resort, and an accumulation of usurpations and abuses, rendering passive obedience and non-resistance a greater evil, than resistance and revolution, there can remain but one resort, the last of all; an appeal from the cancelled obligations of the Constitutional compact, to original rights and the law of self preservation. This is the ultima ratio under all Governments, whether consolidated, confederated, or a compound of both; and it cannot be doubted that a single member of the Union, in the extremity supposed, but in that only, would have a right, as an extra and ultra constitutional right, to make the appeal.

This brings us to the expedient lately advanced, which claims for a single State, a right to appeal against an exercise of power by the Government of the United States decided by the State to be unconstitutional, to the parties to the Constitutional compact: the decision of the State to have the effect of nullifying the act of the Government of the United States, unless the decision of the States be reversed by three fourths of the parties. . . .

Can more be necessary to demonstrate the inadmissibility of such a doctrine, than that it puts in the power of the smallest fraction over one fourth of the United States, that is, of seven states out of twenty four, to give the law, and even the Constitution to seventeen States; each of the seventeen having as parties to the Constitution, an equal right with each of the seven, to expound it, and to insist on the exposition. That the seven might, in particular instances be right, and the seventeen wrong, is more than possible. But to establish a positive and permanent rule giving such a power, to such a minority, over such a majority, would overturn the first principle of free government, and in practice necessarily overturn the government itself. . . .

In favor of the nullifying claim for the States, individually, it appears . . . that the proceedings of the Legislature of Virginia in 98 & 99 against the Alien and Sedition Acts, are much dwelt upon.

That the Legislature could not have intended to sanction such a doctrine, is to be inferred from the debates in the House of Delegates, and from the address of the two Houses, to their Constituents, on the subject of the Resolutions. The tenor of the debates, which were ably conducted and are understood to have been revised for the press by most if not all of the speakers, discloses no reference whatever to a constitutional right in an individual State, to arrest by force the operation of a law of the United States. Concert among the States for redress against the Alien and Sedition Laws, as acts of usurped power, was a leading sentiment; and the attainment of a concert, the immediate object of the course adopted by the Legislature, which was that of inviting the other States "to *concur,* in declaring the acts to be unconstitutional, and to *co-operate* by the necessary and proper measures; in maintaining unimpaired the authorities rights and liberties reserved to the States respectively and to the people." That by the necessary and proper measure to be *concurrently* and *co-operatively* taken, were meant measures known to the Constitution, particularly the ordinary controul of the people and Legislatures of the States, over the Government of the United States, cannot be doubted; and *the interposition* of this controul, as the event shewed, was equal to the occasion. It is worthy of remark, and explanatory of the intentions of the Legislature, that the words "not law, but utterly null, void, and of no force or effect" which had followed, in one of the Resolutions, the word "unconstitutional," were struck out by common consent. Tho the words were in fact but synonomous with "unconstitutional"; yet to guard against a misunderstanding of this phrase as more than declaratory of opinion, the word unconstitutional, alone was retained, as not liable to that danger.

The letter to Everett demolished nullification as a theory and may have contributed to its actual defeat in 1833. Although he approved the action, Madison also labeled "heretical" the strident nationalism of President Jackson's proclamation against South Carolina's attempt to nullify the tariff. The last act of the drama was Henry Clay's Compromise Tariff of 1833. Madison applauded it heartily as going some way toward meeting the just objections of the South without impairing the foundations of the Union.

All through this crisis Madison was a semi-invalid at Montpelier. Rheumatism crippled his wrists and hands until he was forced to dictate many of his letters. The disease let up in 1833 but the body slowly gave out. The next year he resigned as rector of the university. Those who saw him in these last years testify that his mind and spirits were as lively as ever. He could not shake his anxiety over the fate of the Union. And he worried over the deterioration of his estate. For several years he had been forced to sell land and slaves to keep afloat. The economic depression of Virginia

Last page of Madison's will, 1835

Dolley Madison lived until 1849. This mutilated daguerrotype was made during her last decade.

agriculture had finally caught up with him, though it had been helped along by the constant drain of dollars—$40,000 during twenty years—to pay the debts of his profligate stepson, Payne Todd. Madison had hoped to emancipate and colonize the Montpelier slaves by his will. But with bankruptcy staring him in the face, this became quite impossible.

He died quietly and serenely at Montpelier on June 28, 1836, at the age of eighty-five. That morning breakfast had been brought to him in bed. His niece, noticing that he could not swallow, asked him what was wrong, to which the former President replied, "Nothing more than a change of *mind*, my dear." Then, according to his servant, "His head instantly dropped, and he ceased breathing as quietly as the snuff of a candle goes out." He was buried the next day in the family burial ground half a mile south of his house. Soon afterward, Dolley moved back to Washington where, although plagued by debts, she reigned for another decade as the grande dame of the capital's social life. She died in 1849, at the age of eighty-one.

Having served his country and his fellow man for sixty years, Madison had to be forgiven nothing and nothing had to be mourned in his death. He was not a religious man in the conventional sense. His life was given up to a political religion, what Harriet Martineau called "his inexhaustible faith that a well-founded commonwealth may ... be immortal; not only because the people, its constituency, never die, but because the principles

405

of justice in which such a commonwealth originates never die out of the people's heart and mind." Since his youth he had seldom speculated on religious questions. In 1825 an evangelical minister tried to press these questions upon him. Madison replied to the Reverend Frederick Beasley.

Unsigned note announcing the death of James Madison on June 28, 1836

Montpr. Novr. 29, 1825

I have duly recd. the copy of your little tract on the proofs of the Being & Attributes of God. To do full justice to it, would require not only a more critical attention than I have been able to bestow on it, but a resort to the celebrated work of Dr. [Samuel] Clarke, which I read fifty years ago only, and to that of Dr. [Daniel] Waterland [who argued with Clarke about the Trinity in 1712] also which I never read.

The reasoning that could satisfy such a mind as that of Clarke ought certainly not to be slighted in the discussion. And the belief in a God All Powerful wise & good, is so essential to the moral order of the world & to the happiness of man, that arguments which enforce it cannot be drawn from too many sources nor adopted with too much solicitude to the different characters & capacities to be impressed with it.

But whatever effect may be produced on some minds by the more abstract train of ideas which you strongly support, it will probably always be found that the course of reasoning from the effect to the cause, "from nature to nature's God," will be of the more universal & more persuasive application.

The finiteness of the Human understanding betrays itself on all subjects, but more especially when it contemplates such as involve infinity. What may safely be said seems to be that the infinity of time & space forces itself on our conception, a limitation of either being unconceivable: that the mind prefers at once the idea of a self-existing cause to that of an infinite series of causes & effects which augments, instead of avoiding the difficulty: and that it finds more facility in assenting to the self-existence of an invisible cause possessing infinite power, wisdom & goodness, than to the self-existence of the universe visibly destitute of those attributes and which may be [the] effect of them. In this comparative facility of conception & belief, all philosophical reasoning on the subject must perhaps terminate. But that I may not get farther beyond my depth, and without the resources which bear you up in fathoming efforts, I hasten to thank you for the favour which has made me your debtor, and to assure you of my esteem & my respectful regards.

In the end, faith in the Union had become the core of Madison's political religion. The crisis of nullification had passed, but other dangers, above all slavery, threatened to destroy the Union and with it the world's best hope for liberty and self-government. In 1834, when eighty-three years old, Madison penned a solemn appeal to his countrymen to cherish the Union. It was the political testament of the last Founding Father.

"Advice To My Country" [Fall of 1834]

As this advice, if it ever see the light will not do it till I am no more, it may be considered as issuing from the tomb, where truth alone can be respected, and the happiness of man alone consulted. It will be entitled therefore to whatever weight can be derived from good intentions, and from the experience of one who has served his country in various stations through a period of forty years, who espoused in his youth and adhered through his life to the cause of its liberty, and who has borne a part in most of the great transactions which will constitute epochs of its destiny.

The advice nearest to my heart and deepest in my convictions is that the Union of the States be cherished and perpetuated. Let the open enemy to it be regarded as a Pandora with her box opened; and the disguised one, as the Serpent creeping with his deadly wiles into Paradise.

Following Madison's death, Congress resolved to shroud chairs of Speaker and Senate president in black and to wear crepe armbands for thirty days.

Selected Bibliography

Adams, Henry. *History of the United States During the Administrations of Jefferson and Madison.* 9 vols. New York: Charles Scribner's Sons, 1889–91.

Beirne, Francis F. *The War of 1812.* New York: E. P. Dutton, 1949.

Brant, Irving. *The Fourth President: A Life of James Madison.* Indianapolis: Bobbs-Merrill, 1970.

————. *James Madison.* 6 vols. Indianapolis: Bobbs-Merrill, 1941–61.

————. *James Madison and American Nationalism.* Princeton: Van Nostrand, 1968.

Burns, Edward McNall. *James Madison: A Philosopher of the Constitution.* rev. ed. New York: Octagon Books, 1968.

Clark, Allen Culling. *Life and Letters of Dolly Madison.* Washington: W.F. Roberts, 1914.

Cunningham, Noble E., Jr. *The Jeffersonian Republicans in Power: The Formation of Party Organization, 1789–1801.* Chapel Hill: University of North Carolina Press, 1957.

Dangerfield, George. *The Era of Good Feelings.* New York: Harcourt, Brace, 1952.

De Conde, Alexander. *Entangling Alliance: Politics and Diplomacy under George Washington.* Durham: Duke University Press, 1958.

Farrand, Max, ed. *The Records of the Federal Convention of 1787.* rev. ed. 4 vols. New Haven: Yale University Press, 1937.

Hunt, Gaillard. *The Life of James Madison.* New York: Doubleday, Page, 1902.

Ketcham, Ralph. *James Madison: A Biography.* New York: Macmillan, 1971.

Koch, Adrienne. *Jefferson and Madison: The Great Collaboration.* New York: Alfred A. Knopf, 1950.

————. *Madison's "Advice to My Country."* Princeton: Princeton University Press, 1966.

Lord, Walter. *The Dawn's Early Light.* New York: W.W. Norton, 1972.

Madison, James. *Letters and Other Writings of James Madison, Fourth President of the United States.* Edited by William C. Rives and Philip R. Fendall. 4 vols. Philadelphia: J.B. Lippincott, 1865.

————. *The Papers of James Madison.* Vols. 1–7, Edited by William T. Hutchinson and William M.E. Rachal et al. Vol. 8–, Edited by Robert A. Rutland and William M.E. Rachal et al. Chicago: University of Chicago Press, 1962–.

————. *The Papers of James Madison Purchased by Order of Congress...* Edited by Henry D. Gilpin. 3 vols. Washington: Langtree & O'Sullivan, 1840.

————. *The Writings of James Madison, Comprising His Public Papers and His Private Correspondence.* Edited by Gaillard Hunt. 9 vols. New York: G.P. Putnam's Sons, 1900–1910.

Padover, Saul, ed. *The Complete Madison: His Basic Writings.* New York: Harper, 1953. Republished as *The Forging of American Federalism: Selected Writings of James Madison.* New York: Harper & Row, 1965.

Perkins, Bradford. *The First Rapprochement: England and the United States, 1795–1805.* Philadelphia: University of Pennsylvania Press, 1955.

————. *Prologue to War: England and the United States, 1805–1812.* Berkeley: University of California Press, 1961.

Riemer, Neal. *James Madison.* New York: Washington Square Press, 1968.

Rives, William C. *History of the Life and Times of James Madison.* 3 vols. Boston: Little, Brown, 1859–68.

Rossiter, Clinton. *1787: The Grand Convention.* New York: Macmillan, 1966.

Smelser, Marshall. *The Democratic Republic, 1801–1815.* New York: Harper, 1954.

Smith, Margaret Bayard. *The First Forty Years of Washington Society.* Edited by Gaillard Hunt. New York: Charles Scribner's Sons, 1906.

White, Leonard D. *The Jeffersonians: A Study in Administrative History, 1801–1829.* New York: Macmillan, 1951.

Acknowledgments

Unless otherwise specifically credited below, all documents reproduced in this volume are from the James Madison Papers, Library of Congress, Washington, D.C., the greatest collection of Madison documents in existence. In addition the Editors would like to thank the following individuals and institutions for permission to reprint documents in their possession:

American Art Association, Anderson Galleries catalogue, 1936, page 344(bottom)–345
George B. Cutts, Brookline, Mass., pages 251(bottom), 252–53(top), 365–66
Mrs. Theodore P. Dixon, Jr., Darien, Conn., pages 267(bottom), 268, 271–72, 282–83
Greensboro, N.C., Historical Museum, page 253(center)
Historical Society of Pennsylvania, Philadelphia, pages 22–39, 202(bottom)–203, 250(bottom)–251(top), 280(bottom)–281(top)
Massachusetts Historical Society, Boston, pages 238, 352–53(top), 359(bottom)–360, 381(bottom)–382(top), 398(bottom)–404(top)
National Archives, Washington, D.C., pages 58(bottom)–61, 239–43(top), 244(bottom)–247, 254–57, 261(bottom)–267(top), 269–70, 330(bottom)–331(top), 338–40, 354(bottom)–359(top), 361–62
New-York Historical Society, New York, N.Y., pages 279(bottom)–280(top), 334(center), 343(bottom)–344(top)
Pierpont Morgan Library, New York, N.Y., pages 323–25(top), 394(bottom)–396(top)
Princeton University, Princeton, N.J., page 258
University of Virginia Library, Charlottesville, page 251(center)
Virginia State Library, Richmond, pages 91–94

The Editors also make grateful acknowledgment for the use of documents from the following works:

Davis, Richard Beale, ed. *Jeffersonian America, Notes on the United States of America Collected in the Years 1805–6–7 and 11–12 by Sir Augustus John Foster.* San Marino, Cal., 1954. Pages 214(bottom)–217
Gilpin, Henry D., ed. *The Papers of James Madison.* 3 vols. Washington, D.C., 1840. Pages 72(bottom)–73(top)
Hillard, George S., ed. *Life, Letters, and Journals of George Ticknor.* 2 vols. Boston, 1876. Pages 367–68(top)
Hunt, Gaillard, ed. *The First Forty Years of Washington Society.* New York, 1906. Pages 273–76(top)
———. *The Writings of James Madison.* 9 vols. New York, 1900–1910. Pages 223(bottom)–229(top), 363–64
Proceedings and Debates of the Virginia Convention... 1829–30. Winchester, Va., 1830. Pages 389–92(top)
Martineau, Harriet. *Retrospect of Western Travel.* 3 vols. London, 1838. Pages 377–79(top)
Richardson, James D., ed. *A Compilation of the Messages and Papers of the Presidents.* Washington, D.C., 1907. Pages 298–301(top)
Robertson, David, comp. *Debates and Other Proceedings of the Convention of Virginia... June, 1788...* Richmond, 1805. Pages 157–61

The Editors also wish to express their appreciation to the many institutions and individuals who made available their pictorial materials for use in this volume. In particular the Editors are grateful to:

American Antiquarian Society, Worcester, Mass.—Georgia B. Bumgardner
Anne S. K. Brown Military Collection, Brown University, Providence, R.I.
Library of Congress, Manuscript Division, Washington, D.C.—Carolyn H. Sung
Maryland Historical Society, Baltimore
National Archives, Washington, D.C.
New-York Historical Society, New York, N.Y.—Wilson G. Duprey
New York Public Library, New York, N.Y.
The Papers of the Continental Congress, National Archives, Washington, D.C.—Kenneth E. Harris
The Papers of James Madison, University of Virginia, Charlottesville, Va.
Presbyterian Historical Society, Philadelphia, Pa.
Princeton University Archives, Princeton, N.J.—Nancy Graham
Virginia Historical Society, Richmond—Mary S. Southall
Yale University Art Gallery, New Haven, Conn.

Finally, the Editors would like to thank Russell Ash in London and John D. Knowlton in Washington, D.C., for advice and assistance in obtaining pictorial material, Thomas Froncek for editing, and Mary-Jo Kline for compiling the chronology and bibliography.

Index

Boldface indicates pages on
which illustrations appear.

416

B
MADISON   1454

Madison, James
James Madison
Volume 2

B   Madison, James
MADISON   **Date Due**   1454
James Madison – Volume 2

BRODART, INC.   Cat. No. 23 231   Printed in U.S.A.

unsuccessful untill a few days a[...]

of them which I now enclose. They [...]

for England, who will either carry [...]

the care of Mr. Adams. I do not y[...]

the full quantity which you wishe[...]

successful as to the seed of the Sug[...]

proceed for the purpose. — I have [...]

allotted for this conveyance, but th[...]

writing in Cypher, and several mes[...]

whether I shall be able to finish [...]

fear of losing the opportunity for b[...]

The Fundamentals of Fashion Design

Richard Sorger/Jenny Udale

2nd edition

ava
academia

An AVA Book

Published by AVA Publishing SA
Rue des Fontenailles 16
Case Postale
1000 Lausanne 6
Switzerland
Tel: +41 786 005 109
Email: enquiries@avabooks.com

Distributed by Thames & Hudson (ex-North America)
181a High Holborn
London WC1V 7QX
United Kingdom
Tel: +44 20 7845 5000
Fax: +44 20 7845 5055
Email: sales@thameshudson.co.uk
www.thamesandhudson.com

Distributed in the USA & Canada by:
Ingram Publisher Services Inc.
1 Ingram Blvd.
La Vergne TN 37086
USA
Tel: +1 866 400 5351
Fax: +1 800 838 1149
Email: customer.service@ingrampublisherservices.com

English Language Support Office
AVA Publishing (UK) Ltd.
Tel: +44 1903 204 455
Email: enquiries@avabooks.com

Second edition © AVA Publishing SA 2012
First published in 2006

ISBN 978-2-940411-78-8

Library of Congress Cataloguing-in-Publication Data
Sorger, Richard; Udale, Jenny.
The Fundamentals of Fashion Design / Richard Sorger, Jenny Udale p. cm.
Includes bibliographical references and index.
ISBN: 9782940411788 (pbk. :alk. paper)
eISBN: 9782940447404
1. Fashion design. 2. Fashion design -- Study and teaching.
TT507 .S675 2012

10 9 8 7 6 5 4 3 2 1

Design by Luke Herriott, Studio Ink

Production by AVA Book Production Pte. Ltd., Singapore
Tel: +65 6334 8173
Fax: +65 6259 9830
Email: production@avabooks.com.sg